DAREDEVIL
PSYCHOLOGY

The Devil You Know

FOREWORD BY
STAN LEE
EDITED BY TRAVIS LANGLEY

#DDpsych#PsychGeeks

STERLING
New York

STERLING
New York

An Imprint of Sterling Publishing Co., Inc.
1166 Avenue of the Americas
New York, NY 10036

ISBN 978-1-4549-3011-2

Distributed in Canada by Sterling Publishing Co., Inc.
^{c}/o Canadian Manda Group, 664 Annette Street
Toronto, Ontario M6S 2C8, Canada
Distributed in the United Kingdom by GMC Distribution Services
Castle Place, 166 High Street, Lewes, East Sussex BN7 1XU, England
Distributed in Australia by NewSouth Books
45 Beach Street, Coogee, NSW 2034, Australia

For information about custom editions, special sales, and premium and corporate purchases,
please contact Sterling Special Sales at 800-805-5489 or specialsales@sterlingpublishing.com.

Manufactured in Canada

2 4 6 8 10 9 7 5 3 1

sterlingpublishing.com

Cover design by Igor Satanovsky
Cover Photograph by AWL Images Ltd / Shutterstock

Photo Credits
iStock: © 4x6: 8, 212; © A-Digit: 80, 138; © AdrianHillman: 199; © Alex Langley: xi; © blamb: 226;
© Michal Boubin: 187; © DeCe_X: 125; © Jeffrey Henderson: xiii; © jennyhorne: 64; © JPLDesign: 113;
© Leontura: 152; © leremy: 163; © MarinaMariya: 30; © pixitive: 101; © PiXXart Photography: 175;
© SongSpeckels: 53; © Vectorig: 18; © Ylivdesign: 93

Shutterstock: © Piter Kidanchuk: 40; © Marble background: 50; © Petrafler: throughout;
© Pavlenko Volodymyr: 90, 122, 172

Dedication

To Randy Duncan
for daring to leap first

CONTENTS

ACKNOWLEDGMENTS:

PARTNERS & ASSOCIATES

TRAVIS LANGLEY

Randy Duncan paved the way—or, perhaps more accurately, revealed hidden paths worth taking. Long before any of us who have worked on this book, Randy became a comics scholar, and a prominent one at that. As a professor of communication at Henderson State University, he began teaching his Comics as Communication course, brought comic book writers and artists to speak on campus, initiated the creation and expansion of our library's graphic novel reading room with the help of librarian Lea Ann Alexander, and founded our students' Comics Arts Club. His activities, in turn, inspired David Stoddard, Scott McKinnon, Steve Listopad, Michelle Johnson, Matthew Sutherlin, Michael Taylor, countless students, and me to trek into comics studies, too. With Matthew Smith, Randy has written and edited books on comics, including one that earned them an Eisner Award nomination. With Peter Coogan, Randy co-founded the Comics Arts Conference, which Kathleen McClancy chairs today. My son Nicholas's participation in both Matt's research and that conference introduced me to the community of comics scholars. Thank you, Randy, for the many ways you helped me find this path (and for knowing Daredevil's costume needs to stay red).

We are fortunate to teach at a university that values this kind of work. Our administrators—President Glendell Jones, Provost Steve Adkison, Dean Angela Boswell—encourage creative ways of teaching. Library director Lea Ann Alexander looks forward to my next strange request so she and her staff can keep the shelves full of unusual resources, and Lea Ann deserves credit for consistently encouraging us to develop the comics studies minor that we have in place today. David Bateman, Lecia Franklin, Carolyn Hatley, Ermatine Johnson, and Salina Smith help us and our students go all the places we need to go (when it's in the budget). Latrena Beasley, Millie Bowden, Renee Davis, Sandra D. Johnson, and many other staff members make sure other essentials get done. Beth Taggard brought section V's opening Shakespeare quote to my attention. My fellow psychology department members provide encouragement and put up with my crazy schedule, much like the communication and theatre arts department backs Randy. Our faculty writers' group (Anji Boswell, Matthew Bowman, Jennifer Dawes, Brian George, Nydia Jeffers, Suzanne Tartamella, Mike Taylor) reviewed portions of this manuscript. Through groups such as our Comic Arts Club and the Legion of Nerds (the largest organization on campus!), our students prove that nerdy passions belong in higher education. They seem to enjoy the fact that some of their professors are professional nerds, and we enjoy bragging on them.

I met many of our chapter contributors, along with relevant writers, artists, editors, actors, filmmakers, propmakers, and more, through fan conventions, beginning with the afore-mentioned Comics Arts Conference which Randy Duncan co-founded. Therefore, I must thank the organizers who work hard to put the cons together. Most germane for this particular collection are those who help us at San Diego Comic-Con International (Eddie Ibrahim, Gary Sassaman, Cathy Dalton, Sue Lord, Adam Neese, Amy Ramirez, Chris Sturhann), ComiCon-way (Jimmy Dyer, Kara Rimmer Dyer), the Hero Round Table (Matt Langdon), and many Wizard World conventions over the years (Ryan Ball, Donna Chin, Kate Gloss, Chris Jansen, Peter Katz, Jerry Milani, Mai Nguyen,

Kayce Schulte, Brittany Walloch-Key). Danny Fingeroth, who has often led or joined convention panels with me, wrote the book *Superman on the Couch* which first inspired me to write this kind of book.

Daredevil Psychology: The Devil You Know would not be before you right now if not for the diligence of my literary agent, Evan Gregory of the Ethan Ellenberg Literary Agency. Publicists Blanca Oliviery, Ardi Alspach, Sari Lampert, and Lauren Tambini do so much to help me and to promote these projects. Kate Zimmermann is an outstanding editor. My previous editor, Connie Santisteban, continues to help as consultant, teammate, and friend.

For serving as our devil's advocates, muses, founts of knowledge, associates, and partners in many things, our writers thank Dave Adams, Ginny D'Angelo, Eli Mastin, Dustin McGinnis, Brian Edward Therens, Anne Ramage, Amy Ray, and the Johnson Family Zoo. Jeff Henderson, Daniel Thompson, FirstGlance Photography's Bill Ostroff, and others shot our author photos. Paul Benjamin, Rafael and Beverly Bejarano, Katrina Hill, Clare Kramer, Alex Langley, Travis Sr. and Lynda Langley, Sharon Manning, Marc Nadel, Ed O'Neil, Kaja Perina, Amy Ray, Eliot Sirota, Karl Southgate, Tim Stevens, and Michael Uslan deserve mention for reasons diverse and sometimes hard to explain. Alan "Sizzler" Kistler, a walking encyclopedia of comic book knowledge, helped a number of our writers find the right examples to help them make their points. Rebecca Manning Langley gets my greatest appreciation, adoration, respect, and love for being my superhero—my wife, best friend, colleague, managing partner, and co-founder of the firm.

Online databases can be precious resources helpful for pointing us toward the correct issues or episodes when we need to double-check the original material, and so we thank the many volunteer editors and other contributors at Comic

Vine, comics.org, WikiProject Comics, marvel.wikia.com, and more. Great guides to Daredevil online with their own thoughtful analyses include ManWithoutFear.com and TheOtherMurdockPapers.com, maintained respectively by Kuljit Mithra and Christine Hanefalk who both offered us direct assistance along the way. A Twitter army including James Monge, Chris Murrin, Brian Leahy, Jamie Walton, and so many have helped us check facts or field interest.

Legion of Leia founder Jenna Busch is a valuable editorial assistant and a fun person to have on the team. Thank you, Jenna, for discussing Daredevil with executive producer Steven S. DeKnight, along with so much more. Thank you, Steven, for that discussion. Jenna previously worked for Stan Lee, co-hosting "Cocktails with Stan" on YouTube, and they've remained close. She discussed this book with him, and the thoughts he shared then became the basis for his fantastic foreword. We thank Darren Passarello and Yuka Kobayashi for helping set that up, and we certainly thank the man born Stanley Lieber for the foreword itself—his second in this series! Our first multi-foreword author happens to be Stan "the Man" himself, and it is an honor.

Stan Lee also deserves credit for creating Daredevil with artist Bill Everett in the first place, aided by Jack "King" Kirby. Artist Wally Wood designed the definitive Daredevil costume. Gene Colan established the fluid motion that would influence Daredevil artists for years to come, including Klaus Janson, Michael Lark, Alex Maleev, David Mazzucchelli, Joe Quesada, John Romita, Jr., Tim Sale, Paola Rivera, Chris Samnee, and Bill Sienkiewicz. Writers Brian Michael Bendis, Ed Brubaker, D. G. Chichester, Gerry Conway, Karl Kesel, Kevin Smith, Mark Waid, and more have kept telling the tales. We particularly thank inustry pros Tony Isabella, Thomas Jane, David Mack, Ann Nocenti, Denny O'Neil, Mark Waid, Len Wein, and Marv Wolfman for speaking with us at different times, with special thanks to Annie for letting us include her interview about the villain Typhoid. Let's not forget the actors who have brought the Devil of Hell's Kitchen to life onscreen (Rex Smith, Ben Affleck, Charlie Cox), along with everyone else who works on their movies and shows. Anyone who knows much about Daredevil, though, knows it was Frank Miller's work as storyteller at different points in the 1980s that turned this already-troubled hero into the tormented soul worthy of elaborate psychological analysis today. So for making Matt Murdock more complex than ever before, we thank Frank.

Finally, we thank *you* for joining us in our descent into Hell's Kitchen as we try to know its guardian devil, "the Man without Fear."

Stan Lee and our editor Travis Langley share a laugh at a comic con.

THE DEVIL YOU KNOW

STAN LEE

The Fantastic Four had taken their fateful flight, the Avengers had assembled, the X-Men had started school, and Spider-Man had learned his hard lesson about power and responsibility. They all had problems. I wanted a new super-hero who had a different problem, a serious problem that would floor almost anybody else: Daredevil was blind. But I wanted to show that even somebody with that kind of a problem could find a way to work through it and succeed. He could be "the Man without Fear." And I'm happy to say, we received so many letters and calls from different charities for blind people, saying they thought it was great to have a blind superhero, so I'm glad we did it.

Matt Murdock's more of a loner than other superheroes. Even Spider-Man tried to join the Fantastic Four. I just couldn't see Daredevil as part of a gang. It occurred to me that having one hero who is a lawyer and has his power and gets involved was great. I thought that his blindness and the way he overcame it in fighting the villains were interesting enough without need-ing other characters. So he barely had a supporting cast—little more than Foggy and Karen for years, the same characters you see with him today on TV.

Frank Miller and other writers made Daredevil even more troubled than we did in the beginning. Did they make a mistake? No, I don't think so. The more troubled you make a character, the more interesting he gets to the readers, so I don't mind at all. Matt Murdock keeps going no matter how many troubles he has or how much he hurts. That's why he's a superhero, that's why he's the good guy, and that's why it doesn't matter how tough things are. He has something he wants to accomplish and he's going to accomplish it, no matter what. He thinks it's his destiny.

Can a superhero like Daredevil inspire real people? I would certainly hope so! I've received so many letters, as I say, from charities for the blind and even from people who say they don't see as well as they used to, and reading these stories just made them feel so good. I think he would inspire anyone because everybody has troubles. The most important thing someone can learn from Daredevil is that no matter what your difficulty is, you should try to overcome it and make something good out of your life—which we all should try to do whether impaired or not. A person definitely should just try to do the best he or she can and try to overcome any obstacle to whatever degree he or she can.

So sit back and marvel at *Daredevil Psychology: The Devil You Know* as these experts look at the Daredevil we know and, through him, maybe we can learn about a few things that hold true for us all.

Excelsior!

Pictured: Stan Lee with our own Jenna Busch.

STARRING. . .
DAREDEVIL

Creators: Stan Lee & Bill Everett.

Additional Design: Jack Kirby & Wally Wood.

Debut: *Daredevil* #1 (1964). "The Origin of Daredevil." Script: Stan Lee. Art: Bill Everett, Steve Ditko, & Sol Brodsky.

First Television Appearance: *Spider-Man and His Amazing Friends* (animated series), episode 3–4, "Attack of the Arachnoid" (October 8, 1983). Voiced by Frank Welker.

First Live Action Appearance: *The Trial of the Incredible Hulk* (1989 television movie). Played by Rex Smith.

First Theatrical Appearance: *Daredevil* (2003 motion picture). Played by Scott Terra (child), Ben Affleck (adult).

First Television Series: *Daredevil*, also called *Marvel's Daredevil* (and identified as such in our chapter notes to reduce confusion), beginning with episode 1–1, "Into the Ring" (April 10, 2015). Played by Skylar Gaertner (child), Charlie Cox (adult).

THE DEVIL YOU DON'T

TRAVIS LANGLEY

Who in Hell's Kitchen is Daredevil?

Daredevil differs from other superheroes in many ways, even aside from the obvious fact that in his usually secret identity, Matthew Murdock is a blind lawyer. He is the superhero whose superpowers are not visible to others: his superhumanly enhanced physical senses. Because his powers are sensory, observers aren't sure whether he has powers at all. This adds to his mystery, not only to the public and to his opponents but even to his heroic peers. When Stan Lee, Bill Everett, and company created this character, they wove together a unique combination of occupation, limitation, power, personality, and theme.

Occupation + limitation: Lawyer Matt Murdock cannot see. Justice is blind.

Limitation + superpower: The accident that blinds Matt enhances his other senses.

Superpower + personality: Supersenses let the fearless boy become a daredevil.

Personality + theme: The latter part of his superhero name inspires his costume's devil theme, which eventually ties back to another personality feature, his pervasive guilt.

His devil theme, in his fiery red costume with horns, is unusual for a superhero. Others who adopt Halloween themes incorporate animals that many people fear—a bat or spider, creepy perhaps but not plainly evil. Like them, Matt is driven by guilt over a parent's death,[1] and perhaps those frightening symbols suggest how they feel about themselves. Batman and Spider-Man feel guilty for things they haven't done with regard to random crime: Bruce Wayne as a child cannot stop a mugger from killing his parents, and Peter Parker in his teens chooses not to stop the burglar who later happens to murder Pete's Uncle Ben. Matt feels responsible for something he has done, if indirectly, that leads to a crime with nothing random about it: Matt's actions and his faith in his father "Battlin'" Jack Murdock inspire Jack to stand up to mobsters, to refuse to throw a boxing match, and for that the criminals kill him.[2] Like Batman and Spider-Man, Daredevil reaches into his own inner darkness to channel his pain into a mission that he hopes will keep others from suffering as he has. Whereas the truest friend Daredevil has among superheroes might be Spider-Man, he and Batman do not get along the few times they cross paths.[3] Even though people tend to prefer others who are similar to themselves, similarities might be why Marvel's "red Batman"[4] and the actual Dark Knight dislike each other if, at heart, they do not like themselves.

Like them, Daredevil feels that he is not a basically good person. Unlike them, though, he adorns himself with a symbol that represents evil in the minds of many—the supernatural figure who lures people into his domain through temptation and, the part perhaps more pertinent to Matt's mission, administers punishment to the wicked. Echoing the Lord of Hell, Matt Murdock punishes evil in the Hell's Kitchen neighborhood of New York. He also punishes himself while trying to make sure that what he does will serve justice. The judgment suggested by Matt's motif is about what's right or wrong deep inside each soul,[5] and it's something he has learned as part of ethical and religious principles that value forgiveness, too.[6]

Among superheroes and to the people in his life, he is the devil you don't know. Out of all major Marvel heroes, Daredevil may be the one least ready to team up with others and the one least prone to divulge secrets. Even when he works with other heroes, he tends to be the least forthcoming with information about himself.[7] As Matt, he can be distant in his personal life as well. In the *Daredevil* comic book's early years, the ongoing supporting cast consisted of Matt's law partner Foggy Nelson and their secretary Karen Page. At times in Daredevil's history, the list has consisted only of Foggy.

Every aspect of the unique combination that Lee, Everett, and colleagues stirred together in Daredevil can be off-putting, distancing him from others as both Daredevil and Matt.

Occupation: Negative attitudes toward lawyers are common—hence, the proliferation of disparaging lawyer jokes.[8]

Limitation: Disability can be stigmatizing and can lead to stereotyping.[9] Daredevil's particular disability, despite his many advantages, keeps him from knowing details as basic as color.

Superpower: People can be wary of those with insight or knowledge they themselves do not have (e.g., anti-intellectualism[10]).

Personality: Prioritizing life goals over short-term interaction and agonizing over guilt are but two of the many traits that distance him from others.[11]

Theme: Not everyone wants to get friendly with the guy in the scary costume, the one that evokes associations with judgment and damnation.[12]

Matt Murdock is not a devil, though. The character is a man. So let's look past the disguise. Like him, let's try to perceive more than eyes can reveal. To understand "the Man without Fear," the people around us, and maybe ourselves, too, let's see without seeing.

Let's dare.

> *"We are each our own devil . . ."*
> —playwright Oscar Wilde[13]

> *"Just sit back and take this in. Ya might learn something."*
> —Stick[14]

NOTES

1. *Amazing Fantasy* #15 (1962); *Detective Comics* #33 (1939); *Daredevil* #1 (1964).
2. *Daredevil* #1 (1964); *Daredevil: Battlin' Jack Murdock* #3–4 (2007); *Daredevil: The Man without Fear* #1 (1993).
3. *Daredevil and Batman* (1997); *Batman/Daredevil* (2000).
4. *Daredevil* #24 (2013).
5. Matthew 6: 12-15.
6. First mentioned in *Daredevil* #119 (1975), the personal importance of Matt Murdock's Catholic faith would feature more overtly in later comics such as "Born Again" *Daredevil* #227–231 (1986) and "Guardian Devil" *Daredevil* #1–8 (1998–1999); the motion picture *Daredevil* (2003); and *Marvel's Daredevil,* starting with episo de 1–1, "Into the Ring" (April 10, 2015). See Judge (2014); Miner (2015).
7. *The Defenders* #1 (2017); *Marvel's The Defenders*, episode 1–4, "Royal Dragon" (August 18, 2017).
8. Hodben & Olson (1994).
9. Lalvani (2015); Trani et al. (2016).
10. Bosson et al. (2012); Cobrinik et al. (1953); Dixon (2015); Juvonen & Murdock (1993); Kerr (1954); Marques et al. (2017); May (1955); Rentzsch et al. (2011); Shaffer et al (1977); Thompson (1955).
11. As previously noted in Langley (2017).
12. Dorella (2010).
13. Wilde (1883/2007), p. 479.
14. *Daredevil* #188 (1982).

THE PUBLISHER:
IT'S ALL MARVEL

Daredevil and related Marvel Universe characters originate in publications from Marvel Comics. The company has undergone several name changes during its history.

Timely Publications: Founded in 1939, soon renamed **Timely Comics.**

Atlas Comics: New company name starting in 1951.

Marvel Comics: Rebranded in summer, 1961. Official company name has been **Marvel Publishing**, **Marvel Comics Group**, and **Marvel Worldwide**.

Parent Company: Marvel Enterprises, then **Marvel Entertainment** (part of **The Walt Disney Company** as of 2009).

Location: New York, NY.

Because Marvel published most of the comics cited herein, references will identify a comic book's publisher only for the few instances in which an outside company (such as DC Comics or Lev Gleason Publications) published the work.

Marvel's Daredevil is unrelated to a Lev Gleason Publications superhero also called Daredevil, created by Jack Binder for *Silver Streak Comics* #6 (1940) and revised by Jack Cole in #7 (1941). The Lev Gleason character is now in the public domain.

Marvel Comics has reset *Daredevil*'s numbering repeatedly, so the comic book series has had #1 issues published in 1964, 1998, 2011, 2014, and 2015. Even though fans assign volume numbers, Marvel typically does not. Publication dates therefore indicate story order better than issue numbers do.

I

SUMMONS

"Speak of the devil and he shall appear."
—*idiom*

SUMMONING THE DAREDEVIL

Summons *(noun)*. 1. A writ ordering an individual to appear in court. 2. A request, demand, or calling.

The most famous studies in psychology have often looked at what brings out the worst in people: When will good people follow evil commands, join in cruelty initiated by others, turn vicious on their own, blame victims for their distress, or merely stand by, doing nothing, while innocents suffer?[1] And when do the victims lose all hope?[2] After spending much of his career looking at how inescapable misery can lead to learned helplessness and depression, one experimental psychologist said that psychologists need to do more to study the better side of human nature, to find strengths and virtues in the midst of weaknesses and failings—and so began *positive psychology*.[3]

Another prominent researcher, a social psychologist made famous by his prison simulation study that went wrong,[4] spent more than thirty years trying to understand the factors that lead good people to commit acts of evil. He named this transformation *the Lucifer effect* "after God's favorite angel, Lucifer, who fell from grace and ultimately became Satan."[5] Like the one who founded positive psychology, though, this social psychologist then turned his attention to the better side of human nature, too. He wanted to understand heroism, to learn where it comes from as well.[6] When some might take the evil turn or tolerate evil in others, what about the individuals in those same dark places who instead dare to try to do right?

If an angel can fall, can a devil rise? How does a flawed and imperfect human being who carries the potential for evil answer a higher calling, a summons for the hero who's in there, too?

—T.L.

NOTES

1. e.g., Bandura (1962); Darley & Latané (1970); Lerner (1970); Milgram (1963); Zimbardo (1971).
2. e.g., Seligman (1972).
3. Seligman (1998).
4. Zimbardo (1971).
5. Zimbardo (n.d.).
6. Hero Construction Company (2015).

CHAPTER 1

LEARNING TO SEE THE HERO YOU ARE: POSTTRAUMATIC GROWTH AFTER PHYSICAL INJURY

JANINA SCARLET & TRAVIS ADAMS

> *"Just as our bodies get stronger when we push ourselves*
> *physically, our personal strengths also develop*
> *when we challenge ourselves psychologically."*
> —morality researcher Ronnie Janoff-Bulman[1]

> *"What does it mean to be a hero?*
> *Look in the mirror and you'll know."*
> —Karen Page[2]

People often do not fully understand their own abilities. Sometimes a realization of our own ignorance occurs following a traumatic event, which can scar people mentally or physically. Physical injury because of an accident can sometimes lead to a long-term disability, such as a loss of movement or a visual impairment. Some people can develop mental health disorders and other struggles due to their loss of function. Other people, such as Matthew Murdock, might display resilience and posttraumatic growth, finding purpose in life and growing as a human or even a superhuman. Which individuals develop mental health disorders after a significant loss of function, and who follows a path of posttraumatic growth? Does Daredevil fit either pattern, and it is possible for him to vacillate between both?

PSYCHOLOGICAL DISTRESS AFTER IMPAIRMENT

Not only do accidental injuries tend to be the leading causes of death among children, they are also the leading cause of disabilities for them as well.[3] Children who experience trauma such as being hit by a truck (as young Matt is while saving an elderly man)[4] or impairment in functioning (which Matt experiences when he loses his eyesight as a result of the accident) might develop posttraumatic stress disorder (PTSD), anxiety, or depression, whether their impairment is temporary or (like Matt's) permanent.[5] About one-fifth of children meet the criteria for PTSD after an injury brought on by an accident, and another one-fourth might also meet partial criteria for the condition. Common PTSD symptoms might include flashbacks, nightmares, avoidance of trauma reminders, mood changes, and *hypervigilance* (excessive alertness to danger).[6] Following Matt's exposure to the truck's radioactive waste, he develops heightened senses and becomes hyperaware of his surroundings. This *hypersensitivity* is so overwhelming to him that he wishes he could die. It is only after his training with Stick, a blind martial artist, that Matt is able to focus his senses, eventually allowing him to become Daredevil.[7]

Children who suffer accidental injury might also experience anxiety and depression. Approximately 30 percent of people with persistent physical disability, such as visual impairment, might experience depression, panic attacks or panic disorder, *agoraphobia* (extreme, unrealistic fear of being far away from a safe location or person), or *generalized anxiety disorder* (overwhelming, uncontrollable worry about a number of different situations).[8] These symptoms might appear months after the initial injury.[9] At one point, Matt speaks to his client, Aaron, a teenager who loses his ability to walk, about his experiences. Matt informs Aaron that he will have many people, including doctors, family members, and therapists, telling him to stay positive. Aaron shares that after his injury, he felt angry at everyone and wanted his old life back.[10]

In some situations, the child's risk of developing a mental health disorder after an accidental injury or trauma can increase. The biggest contributors to depression in people with physical disabilities, specifically those with visual impairments, appear to be low levels of socialization and their perceived levels of disability.[11] As a child, Matt does not talk or play with other kids, focusing on his studies and telling himself, "I've got to be the son he wants me to be."[12] Another boy gives Matt the nickname "daredevil," not to recognize him for being a risk-taker but to mock him for isolating himself from others and focusing on his studies instead of joining the neighborhood kids in play.[13] Individuals like Matt who have less frequent social interactions with others are likely to have higher levels of depression compared to individuals with higher levels of socialization.[14] Following his accident, Matt spends more time alone, believing himself to be useless while feeling both furious and tearful.[15]

In addition, levels of *hope* (as may be indicated by an individual's sense of determination and planning to meet one's goals) also contribute to the degree of depression one might experience.[16] People with lower levels of hope (those who are less determined to meet their goals, for example) are more likely to experience depression than those with a higher degree of hope.[17] After his father's death, Matt spends more time training at the gym.[18] He pushes himself, adapting to his newfound abilities, realizing that he can make a difference. Through this experience, his depressive symptoms abate as he finds hope and meaning.[19]

Individuals with visual impairments are prone to have fewer friends, go on fewer dates, and experience greater loneliness, compared to fully sighted individuals. Even though many struggle with lower self-esteem and might demonstrate poorer school achievement,[20] this is certainly not the case for all. It isn't for Matt Murdock, who promises his father that he will focus on school and become a doctor or a lawyer.[21] Matt receives straight A's in school,[22] becomes valedictorian,[23] and eventually opens Nelson & Murdock, a legal firm with his college roommate Foggy, fulfilling his promise to his dad.[24]

HOPE AND HEALING

Immediately after trauma, most people will display some symptoms of posttraumatic stress but not the full disorder.[25] Although approximately 20–25 percent of individuals exposed to trauma might develop PTSD or some symptoms of PTSD later, 75 percent recover naturally over time. Some who experience a loss of function due to an accident might actually develop *posttraumatic growth* (PTG, a new sense of meaning and growth after exposure to a traumatic event).[26] Among the most notable factors contributing to the development of posttraumatic growth are socialization, hope, self-efficacy, locus of control, and meaning making.[27]

BECOMING ABLE BY
CHANGING MALADAPTIVE THOUGHTS

Changes in people's ability can also affect how they perceive themselves.[28] For example, after a traumatic event people might perceive themselves to be "not good enough," "broken," or "incapable."[29] Throughout Matt's life he experiences many instances in which he feels that he is letting others down. When he is struggling, Matt tells himself that he is "useless,"[30] that he "can't help anybody,"[31] and that he is "crazy," "stupid," or "reckless."[32] These thoughts are examples of unhelpful beliefs.[33]

Maladaptive beliefs are especially problematic because they keep people "stuck," preventing them from recovering. In order to adjust these maladaptive thoughts, therapists who specialize in treating people with PTSD, depression, or anxiety might teach the individuals to challenge their beliefs by examining the evidence for and against each of these thoughts.[34] Angry over his losses, Matt struggles with his sense of purpose, not being able to find relief even at his favorite location, the gym. When Stick finds Matt, he tells the boy to "quit feeling sorry" for himself.[35] With Stick's guidance, Matt begins training in acrobatics and martial arts, allowing him to change his beliefs and see that he is capable.[36] Challenging maladaptive beliefs in this way can help individuals with disabilities to reduce shame and stigma some of them may feel about their condition, as well as to engage in helpful prosocial behaviors. In addition, such cognitive changes can also lead to decreased depression, decreased trauma symptoms, and improved sense of self.[37]

Just as low levels of hope can contribute to higher levels of depression, higher levels of hope can lead to lower levels of depression and increase the likelihood of PTG.[38] At one point in the comic book series, Karen asks Matt to promise that he will never quit being Daredevil.[39] After the assassin Bullseye murders her,[40] Matt starts drinking, fighting, and considering suicide. However, the memory of his promise to her and the realization of the impact he has on the people of Hell's Kitchen cause Matt to reconsider his behaviors and reclaim his role as Daredevil.[41]

Related to hope, *self-efficacy* is the belief in one's own ability to succeed. It is also related to posttraumatic growth after an exposure to accidental injury.[42] Higher levels of self-efficacy are associated with improved task completion as well as protective factors against depression. Inspired by his son Matt's strength, Jack Murdock believes himself to be capable and wins a fight that he seemed unlikely to win.[43] A sense of self-efficacy appears to also be related to a person's *locus of control*,[44] the general expectation that events in life are driven by the individual's own behavior (*internal*) or caused by things beyond that person's control, such as luck, fate, or other people (*external*). People with an internal locus of control and a strong sense of self-efficacy are more likely to experience posttraumatic growth after a trauma.[45]

Finally, by finding a sense of purpose, people who have undergone traumatic events might also be able to experience posttraumatic growth. Through posttraumatic growth, these people might be able to make sense of the event and use their struggles to find a path for healing. Matt Murdock, using his heightened senses, actively makes a difference in others' lives, adapting to his disability and turning it into an extraordinary ability.[46] Utilizing their experiences, individuals who have experienced trauma may regain a sense of ability, build relationships with others, find new possibilities in life, and increase personal strength.[47]

DEFENDERS WHO
STICK TOGETHER HEAL TOGETHER

By the time the Defenders find one another, each has endured various traumatic experiences, events that they have used to grow and pursue a life of service, helping those in need. Hunted by villains (the Hand on television, Diamondback in the comics[48]), Daredevil joins Jessica Jones, Luke Cage, and Iron Fist. Together they decide to fight together in an attempt to defend their city.[49] In realizing that together they can make a difference and choosing to take action to make things better, these superheroes are utilizing an internal locus of control.[50]

THE BLIND SIDE OF TRAUMA

Following traumatic events, a person's worldview can shift.[51] In Matt Murdock's case, he loses his sight but gains an ability to save others despite his physical injury.[52] Through hope, social support, and resiliency, people can significantly boost their adaptability to change and make an impact on the world in which they live.[53] Matt follows his passion for helping people despite this visual impairment.[54] By focusing on his abilities instead of his perceived disability, Matt utilizes both self-efficacy and internal locus of control. Both of these factors play a role in helping individuals establish a sense of post-traumatic growth.[55] With the aid and support of his friends, Matt not only overcomes many obstacles, but grows from his traumatic experience.[56]

NOTES

1. Janoff-Bulman (2004), p. 31.
2. *Marvel's Daredevil*, episode 2–13, "A Cold Day in Hell's Kitchen" (March 18, 2016).
3. Le Brocque et al. (2009).
4. *Daredevil* #1 (1964).
5. De Vries at al. (1999); Ehlers et al. (1998); Holmes et al. (2014); Jackson et al. (1998).
6. Le Brocque et al. (2009).
7. *Daredevil: The Man without Fear* #1 (1993).
8. Bryant et al. (2010); Holmes et al. (2014); Jackson et al. (1998).
9. Bryant et al. (2010); Holmes et al. (2014); Jackson et al. (1998).
10. *Marvel's The Defenders*, episode 1–1, "The H Word" (August 18, 2017).
11. Jackson et al. (1998).
12. *Daredevil* #1 (1964).
13. *Daredevil* #1 (1964); *Daredevil* #28 (2013).
14. Jackson et al. (1998).
15. *Daredevil: The Man without Fear* #1 (1993).
16. Jackson et al. (1998).
17. Jackson et al. (1998).
18. *Daredevil* #1 (1964).
19. *Daredevil: The Man without Fear* #2 (1993).
20. Huurre & Aro (1998).
21. *Daredevil* #164 (1980).
22. *Marvel's Daredevil*, episode 1–2, "Cut Man" (April 10, 2015).
23. *Daredevil* #1 (1964).
24. *Marvel's* Daredevil, episode 1–1, "Into the Ring" (April 10, 2015).
25. Vaiva et al. (2003).
26. Collicutt & Linley (2006); Pollard & Kennedy (2007).
27. Batool & Nawaz (2016); Byrne (2012); Elliott et al. (1991); Le Brocque et al. (2009).
28. Levins et al. (2004).
29. Bogart et al. (2017); McCormack & Thomson (2017).
30. *Daredevil: The Man without Fear* #1 (1993).
31. *Daredevil: Reborn* #1 (2011).
32. *Daredevil: Reborn* #3 (2011).
33. McCormack & Thomson (2017); Wheatley et al. (2007).
34. Blanchard et al. (2003).
35. *Daredevil: The Man without Fear* #1 (1993).
36. *Daredevil: The Man without Fear* #1 (1993).
37. Blanchard et al. (2003); McCormack & Thomson (2017); Wheatley et al. (2007).
38. Le Brocque et al. (2009); Elliott et al. (1991).
39. *Daredevil* #6 (1999).
40. *Daredevil* #5 (1999).
41. *Daredevil* #6 (1999).
42. Batool & Nawaz (2016).
43. *Daredevil: Battlin' Jack Murdock* #4 (2007).
44. Byrne (2012).
45. Byrne (2012).
46. Collier (2016).
47. Bryant et al. (2010).

48. *Marvel's The Defenders*, episode 1–3, "Worst Behavior" (August 18, 2017); *The Defenders* #1–2 (2017).

49. *Marvel's The Defenders*, episode 1–5, "Take Shelter" (August 18, 2017).

50. *Marvel's The Defenders*, episode 1–4, "Royal Dragon" (August 18, 2017).

51. *Marvel's Daredevil*, episode 1–13, "Daredevil" (April 10, 2015).

52. *Daredevil* #1 (1964).

53. Batool & Nawaz (2016); Byrne (2012).

54. *Marvel's The Defenders*, episode 1–1, "The H Word" (August 18, 2017).

55. Batool & Nawaz (2016); Byrne (2012).

56. *Marvel's The Defenders*, episode 1–8, "The Defenders" (August 18, 2017).

CHAPTER 2

THE TRUTH ABOUT THE DARE: WHO SEEKS THRILLS AND CHILLS?

TRAVIS LANGLEY & CHRISTINE HANEFALK

"Daredevil? Sounds like he's gonna jump Snake River Canyon on his rocket cycle."
—Foggy Nelson, comparing Daredevil to Evel Knievel[1]

"I did everything by the seat of my pants. That's why I got hurt so much."
—motorcycle daredevil Evel Knievel[2]

Superheroes tend to be named for their abilities (Spider-Man, Storm) or for how they look to others, whether that means physical appearance (the Hulk, the Thing), symbol or motif (Batman, Captain America), or reactions they inspire (Wonder Woman, Captain Marvel). Unusual among his peers, though, Daredevil derives his superhero moniker from a psychological trait—for being a bold, death-defying daredevil, "the Man without Fear."[3] While his costume's devil horns and fiery red color underline the *devil* part of the word, it is the name that inspires the costume and not the other way around, and that word begins with *dare*.

Even though other kids tease young Matt Murdock by calling him "Daredevil" as a taunt when he won't come out and play, the irony is that he is already a daredevil at heart. He struggles to suppress his inherent nature in order to concentrate on his studies to satisfy the father he admires.[4] As a superhero, he seeks danger, but why? Why does anyone engage in death-defying activities, whether recreational or occupational?[5] What kind of person deliberately enters dangerous situations and engages in risky behavior, whether that means jumping a motorcycle over a dozen buses, rushing into a burning building, or swinging through a city in search of criminals to punch? Who dares?

SENSATION SEEKING

The moment that reveals young Matt to be a daredevil is also the moment that gives him the power to become Daredevil.[6] As the adult lawyer whom Matt becomes might put it, an accident gives him the *means* to become a superhero and his father's murder provides the *motive*.[7] Neither, though, adequately explains why he puts himself and those around him in so much danger. The manner in which he pursues vigilante justice directly violates the rules that govern his work as a lawyer. When he worries that administering justice with his fists while wearing a mask makes him a hypocrite, he's experiencing *cognitive dissonance*, the anxiety that arises when we realize our actions and attitudes contradict each other.[8] A so-called "adrenaline junkie," though, might not feel as bothered by such a source of distress and could conceivably find some kind of reinforcement from living on a personal edge.[9]

At times, Daredevil shows sheer joy from simply running and jumping around the city for no other reason than that it feels good.[10] Matt thrives on risk, and that "kick" may become something of an addiction. Is the word *addiction* appropriate for behaviors that do not involve addictive substances? Neurologically, it might be. The nervous system reacts similarly, regardless of whether the source of adrenaline elevation is a substance or an activity. For example, a study on whether "adrenaline junkies" truly show defining features of addiction indicated that periods of abstaining from rock climbing would cause the most experienced rock climbers to show signs of withdrawal, such as *anhedonia* (inability to experience pleasure) or strong cravings to climb again. Matt has quit being Daredevil more than once, and yet he quickly feels the itch and goes right back to that lifestyle.[11]

Sensation seeking, the need for variety or excitement and the accompanying willingness "to take physical and social risks for the sake of such experiences,"[12] was described as a distinct trait by psychologist Marvin Zuckerman. He measured it in people with a test first published the year that Daredevil debuted[13] and then repeatedly revised as he and his colleagues learned more about it.[14] Elaborating on the work of previous psychologists who'd listed excitement and stimulation among the many psychological needs that might drive people,[15] Zuckerman sought to understand people who, like himself, yearn for arousal beyond the levels that most people find optimal. Trying to understand himself, he looked at why some people sought out the dares that others would prefer to avoid. Like superhero Matt Murdock, psychologist Marvin Zuckerman pondered his own risky behavior.

Not all sensation-seekers are active risk-takers. While all kinds of sensation-seekers accept or underestimate the risks associated with the experiences they want, some simply view risk as the price to pay for a desired experience, rather than something to be maximized for its own sake.[16] Most of Matt's endeavors as Daredevil seem directed toward those physical, high-risk activities associated with the comic book vigilante lifestyle—which are even riskier for him, given that he has neither visible superpowers nor sci-fi gadgets to fall back on if something goes wrong during dangerous activities, such as swinging through the city from one skyscraper to another.

Later versions of the Sensation Seeking Scale therefore included subscales in order to paint a more detailed picture by identifying different kinds of sensations sought.[17] How might Matt Murdock score in all four subcategories, not just the ones that involve physical risk?

THRILL AND ADVENTURE SEEKING

Any daredevil activities (which include superheroing) by definition include adventuring. "Feel your heartbeat racing? That's what life's about. That's what you helped teach me—diving into lakes, running off rooftops," Daredevil tells Elektra after discovering that she has found peace atop a mountain after coming back from the dead. "Life's not peace on a mountain or in a grave! It's passion—vitality!"[18] *The thrill- and adventure-seeker* is the sensation-seeker most out for the so-called adrenaline rush. Aficionados of extreme sports and other physically risky behaviors do incur physical injuries and some die while doing the dangerous things they love,[19] though perhaps less often than some might assume because these enthusiasts may gain knowledge and skills along the way that can help them reduce the risks.[20] Because reducing the risk can reduce the rush, though, some escalate the risks as they "take it to the next level."[21] This is the form of sensation seeking that defines a *daredevil*.

Counterintuitive as it might seem, the kind of sensation seeking that psychologist Marvin Zuckerman wrote about can potentially help a person manage sensory overload. Because arousal reduces the number of details that reach conscious attention, an exciting activity can help the person focus on priorities,[22] especially if that individual has the relevant skills or personality.

EXPERIENCE SEEKING

Some sensation-seekers seek aesthetics over adrenaline. They like variety.[23] Matt probably would score somewhat above average on *experience seeking*. Individuals of the experience-seeking type wish to engage in activities that stimulate the mind and the senses more so than the body. This subcategory reflects a general attraction to travel, art, food, and unusual people. The fact that Matt at one time maintained a sculpture room in his brownstone apartment shows that he has an appreciation for sculpted art strong enough that he devotes a meaningful part of his home to it,[24] and yet the fact that characters rarely mention this room suggests that the interest does not extend to preoccupation.

DISINHIBITION

Overcontrolled individuals can carry considerable hostility within themselves.[25] Crime-fighting is Daredevil's outlet for his hostility. When fatigued and stressed to the point of breaking, he can lose control, and yet he pushes himself to regain it.[26] People who score high on the *disinhibition* subscale are more likely to gamble, abuse alcohol and other drugs, and engage in unsafe sex in the course of losing their inhibitions. While some might point to Matt Murdock's relatively long list of past loves, his sexual behavior is more that of a serial monogamist than of someone who engages in high-risk sex for its own sake. He has never willingly taken narcotics and rarely drinks.[27] Much as he still continues to love thrills and adventure,[28] aspects of those that he and Elektra share in their younger days leave a sour taste because he believes in boundaries. He will walk the edge, he

THE DEVIL'S BREW

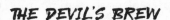

Despite all the booze that flows in Daredevil's TV series,[29] Matt Murdock in the comics has never been much of a drinker.[30] "I don't drink," he thinks one morning when puzzled by a hangover-like feeling, "I didn't drink last night." Even when he spends Christmas evening in a bar chatting with Mephisto, the devil in disguise teases Daredevil for sitting alone and simply nursing one beer.[31] Across the world and throughout history, people have used alcohol and many other substances in order to reduce sensory, cognitive, and emotional experience, to feel *less*,[32] so why won't the man whose hypersenses threaten to engulf him at any time indulge?

When alcohol reduces central nervous system activity, the same *CNS depressant* effect that can make people feel comfortably numb also impairs self-regulation.[33] Due to Daredevil's dread of losing *behavioral self-control* (management of his own actions), he might avoid alcohol because he does not want to impair his *perceptual self-control* (management of his own senses). An individual bombarded by stimuli may prefer to cling to the ability to regulate the vast volume of sensory signals coming at him or her from every direction. Weakening some signals does little good if they all flood into perception. So Matt might feel the indulgence in alcohol would not be worth the risk.

will run it, but he does not want to throw all caution to the wind and fall into chaos.

Donning a mask can be liberating.[34] Under different circumstances and for different people, anonymity and other sources of disinhibition might unleash the very worst of what they normally hide about themselves.[35] Behind the anonymity of the internet, for example, individuals who are nice to others in their everyday lives can turn into trolls while others too shy

PERSONALITY FACTORS AND SENSATION SEEKING

Sensation seeking and certain other well-known traits appear together in people at rates higher than chance (a *positive correlation*). For example, high sensation-seekers show a greater tendency to be extraverts than introverts.[36] *Extraverson* is a set of traits that includes assertiveness, boldness, boredom when alone, external focus, risk taking, and outgoing behavior, as opposed to *introversion* at the opposite end of the same dimension.[37] Few people are completely extraverted or introverted, even those strongly inclined toward one or the other. Despite some introverted traits such as comfort at being alone, Matt Murdock is certainly an assertive and bold risk-taker.[38] Extraverts also show a greater tendency toward fearlessness, and he is the "Man without Fear."[39]

Sensation seeking correlates positively with *psychoticism*, an ominous-sounding and inaccurately named personality factor.[40] Traits in the psychoticism set include aggressiveness, antisociality, creativity, egocentrism, impulsivity, to stand up to bullies IRL might fight for others through their avatars. Anonymity can lessen inhibitions not only by lowering the likelihood of consequences for actions but also because it can produce *deindividuation*, reduced awareness of oneself as an individual. A mask might not deindividuate when it's part of a role or identity the individual takes personally, and Matt cares how the public views Daredevil. Still, that mask lets him unleash the daredevil side he long ago learned to hide.

tough-mindedness, rigidity, and lack of cooperation.[41] The number of traits involving creativity in the personality factor inspired the psychologist who first identified the factor to name it psychoticism because he believed that creativity and madness go hand in hand, and yet empirical evidence does not support the assumption that these traits predict clinical *psychosis*—severe detachment from reality. Because psychosis does not appear to tie these traits together, other researchers call the factor by other names (such as *impulse control* for the low-psychoticism end of the dimension[42]), while still others suggest that its traits actually belong to other dimensions entirely. Whatever it means, Daredevil does show many of these traits, particularly during times of stress—for example, when his behavior takes a violent turn and he acts rashly and recklessly after an enemy, Mister Fear, releases a toxin that causes Matt's wife Milla to suffer a deteriorating mental state.[43] The correlation between sensation seeking and psychoticism may depend on the individual's particular type of sensation-seeking behavior.[44]

BOREDOM SUSCEPTIBILITY

Even a person who easily grows bored might not be motivated by tedium to seek change for its own sake or to take great risks simply to alleviate boredom. If escaping tedium is not a major motivator in a person's life and if it does not drive the individual to seek sensations much more so than others might, then boredom alone does not make that person score high in sensation seeking. The vigilante lifestyle certainly offers such a change of pace for Matt that he appears to have little additional need for a constant and varying flow of new external stimuli in the form of social interactions or entertainment. Actively seeking something out because it is fun and mentally rewarding is different from constantly keeping busy to stave off boredom. Matt maintains consistency in many areas of his life, such as when he keeps moving into similar brownstones[45] after losing his homes to eviction or detonation.[46] When he seeks change, he does so with purpose. If Matt Murdock had a high degree of *boredom susceptibility*, he would probably not keep the same steady friend throughout his adult life, show the same level of engaged and patient interest in both his clients and the people who live in his neighborhood, or patrol the same few blocks nearly every night. Individuals who score high on boredom susceptibility have little patience for monotonous routines and familiar surroundings.

TRUTH AND DARE

Considerable evidence suggests that the greatest sensation-seekers are biologically and hereditarily predisposed toward their pursuit of excitement.[47] In Matt's case, this might stem from the fact that both of his parents are big risk-takers: his father, the boxer whose violent lifestyle and eventual defiance of mobsters gets him killed, and his mother, the nun who repeatedly gets herself arrested for activist exploits. One raises him and the other does not, and yet all three chase trouble.

As an attorney, Matt Murdock is a gifted speaker, with charisma, analytical ability, and knowledge of the law, capable of achieving great things and possibly changing the law or society itself as one of the leading legal minds of his time. Though he accomplishes much as an attorney, his other life as Daredevil causes him to miss court and take on fewer cases, often inconveniencing others as he becomes the unreliable half of Nelson & Murdock, Attorneys at Law. So why charge out into the night to beat up criminals at odd hours? Anger toward criminals drives him, to be sure, as does his great empathy. Empathy can keep a person from ignoring those in need,[48] and he hears everyone. He cannot rest. He cannot ignore the city's sirens and the victims' outcries. Anger and empathy are still not the full story, though. His daring activities energize him. Guilt-prone Matt Murdock worries about the accusation his law partner sometimes hurls his way—that he might not be doing what he does solely for the "right" reasons, that he might be getting such a kick out of it that seeking the kick becomes an unhealthy addiction.[49]

> "I thought I was bulletproof or Superman there for a while.
> I thought I'd never run out of nerve. Never."
> —Evel Knievel[50]

> "Okay, then let's say I'm the new Evel Knievel."
> —Foggy Nelson[51]

NOTES

1. *Marvel's Daredevil*, episode 1–13, "Daredevil" (April 10, 2015).
2. Quoted by Barker (2004/2008), p. 56.
3. Starting with *Daredevil* #1 (1964).
4. *Daredevil: The Man without Fear* #1 (1993); *Daredevil* #28 (2013).
5. Yar (2015).
6. *Daredevil* #1 (1964).
7. *Daredevil* #164 (1980).
8. Festinger (1957).
9. Delahunt & Mellsop (1987).
10. *Daredevil* #170 (1981); *Daredevil* #178 (1982).
11. e.g., *Daredevil* #49 (1969); *Marvel's The Defenders*, season 1 (August 18, 2017).
12. Zuckerman (1979), p. 10.
13. Zuckerman et al. (1964).
14. Zuckerman (1971); Zuckerman & Link (1968); Zuckerman et al. (1978).
15. Fromm (1941); Murray (1938).
16. Zuckerman (1994).
17. Zuckerman (1971).
18. *Daredevil* #325 (1994).
19. Loria (2016).
20. Wishart et al. (2017).
21. Butler (2017).
22. Easterbrook (1959); Zajonc (1965).
23. Farley (1971).
24. *Daredevil* #206 (1984).
25. White (1975).
26. *Daredevil* #228 (1986).
27. *Daredevil* #227 (1986).
28. *Daredevil: The Man without Fear* #2–3 (1993); *Marvel's Daredevil*, episode 2–5, "Kimbaku" (all March 18, 2016).
29. e.g., *Marvel's Daredevil*, episodes 1–9, "Speak of the Devil," 1–10, "Nelson v. Murdock," 1–11, "The Path of the Righteous" (all April 10, 2015); 2–1 "Bang," 2–4, "Penny and Dime," 2–5, "Kimbaku" (all March 18, 2016).
30. As noted by Hanefalk (2016).
31. *Daredevil* #266 (1989).
32. Jung (2000).
33. Dagher (2014).
34. Langley (2012) elaborates on ideas shared in this paragraph in chapter 4, "Why the Mask?"
35. Johnson & Downing (1979).
36. Eysenck & Zuckerman (1978).
37. Loo (1979).
38. *Marvel Knights* #15 (2001).
39. Called that from *Daredevil* #1 (1964) onward.
40. Eysenck & Zuckerman (1978).
41. Eysenck (1992); Heath & Martin (1990); Howarth (1986).
42. Costa & McCrae (1992).
43. *Daredevil* #100 (2007) through #105 (2008).
44. Glicksohn & Abulafia (1998).

45. *Daredevil* #93 (2007).
46. *Daredevil* #227–228 (1986).
47. e.g., Fulker et al. (1980).
48. Abbot & Cameron (2014).
49. Heirene et al. (2016).
50. Quoted by Barker (2004/2008), p. 260.
51. *Daredevil* #120 (1975).

CHAPTER 3

MORE THAN A MONTAGE: DEVELOPMENT OF A SUPER IDENTITY

JEREMY JOHNSON, LISA JOHNSON, & ERIN CURRIE

"Identity provides . . . a sense of integration of the self . . . the confluence of physical, cognitive and social aspects of development allow one to construct this identity."
—psychologist Jerome Dusek[1]

"Promise me you'll be the somebody I never could. Make me proud, son."
—"Battlin' " Jack Murdock[2]

When it comes to understanding superheroes, it is tempting to be satisfied with *superpowers + motivation to do good = superhero*. However, the journey is more important than the destination, and there is more to superhero development than a fighting skills–training montage. The process of developing a super identity and the underlying superpowers is not easy.

It often involves a fair amount of frustration and struggle as society challenges the development of the superhero's identity and villains challenge the hero's skill development. The fields of educational psychology and identity development cast light on the process of Matt Murdock's development, his development into Daredevil, and how individual superheroes develop into a team.

SUPER SKILLS DEVELOPMENT

Children do not need to be taught how to see, hear, touch, taste, or smell. Unless there is an injury to—or lack of in-utero development of—the sensory organs and certain brain regions that infants automatically use their senses to learn about their world.[3] Just like other children, as a child Matt doesn't need to be taught to use his normal human sensory capabilities. Later, after his exposure to the radioactive materials, his super sensory capabilities also developed without any initial effort on his part.[4]

Similarly, infants automatically move their bodies in ways that we interpret as hitting and kicking, even head-butting. These rudimentary reflexive actions eventually become deliberate and refined skills and abilities through simple trial-and-error interactions with their environment.[5] Matt is no different as a child. He is able to hit, kick, and jump as needed without combat training.[6] However, developmental theorists who emphasize social learning would point out that observation of another's skilled behavior is enough to provide guidance that a child can use to improve his or her skills. In that way, Matt may have learned some fighting skills through watching his father, Jack, in the boxing ring.[7]

As the skills and abilities needed to be effective in our environment become more advanced, some active instruction is necessary. Even though Matt has super senses after the accident, it takes his mentor Stick to teach him how to use them effectively. Increasingly abstract and complex skills have evolved in human society, as they have been passed down over time and refined by smaller cultural communities, based on their specific needs. The people in the community who have mastered the skills teach them to the next generation.[8] So Stick, being blind and having already developed his other senses, teaches Matt to understand and use the stimuli that only they can sense. He also teaches him fighting skills that use his super senses.

There are two levels of development that must be attended to when one is teaching the next generation the advanced skills of the culture. First, the *actual developmental level* is the level at which one has mastered the skills that are necessary to accomplish a task without any help. Prior to the accident, Matt had already been taught the necessary sensory skills to autonomously manage his environment at the level expected for a child his age. Losing his sight and gaining super senses changes the skills he needs to manage his environment, and he needs help to learn these new skills.

Second is *proximal developmental level,* which is the level of development of a skill that is nearly complete, but still needs teaching or guidance in order to be successfully performed.[9] Without training, Matt does not quite have the ability to focus his super senses enough to pick out the same information that Stick is able to sense.[10] The best teachers know the proximal developmental level of their students and provide them the most appropriate advanced challenge and just enough guidance for the student to meet the challenge.[11] All it takes for Matt to start using his super senses is for Stick to point out the underlying tastes within the vanilla ice cream they are both eating, including the remnants of garden dirt on the hands of the person who served the ice cream. Matt quickly takes it from there, expanding to use other super senses, which shows that Stick has correctly assessed Matt's proximal developmental level.[12]

In addition to understanding Matt's developmental levels, Stick is the ideal teacher for Matt Murdock because he teaches him the limitations of vision. The development of the ability to create a mental visual representation of our environment is a developmental milestone that sets us apart from our closest primate relatives. The ability of an ape to solve problems is limited by what is available in its visual field. By contrast, a human child is capable of developing the ability to imagine his or her environment and its likely contents without actively looking at it: As a result, people have larger tool selection to aid in problem solving.[13] Matt and Stick take this development one step further. Instead of their super fighting skills developing in spite of the lack of eyesight, their development is facilitated by it. Moment to moment, human vision still perceives less than half of the environment at a time, based on where the eyes are focused. Matt and Stick are able to focus on hearing, touch, and smell, which allow three-dimensional awareness of unfamiliar environments, including what is happening on the other side of walls.[14]

COGNITIVE DEVELOPMENT

Like physical skills development, the development of self-*awareness*, or how one comes to know oneself, is directly influenced by the world. People's perception of the world in which they live will inform their self-concepts. A society's stereotypes about different social groups can have a major impact on group members' perceptions of themselves. For people with a disability, society's emphasis on the lack of an ability falsely overshadows the many ways the person functions effectively, if differently, in the world. If the individual internalizes this societal construct, this can cause the development of an inaccurate sense of self.[15] It is unclear to what degree dominant social consciousness has truly impacted how Matt thinks about himself as an adult. As Matt Murdock, attorney at law, he often showcases his blindness, even when he is capable of using other senses to accomplish his goals, but, as his super-hero alter ego, he emphasizes his supersensory abilities with minimal regard for his lack of sight.

The view of disability as a medical problem is a pervasive belief in US society. It encompasses the misconception that people with disabilities are defective and must be fixed if they want to achieve full capacity, and therefore full status, as human beings.[16] Early in the comic book series, girlfriend Karen Page begs Matt to go to a surgeon to try to get his eyesight back. He accedes to her pressure, though he never undergoes the proce-dure because he changes his mind (after villains kidnap the doctor, of course).[17] The view of disability as personal tragedy bleeds pity and focuses on physical and psychological short-comings.[18] At one point Karen comments on what a loss it is that "such a wonderful, handsome man is handicapped."[19] These comments contribute to a view of disability as loss and the view that a human experiencing an impairment is less than whole. Matt Murdock tends to perpetuate, rather than chal-lenge, the public view of disability by seeking help from others for things he is capable of doing independently.

Having positive role models who demonstrate wholeness regardless of disability is important for developing a positive identity that includes the disability.[20] Stick doesn't just teach Matt how to use his super senses and to fight, he teaches him that people without sight can be even stronger and more capa-ble than those with sight. Daredevil confidently uses his super senses to carry out movement and fighting skills that are well beyond the proximal development level of most sighted indi-viduals. Matt even tells Foggy, "He taught me that blindness isn't a disability, that sight is a distraction."[21]

SOCIAL DEVELOPMENT

The ways individuals choose to manage their disability status in everyday life is influenced by the disability, the visibility of the disability to others, the degree of the impairment, and the situation.[22] Moving between various ways of managing oneself and portraying oneself to others results in a complex identity, and it doesn't get much more complex than having a superhero alter ego. When Matt is Daredevil, he attempts to portray himself as nondisabled to the point of overcompensating for the disability by becoming "super." However, when he is being Matt Murdock, attorney at law, he openly shares his disability but hides his super senses, doing things such as pretending to confuse denominations of paper bills, even though he knows which is which through super touch.[23] What better way to hide a superhero identity than by using society's stereotype in his favor? It makes connecting the hero with *super*human fighting abilities with the mild-mannered blind lawyer highly unlikely. However, acting below one's actual developmental level perpetuates negative stereotypes of blindness.[24] So regardless of whether he is underperforming to keep his dual identity secret or because of internalization of negative stereotypes about disability, in the end he is hurting himself and his community.

Hiding core aspects of oneself is hard work, but it may decrease the disadvantages created by negative social perceptions of the general capabilities of those with specific disabilities. Matt benefits from being able to control the way he is perceived by others, including avoiding the idea of having an ability deficit which could diminish his ability to intimidate criminals as Daredevil. However, the consequences of a decision to not embrace one's identity can have traumatic implications.[25] Denying or hiding the true self is unhealthy in the medical sense and the psychological sense as well. By hiding a disability, a person risks experiencing hidden injuries that come from not getting important and helpful resources. Psychologically speaking, rates of social isolation and mental health disorders, such as depression and anxiety, also increase.[26]

GROUP DEVELOPMENT

Peers can be a source of the guidance needed to develop advanced skills. One benefit of *peer group learning* is that each person in the group comes to a challenge with a slightly different set of strengths. If their overall proximal development levels are similar, they can learn from each other's strengths to overcome their skills gaps and meet the challenge they couldn't have overcome on their own.[27] Elektra's greater experience fighting the Hand proves helpful when Daredevil's usual tactic of sensing his enemies through their heartbeats is thwarted by the Hand's ability to mask their heartbeats. She tells him to listen for the sounds of their weapons instead.[28]

Unfortunately, attitudes toward group work in academic settings and employment settings are often negative, due to personal experiences of conflict sabotaging group effectiveness. Daredevil rarely works with groups. When he gets together with Jessica Jones and other heroes, conflict over their personal differences almost keeps them from solving the very complex problem of defeating dangerous enemies.[29] So, what is needed to unlock the developmental potential of group work so that they can succeed?

Developing a sense of team identity is vital to group collaboration and learning. However, it takes more than just a team name to create cohesion. One fundamental requirement for effective team development and eventual problem solving is going through the process of creating a common understanding of a shared problem. Developing a common understanding requires effective communication by all partners of

SUPER SELF-CONCEPT

People have complex self-concepts that involve multiple roles and relationships, and these aspects will eventually conflict. Psychologists argue that we are motivated to satisfy these complex roles while still maintaining a coherent (and positive) sense of self—a sometimes difficult task that we have to navigate on a daily basis.[33] Daredevil illustrates this struggle by trying to balance the everyday demands of maintaining both his public and his secret identities, as well as by negotiating the internal conflict of being a law-abiding lawyer by day and a vigilante by night. This negotiation is not easy. He often feels ambivalent about using violence to enforce justice when his cherished legal system fails[34] and even people in his life, such as his former wife Milla Donovan and fellow superhero Dr. Strange, have commented on his paradoxical roles.[35]

their individual knowledge and coming to agreement about the situation and appropriate action.[30] At the beginning of group work, each person has unshared knowledge relevant to the problem.[31] For instance, Stick and Matt have information about Elektra that the others don't have. In order to understand the problem fully, all relevant unshared knowledge must be shared. When it becomes clear that knowledge of Elektra and their relationships are important to understanding their shared problem, Matt and Stick share their knowledge with others.[32]

Completely shared knowledge doesn't guarantee that agreement automatically follows. Through the process of questioning and negotiation of shared knowledge, an effective group finds common ground by agreeing on what information is valid and relevant to the problem. When Jessica and Luke Cage question Matt about Elektra, his relationship with her, and whether or not he will be able to be an effective team member when they need to fight her, he is not forthcoming. Tragic losses take place before Matt recognizes the need to share information.[36]

HELPING DEVELOPMENT

Developing one's identity as an individual or a group isn't easy under the best circumstances. Coming to terms with an identity that carries social stigma is exhausting, painful work. Matt has excelled in developing his physical skills and made strides in the cognitive components of his identity with some help from his mentor and friends. However, he still has a long way to go to integrate his social identity and therefore he is still lacking a fully integrated self-concept. Then again, an underdeveloped self-concept may be the ultimate sacrifice that all heroes with a secret identity make, regardless of their abilities. Based on the harmful effects of a false consciousness and a fake portrayal of self to one's community, hopefully Matt will fully develop his identity for the sake of himself, his team, and for the people of Hell's Kitchen.

NOTES

1. Dusek (1987).
2. *Daredevil #167* (1980).
3. Vygotsky (1978).
4. *Daredevil: The Man without Fear #1* (1993).
5. Piaget (1974).
6. *Daredevil: The Man without Fear #1* (1993).
7. Bandura (1977); Vygotsky (1978); *Daredevil: The Man without Fear #1* (1993).
8. Vygotsky (1978).
9. Vygotsky (1978); Marvel's Daredevil, episode 1–7, "Stick" (April 10, 2015).
10. *Daredevil #1* (1993).
11. Vygotsky (1978).
12. *Marvel's Daredevil*, episode 1–7, "Stick" (April 10, 2015).
13. Vygotsky (1978).
14. *Marvel's Daredevil*, episode 2–12, "The Dark End of the Tunnel" (March 18, 2016).
15. Garland-Thomson (2009).
16. Siebers (2008).
17. *Daredevil #8* (1965).
18. Oliver (1996).
19. *Daredevil #1* (1964).
20. Forber-Pratt & Zape (2017).
21. *Marvel's Daredevil*, episode 1–10, "Nelson v. Murdock" (August 18, 2017).
22. Goffman (1963/1986).
23. *Daredevil #1* (2011).
24. Alaniz (2014).
25. Linton (1998).
26. Kumashiro (2002).
27. Barker et al. (2015).
28. *Marvel's Daredevil*, episode 2–7, "Guilty as Sin" (March 18, 2016).
29. *Marvel's The Defenders*, episode 1–4, "Royal Dragon" (August 18, 2017)
30. Barron (2003).
31. Beers et al. (2005).
32. Beers et al. (2005); *Marvel's The Defenders*, episode 1–5, "Take Shelter" (August 18, 2017).
33. Greenwald (1980); Higgens (1987); Jordan & Wesselmann (2015); Steele (1988); Swann et al. (2003).
34. Cavalieri & Cohn (1982); *Daredevil* (2003 motion picture); *Daredevil #191* (1983); *Daredevil #15.1* (2015).
35. *Daredevil #65* (2004).
36. *Marvel's The Defenders*, episode 1–6, "Ashes, Ashes."

CHAPTER 4

INTERVIEW WITH MARVEL'S DAREDEVIL EXECUTIVE PRODUCER STEVEN S. DEKNIGHT: RUNNING THE SHOW IN HELL'S KITCHEN

TRAVIS LANGLEY & JENNA BUSCH

Steven S. DeKnight tells stories about heroes. As a writer, director, and producer, he has worked on *Smallville*, *Buffy the Vampire Slayer*, *Angel*, and *Spartacus*. After *Marvel's Daredevil* showrunner Drew Goddard left the series due to scheduling conflicts, DeKnight took over his duties.[1] We thank season 1 showrunner DeKnight for talking with us about his involvement with the series, the stories, and the superhero known as Daredevil. Let's find out what he thinks about the mind of Matthew Murdock.

Q: Jeph Loeb and others already had the Daredevil TV series in the works when you joined them. What did you bring to the mix?

Steven S. DeKnight: I sat down with Drew Goddard about a year before I signed on. He was gearing up to work on it and he wanted to know if I wanted to collaborate with him and I said, "Oh, I would love to, but I have another year left on my deal with Starz. But I'll be the first one to tune in to the show." And then I think I was on the last couple of months of my deal, I got the call from Jeph [Loeb] and Drew that Drew had to leave to start the Sinister Six/Spider-Man movie a little earlier than expected. They needed someone to come in immediately, to take over and get the show off the ground. So I got there. They pitched me the first season. Drew had the first two scripts written.[2] I in no shape, way, or form wanted to sign up for a TV show at that point, but it sounded so cool, I just couldn't say no. So the first two scripts were written. They had a couple of sentences for the rest of the episodes. So I came and I polished up the first two episodes to get them ready to shoot. I then dove in, exploring each of these episodes in detail and breaking the stories down with my writers' room.

What I was really looking to do was to keep the spirit of what Drew had set out to do completely alive because I loved what he had set up, and just flesh

everything out and really explore the themes that
excite me, particularly the rich and powerful and how
they exploit, which is something I did in *Spartacus* that
carried over into *Daredevil*. We had this huge cast of
characters and we had to figure out where everybody fit,
particularly the villains. When I got Fisk's collection of
villains with Nobu and Madame Gau and the Russians,
it wasn't quite locked in what each one of them was
doing, so we had figure all of that out and figure out
how that all connected. At that time, Madame Gau,
besides being slightly mysterious, didn't have anything
to do with Iron Fist yet, and one of the things that really
excited us in the room was the whole heroin production
thing. It was like, oh, we could use the stamp with the
seal of the serpent and that will be a clue to comic book
fans that she has something to do with Iron Fist. It was
basically a lot of that—making sure the story worked,
making sure we were building something interesting
and keeping alive what Drew had set up, which was just
as much Wilson Fisk's origin story as Kingpin as it was
Matt Murdock's origin story as Daredevil.

Q: *Iron Man* laid the foundation for the Marvel Cinematic
Universe.[3] In a similar way, *Daredevil* established the
reality for the street-level heroes in their dark corner
of that universe. Why Daredevil?

DeKnight: Jeph Loeb had always talked about street-level
heroes and wanted to really explore them and there's no
better place to do it than television. I think the street-
level heroes really, really work well on television. And if
I had to venture a guess, I would say that Daredevil is the
most well-known of the street-level heroes. Any comic
book fan, they know Luke Cage and Danny Rand and
Jessica Jones, but to the public, at least before these shows

came out, you could mention those names and people
would say, "What the hell are you talking about?" So,
I think Daredevil being the most recognizable was a
smart move to kick it off.

Q. As a superhero, what makes Daredevil different from
other superheroes?

DeKnight: It's interesting when we really start to dive
into it. Yes, he has heightened senses, which gives him
the edge, but in all other regards, he's just a normal
man who's pushed himself to the limit, and I think
that's something that makes him very, very different.
It makes him very different from Luke Cage who got his
invulnerability and super strength from experiments that
were done to him in prison,[4] different from Jessica Jones
who from her particular accident became superpowered
with limited flight,[5] and even different from Danny
Rand who is the Immortal Iron Fist.[6] He can channel
incredible amounts of energy. With Matt Murdock, he
lost his sight as a kid. His senses are heightened, but that's
it. And that's something we really wanted to lean heavily
into in the show. Yes, he has heightened senses, but we
really wanted to show that what makes him a hero is
not that. It's a drive. It's a drive to right the wrongs that
happen in the world.

I think the murder of his father had a huge effect
on him. His wanting to help protect the innocent and
the flip side, the dark side of Matt Murdock, were
things that we really wanted to explore. In season 1,
we wanted to blur the line a little bit. Who are you
rooting for? Are you rooting for Matt or are you rooting
for Wilson Fisk? They both want to save the city. They
both make a pretty damn good argument for what
they're doing. Sometimes Wilson Fisk does the right

thing for the wrong reason, and sometimes Matt does the wrong thing for the right reason. But really, Matt Murdock is driven. You see that in the first season after Foggy discovers that he's Daredevil—at that point, the man in the black mask.[7] He doesn't have his name yet. Matt can't quit. It's not like he can just walk away from it. We treated it very much like an addiction. That this is something he has to do. He's compelled to do it. And in the first season he really wrestles with that. How far does he take it? Will he kill someone? And at one point he tries to kill Wilson Fisk. He gets the shit beat out of him. And then he comes around to seeing that's not the way. I think his run-in in season 2 with Frank Castle and his association with Stick really reinforces his belief that murdering is wrong.

Q: Why is Daredevil more of a loner than other heroes? He has one of the smallest supporting casts (often no more than Foggy and maybe one love interest) and he has never been an ongoing member of any established superteam. Even in the comics, the Defenders are not a structured team.

DeKnight: He's a man with a lot of demons and a schism right down the center of his soul. He is one of the most religious characters in the Marvel universe, being Catholic,[8] and he really wrestles with being a good Catholic and what he does. He goes out at night and basically beats up people. Another part of the schism is that he's a lawyer, sworn to uphold the law, and every night he goes out and breaks it. So I think there is always this internal struggle inside of Matt Murdock. I think that's part of what makes him a loner. In a lot of the comics, he's often not the happiest superhero. He's not Spider-Man, swinging around, making jokes.

Which, again, is something we really wanted to hit in season 1. It's no secret that I'm an avowed atheist, but I'm fascinated by religion, and we really wanted to treat Catholicism with respect, especially in relation to Matt. One of my favorite episodes of season 1 was—I believe it was episode 9—where Matt was wrestling with whether or not he's going to kill Wilson Fisk.[9] He has this long conversation with his priest. We really wanted the priest to feel human, Matt to feel human, there to be no easy answers, and to really see the struggle that was going on inside him. I would say, probably, out of the four Defenders, Matt and Jessica are probably the biggest loners. But, yeah, that's why I think Matt is a bit of a loner.

Q: Frank Miller's lasting influence on *Daredevil* is apparent in every live action adaptation.[10] Even *The Trial of the Incredible Hulk* included the Kingpin. Your series features Wilson Fisk, Elektra, Stick, the Hand, the Punisher, Ben Urich, and Miller's "Born Again" story. They weren't all Miller creations or even Daredevil characters originally, but his stories made them integral to how we think of Daredevil.[11] What was it about Miller that made his work so powerful?

DeKnight: Miller, he gets a lot of credit—both for Batman[12] and Daredevil—for bringing a grittier, more down-and-dirty, realistic feel to the characters. That they weren't just swinging around, you know, making jokes and punching bad guys in the jaw. That they were deeply, deeply flawed people. They were vigilantes and really exploring the depth of darkness in each one of their souls, so they weren't just squeaky-clean heroes. That was the biggest revelation from Frank Miller's work for me. I remember I was in college when *The Dark Knight*

Returns came out. That and Alan Moore's *Watchmen*
at that time were such game changers.[13] We got to see
the flawed heroes. Marvel has always been great at
showing the human side of heroes. You can go all the
way back to Spider-Man with the death of Gwen Stacy,
which everybody remembers, but a lot of people don't
remember that, in that run, Harry Osborne was also
battling an addiction at the time.[14] Marvel was really
in the forefront of showing Spider-Man with normal
guy problems, normal teen problems. But Frank Miller
took it to a new level. So Frank Miller was a huge
influence for me, along with Brian Michael Bendis and
Alex Maleev's run on *Daredevil*, which I thought was
gorgeously illustrated and really well-written.[15] We really
wanted to bring that kind of down-to-earth realism
to the character. And we used Alex Maleev's art as a
template for the look of the show.

Q: Is Matt Murdock crazy?

DeKnight: I think, to some extent, you have to be a little
crazy to do what he does. And again, that's something
we explored in the first season. We don't portray him
as a normal, functioning human being. He has serious
problems. As large as his heart is, he has problems
interacting with people. He has problems maintaining
relationships. It's a bit of a joke—they reference him as
being a ladies' man and a womanizer, but that's really
because he can't get close to people. Partly because of his
secret and partly for us for season 1, he was a man who
didn't love himself, and he certainly couldn't love anyone
else. He was extremely self-destructive. To me, it was like
a self-perpetuating cycle of guilt, that he felt compelled
to do these things, but because he was a Catholic, he felt
guilty about it, and it went 'round and 'round and 'round.

Q: What motivates someone like Matt Murdock to keep fighting for others when it hurts him?

DeKnight: You know, again going back to his basis in Catholicism, it's a bit of a redemption story. I think, particularly in our season 1, there's a massive amount of guilt that he feels for his father's death because they have a conversation right before his dad is supposed to throw this boxing match. Young Matt doesn't come right out and say it, but he's pushing his dad not to throw the fight, not to take the dirty money. And that's what really gets to Jack. He wants his son to be proud of him, and I think Matt carries that around with him all the time— that if he hadn't said that, his father would still be alive. For me, that's one of the underpinnings of the character. He's driven to help people, and I think him getting hurt is kind of a bit of self-flagellation. It's the penance he's paying for what he's doing.

Q: Are superheroes such as Daredevil relevant to real-life heroes?

DeKnight: Yeah, I think whenever you show or portray a fictional hero, they can inspire, even in the smallest way. Not that somebody has to dress up and go around saving people at night. Wilson Fisk says in the first season, "A rising tide raises all boats."[16] I think it's the same thing here. When you see stories about people struggling to be good and make a difference, it inspires you to want to make a difference in whatever way you can.

Q: What's inspiring about Daredevil? Is one of the lessons we can learn from Daredevil "the Man without Fear" that things like disabilities, tragic losses, and other difficulties don't have to make a person afraid to do the right thing? To keep going?

DeKnight: Yeah, I think whenever you see someone who doesn't have the standard, inherited advantages of life succeed and excel, it makes you stop and say, "Well, why am I complaining? What are my excuses?" I've been trying to learn the guitar for years and I'm like, ah, I can't play this thing. And then I get on the internet and I see a kid born with no arms who's playing with his feet and I realize I've got no excuse not to practice harder. There is no disadvantage you can't overcome. I think that's really the important lesson.

NOTES

1. Goldberg, L. (2014).
2. *Marvel's Daredevil,* episodes 1–1, "Into the Ring," and 1–2, "Cut Man" (April 10, 2015).
3. *Iron Man* (2008 motion picture).
4. *Luke Cage, Hero for Hire* #1 (1972).
5. *Alias* #22–23 (2003).
6. *Marvel Premiere* #15 (1974).
7. Daredevil first appeared in the simple black costume in *The Trial of the Incredible Hulk* (1989 television movie). This retroactively became part of his history in *Daredevil: The Man without Fear* #4 (1994).
8. First mentioned explicitly in *Daredevil* #119 (1975).
9. *Marvel's Daredevil,* episode 1–9, "Speak of the Devil" (April 10, 2015).
10. *The Trial of the Incredible Hulk* (1989 television movie); *Daredevil* (2003 motion picture); *Marvel's Daredevil,* episodes 1, "Into the Ring" through 1–13, "Daredevil" (April 10, 2015).
11. Miller first drew Daredevil in *Daredevil* #158 (1979) and began writing in the comic book series *Daredevil* #166 (1980).
12. *Batman: The Dark Knight Returns* (1986); *Batman* #404–407 (1987).
13. *Batman: The Dark Knight Returns* (1986); *Watchmen* (1986–1987).
14. Gwen—*Amazing Spider-Man* #121 (1973); Harry—*Amazing Spider-Man* #96–98 (1971).
15. Beginning with *Daredevil* #26 (2001).
16. *Marvel's Daredevil,* episode 1–5, "World on Fire" (April 10, 2015).

II

ADVOCATES

"Playing devil's advocate . . ."
—*figure of speech*

THE DEVIL'S ADVOCATE

Devil's advocate *(noun)*. 1. One who argues against something for the sheer sake of arguing or challenging. 2. The Promoter of the Faith (original meaning).

Historically, the Devil's Advocate (*Advocatus Diaboli*) was the popular name for the Promoter of the Faith, a canon lawyer assigned to contest the canonization of a candidate for sainthood. Well versed in the Catholic Church's laws and principles, this expert was tasked with protecting the church and the faith by identifying a possible saint's character flaws and questioning any evidence that favored canonization.[1]

This practice began under Pope Sixtus V in 1587 and continued until depowered under Pope John Paul II in 1983, the year Frank Miller's original run writing *Daredevil* came to its end with Matt Murdock searching for his soul while playing Russian roulette with Bullseye and an empty gun.[2] In that story, he bears the weight of a tragic fate that has befallen a young boy, apparently as a result of hero-worshipping Daredevil. As a result, Matt plays devil's advocate to himself, questioning his own mission, motives, and worthiness as anyone's hero. He reflects upon how, when he himself was a boy, he had concluded that even his own father, whom he admired, was merely a mortal who needed laws and rules to obey, and this personal epiphany inspires young Matt to work hard to become a lawyer.

As an attorney, Matt Murdock advocates for the innocent. When he's a defense attorney, he tries to represent only clients who are innocent; and when he's a prosecutor, he finds ways to protect the innocent by convicting the guilty.[3] This attorney who finds creative ways to play by the rules breaks some as a vigilante for the sake of true justice because the system does not always work. How does someone reach the point of ethically breaking rules in order to serve greater principles and values? How do any of us develop whatever ethical and moral principles might guide us? We learn from the family that raises us, the family we choose, and many others along life's way. Of course, a devil's advocate might point out the flaws in whatever moral reasoning we try to apply.

—T.L.

NOTES

1. Ryan (2017).
2. *Daredevil* #191 (1983).
3. *Daredevil* #25 (2017).

CHAPTER 5

SYMPATHY FOR THE DEVIL: MORAL CONVICTIONS, EMOTIONS, AND STRUGGLES

ERIC D. WESSELMANN & JORDAN P. LABOUFF

"If you're convinced that I have been in no way compelled to atone for my sins, then you don't know me at all."
—Matt Murdock[1]

"It is a remarkable and encouraging fact about human beings that simply hearing about a good deed, done by a stranger for another stranger, can profoundly affect us."
—social psychologist Jonathan Haidt[2]

Fictional heroes provide us an opportunity to confront our moral struggles in a safe environment, especially those characters we find relatable and engaging.[3] Daredevil is a good example, because even though many of us do not know what it is like to have super senses or to fight crime, we have some sense of what it is like to struggle against life's challenges. Through Daredevil, we can simulate the psychological conflicts we all face when deciding what is "moral" and our feelings when we fail to live up to our moral codes.

MORAL CONVICTIONS AND CONFLICTS: THE DEVIL IS IN THE DETAILS

Daredevil often feels ambivalent about using violence to enforce justice when the legal system fails;[4] this conflict stems from his conceptions of morality. Psychologists argue that our moral worldviews, the guides we use to determine the "rightness" of our and others' behavior, are determined by our social groups, like our families and cultures.[5] As a lawyer, Daredevil relies on what psychologist Lawrence Kohlberg called *conventional* morality—making decisions based upon concrete institutional or cultural rules.[6] Further, he is willing to enforce the law, even if it means bringing those he cares for to justice, such as his former lover Elektra and his uneasy ally the Punisher.[7] Daredevil also takes the legal principle "innocent until proven guilty" seriously and is willing to defend clients he believes to be innocent, even if society views these clients as morally flawed.[8]

Sometimes the legal system fails; the guilty go unpunished or the innocent go to jail. Daredevil created his vigilante identity to pursue justice outside the law when it fails.[9] Kohlberg argued that individuals who make moral decisions favoring abstract ideals (e.g., justice) above institutional authority (e.g., laws) are reasoning at a *post-conventional* level.[10] Daredevil's commitment to justice can be viewed as a *moral conviction*: a belief that supersedes others, is beyond debate, and motivates people to act beyond social norms and laws if necessary—even if that means using violence.[11] Daredevil knows that what he is doing is illegal and that if his secret identity becomes known officially he could lose his license to practice law.[12] However, he firmly believes that "justice is not a sin"[13] and "I'll serve it any way I can."[14]

THE DEVIL HAS FEELINGS, TOO

Daredevil is an introspective character, and audiences are given a privileged view of his emotions as he fights for justice. Emotions are what we experience in response to specific life events.[15] A special group of emotions—the *moral emotions*—are linked to the interests of others or society generally.[16] These emotions can be either negative or positive, and arise when someone's behavior (ours or another's) either violates or upholds our core moral values.[17]

ANGER

Daredevil has unresolved anger toward people who have wronged him: the criminals who murdered his father, his mother who abandoned him, his father who forced him to study and repress his love of fighting, and the various women who have broken his heart.[18] People typically get angry when they believe they have been wronged unjustly.[19] For example, Daredevil expresses anger toward his mother for abandoning him and abdicating her responsibility by joining a convent. He believes his mother tries to justify her past behavior by rein- terpreting it through the lens of her current religious calling.[20]

Daredevil's Roman Catholic faith is important to him, but he sometimes shows ambivalence and anger at God.[21] Many religious individuals experience faith-based struggles through- out their lives.[22] For example, religious people might be angry at their deity during times of suffering, especially when they perceive the suffering as unjust.[23] After a series of misfortunes, Daredevil angrily questions God, "Haven't I had enough

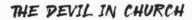

THE DEVIL IN CHURCH

Many people's conceptions of morality and justice are intricately tied to their religious beliefs.[27] Daredevil's Roman Catholic faith is an important guiding principle in his life, not just as a lawyer but also as a crime-fighter.[28] Religious beliefs can influence one's view of justice and attitudes toward punishment and other uses of aggression.[29] Religious individuals can reduce reservations they may have about aggression by using their beliefs to justify the behavior.[30] For example, a psychological experiment demonstrated that religious participants who read a biblical description of divinely approved violence were more likely to punish an opponent aggressively in a competitive game than those who read a secular description of violence— suggesting that religious believers are willing to be violent when they believe God endorses violence.[31] Indeed, Daredevil explicitly refers to fighting crime as "my Father's work" and has several discussions with his priest, arguing that his mission may

pain?"[24] Religious individuals who perceive their deities as cruel also tend to see them as distant and develop religious doubts.[25] Daredevil's anger at his perception of God's injustice makes him question God's existence.[26]

GUILT AND SHAME

Because Daredevil has stringent moral standards, he often falls short of his expectations. When people feel they have failed to uphold their moral standards, they may experience guilt or shame.[40] When people feel *guilt*, they regret their specific actions and seek to make amends, renewing their dedication be a struggle against evil itself (i.e., the devil).[32] By sanctifying his pursuit of justice in this way, Daredevil could reduce any inner turmoil he may have about breaking laws, and bones, in pursuit of justice.

Religious beliefs also influence one's endorsement of the death penalty.[33] Roman Catholic doctrine discourages the death penalty (except in rare cases where there is no other way to protect oneself or others from the perpetrator).[34] Data suggest that, among Roman Catholics, increased religiosity often predicts opposition to the death penalty.[35] Daredevil staunchly opposes killing criminals unless there is no other option. He consistently opposes the Punisher's lethal methods,[36] and the few times he has killed an enemy have been in self-defense.[37] Daredevil has even refused to kill enemies such as Bullseye, the Kingpin, and Mysterio even when these enemies have ruined his life and murdered those close to him.[38] When the Kingpin is confused by Daredevil's refusal to kill him, Daredevil simply responds with "I'm not the bad guy."[39]

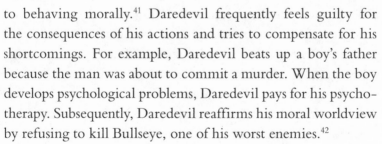

to behaving morally.[41] Daredevil frequently feels guilty for the consequences of his actions and tries to compensate for his shortcomings. For example, Daredevil beats up a boy's father because the man was about to commit a murder. When the boy develops psychological problems, Daredevil pays for his psychotherapy. Subsequently, Daredevil reaffirms his moral worldview by refusing to kill Bullseye, one of his worst enemies.[42]

Like many individuals, Daredevil often dwells on his moral failings obsessively. When individuals feel *shame*, they condemn their identity, rather than their actions (i.e., "I am a failure," instead of "I failed").[43] Whereas guilt can be adaptive because of its prosocial outcomes, shame is often maladaptive because it often promotes anger, helplessness, and social withdrawal.[44] When Daredevil fails to save Elektra's father from assassination, his shame likely motivates him to lash out in anger and break things.[45] Similarly, shamed by the death of Karen Page, he tells Spider-Man that heroes are at best a *temporary* fix for the evils of the world, that "All we offer is false hope." Fortunately, Spider-Man helps Daredevil overcome his shame by reminding him of the most important outcome from their continued struggles—saving lives whenever possible.[46]

COMPASSION AND FORGIVENESS

Some moral emotions are positive—they orient people toward bettering the lives of others and support moral goals.[47] Daredevil's friends, lovers, and even the Kingpin often praise his moral character.[48] Daredevil often feels *compassion* for those who suffer unjustly. When individuals feel compassion (also referred to as sympathy) for another person, they experience a deep concern for that person and their plight.[49] Daredevil values the lives of everyone, even those of his enemies. He believes "in the innate goodness of people."[50] For example, Daredevil worries about the Punisher's safety, even though he finds the Punisher's brutal methods morally repellent.[51] Because Daredevil further recognizes that the Punisher has been traumatized by his family's death, he often holds back when the two fight.[52]

Compassion also motivates individuals to help those who are suffering.[53] Daredevil often shows compassion to his enemies. For example, he saves a wounded criminal instead of chasing down the Punisher.[54] At another point, Daredevil has a broken foot and discovers a derelict in the sewers who has no legs; he gives his crutch to this person and continues on without its aid.[55] Daredevil even says that he will pray for the Kingpin when he realizes the Kingpin is distraught after being left by his wife.[56]

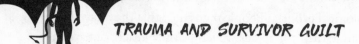

TRAUMA AND SURVIVOR GUILT

BY ERIC D. WESSELMANN
& LEANDRA PARRIS

Two of Daredevil's former lovers die in his arms, Jessica Jones suffers multiple forms of abuse at the hands of Killgrave, and the Punisher's family is murdered in front of him.[57] The list of those in Matt Murdock's world who suffer trauma goes on and on. These traumas emotionally scar these particular characters, driving them to destructive behaviors. People who experience these types of traumas often develop posttraumatic stress symptoms, such as reoccurring images of the trauma, avoiding reminders (i.e., triggers) of the trauma, or prolonged psychological distress.[58] For example, the Punisher continually has nightmares and flashbacks of his family's murder,[59] while Jessica Jones experiences intrusive memories when exposed to triggers (e.g., loud noises and changing lights on a train).[60] After Elektra's death, Daredevil becomes irritable, emotionally distant, and unreliable.[61]

Individuals who experience death-related trauma often develop what psychologists have called *survivor guilt*— guilt either for surviving a traumatic event when others did not or for engaging in morally questionable behaviors in order to survive the trauma.[62] These feelings may ultimately lead to suicidal thoughts and feelings of helplessness.[63] We see examples of survivor guilt in each of our key characters: Daredevil's shame pushes him to attempt suicide after Karen Page is murdered,[64] the Punisher entertains the possibility that he is a failure in his war on crime,[65] and Jessica Jones often struggles with guilt for actions she performed while under Killgrave's control.[66]

A major theme in Daredevil stories is *forgiveness*. Forgiveness is a psychological process: People recognize that they have been harmed, but rather than seek revenge they reach out to the perpetrator with compassion and charity. Both psychologists and theologians argue that forgiveness is crucial for repairing interpersonal relationships.[67] While Daredevil focuses on pursuing justice, he also demonstrates how much he values forgiving those who have wronged him. For example, he forgives Karen Page for selling his secret identity when she was in withdrawal, desperate for drugs, he nurses her back to health, and they rekindle their romantic relationship.[68]

Daredevil also recognizes the importance of asking forgiveness from others when he has wronged them. Asking for forgiveness, especially from one's deity, is an important aspect of many religions.[69] In Roman Catholicism, divine forgiveness is expressed in the sacrament of penance (commonly called *confession*); an acceptable confession requires one to acknowledge wrongdoing, express remorse for one's actions, accept a penance as reparations, and endeavor to avoid sinning in the future.[70] These elements are similar to what psychologists have identified as the key components of an effective apology in interpersonal relationships, and if an apology is missing any of these components it will likely be seen as insincere.[71] Daredevil's priest highlights the importance of expressing remorse and a desire to change in seeking forgiveness when he criticizes Daredevil for coming to confess after letting a criminal die. Without remorse and the desire to change, the priest says that Daredevil is essentially asking for *permission*, not forgiveness. Daredevil later provides a deeply remorseful confession after he fails to save Elektra's father from assassination and questions his own role in perpetrating a cycle of violence.[72]

THE DEVIL INSIDE US ALL

Who is Daredevil? He is compassionate, brave, jealous, depressed, self-critical, and loyal. He is a hero we can relate to, in both his triumphs and his struggles. Cultures often embrace heroes, whether real or fictional, as a way to bind the group together, affirm shared morals, and provide meaning to common experiences.[73] Researchers have found that stories of individuals displaying uncommon goodness or moral heroism inspire us to be our ideal selves and act on the morals central to our identities.[74] In short, the best heroes provide us a mirror to see what we can achieve regardless of our shortcomings. Daredevil embodies the best and worst of our moral struggles, reflecting the moral complexity of the devils inside us all.

NOTES

1. *Daredevil* #21 (2012).
2. Haidt (2003), p. 864.
3. Bal & Veltkamp (2013); Johnson (2012); Mar & Oatley (2008); Rubin (2013).
4. Cavalieri & Cohn (1982); *Daredevil* (2003 motion picture); *Daredevil* #191 (1983); *Daredevil* #15.1 (2015); Johnson (2003).
5. Haidt (2008).
6. Kohlberg (1984).
7. *Daredevil* #175 (1981); *Daredevil* #183 (1982).
8. *Daredevil* #183 (1982); *Daredevil* #69 (2005); *Daredevil Director's Cut* (2012 motion picture Blu-ray); *Daredevil: Redemption* #1 (2005); *Daredevil v. Punisher: Means and Ends* #4 (2005).
9. *Daredevil* (2003 motion picture); *Daredevil* #177 (1981); *Daredevil* #1 (2014).
10. Kohlberg (1984).
11. Skitka (2010); Skitka (2012).
12. *Daredevil* #15.1 (2015); *Daredevil* #43 (2003); *Daredevil Director's Cut* (2012 motion picture Blu-ray).
13. *Daredevil* (2003 motion picture).
14. *Daredevil* #186 (1982).
15. Keltner & Haidt (1999).
16. Haidt (2003); Tangney et al. (2007).
17. Haidt (2003); Weiner (2006).
18. *Daredevil* #177 (1981); *Daredevil* #182 (1982); *Daredevil* #187 (1982); *Daredevil* #4 (1999); *Daredevil* #8 (1999).
19. Haidt (2003); Weiner (2006).
20. *Daredevil* #4 (1999).
21. *Daredevil* #½ (1998); *Daredevil* #1 (1998); *Daredevil* #58 (2004); *Daredevil* #62 (2004); *Daredevil* #16 (2015); *Daredevil* (2003 motion picture); *Daredevil Director's Cut* (2012 motion picture Blu-ray); Miller (2012); Sanderson (1982); Smith (2012).
22. Exline (2013); Exline et al. (2014).
23. Exline et al. (2011); Gray & Wegner (2010).
24. *Daredevil* #2 (1998).
25. Exline et al. (2015).
26. *Daredevil* #1 (1998); *Daredevil* #4 (1999).
27. Cohen (2015); Graham & Haidt (2010); Graziano & Schroeder (2016).
28. *Daredevil* #12 (1998); *Daredevil* #58 (2004); *Daredevil* #62 (2004); *Daredevil* (2003 motion picture); Miller (2012); Sanderson (1982); Smith (2012); *Daredevil* #16 (2015).
29. Grasmick et al. (1993); Laurin & Plaks (2014); Malka & Soto (2011).
30. Ginges et al (2009).
31. Bushman et al. (2007).
32. *Daredevil* #8 (1999); *Daredevil*, episodes 1–1, "Into the Ring" (April 10, 2015); 1–9, "Speak of the Devil" (April 10, 2015).
33. Grasmick et al. (1993); Unnever et al. (2010).
34. *Catholic Church* (1995); United States Conference of Catholic Bishops (2005).
35. Bjarnason & Welch (2004); Perl & McClintock (2001).
36. *Daredevil* #183–184 (1982); *Daredevil vs. the Punisher: Means and Ends* #1 (2005); *Daredevil vs. the Punisher: Means and Ends* #4 (2005); *Marvel Knights* #1 (2000).
37. *Daredevil* #232 (1986); *Daredevil: The Man without Fear* #5 (1994).
38. *Daredevil* #191 (1983); *Daredevil* #7 (1999); *Daredevil* #49 (2003); *Daredevil* #50 (2003).

39. *Daredevil* (2003 motion picture).
40. Haidt (2003); Janoff-Bulman (2012); Tangney et al. (2007).
41. Haidt (2003); Janoff-Bulman (2012); Tangney et al. (2007); Weiner (2006).
42. *Daredevil* #191 (1983).
43. Haidt (2003).
44. Tangney et al. (2007); Weiner (2006).
45. *Daredevil* (2003 motion picture).
46. *Daredevil* #8 (1999).
47. Haidt (2003); Tangney et al. (2007).
48. *Daredevil* #1 (1998); *Daredevil* #8 (1999); *Daredevil* #228 (1986); *Daredevil* #74 (2005).
49. Haidt (2003); Tangney et al. (2007); Weiner (2006).
50. *Daredevil* #7 (1999); *Daredevil* #0.1 (2014); *Daredevil vs. the Punisher: Means and Ends* #3 (2005).
51. *Marvel Knights* #3 (2000).
52. *Ultimate Marvel Team-Up* #8 (2001).
53. Haidt (2003).
54. *Marvel Knights* #1 (2000).
55. *Daredevil* #180 (1982).
56. *Daredevil: Love & War* (1986).
57. *Marvel's Jessica Jones,* episodes 1–1 "AKA Ladies Night" and 1–3 "AKA It's Called Whiskey" (November 20, 2015); *Daredevil* #181 (1982); *Daredevil* #6 (1999).
58. American Psychiatric Association (2013).
59. *Daredevil vs. the Punisher: Means and Ends* #1 & #5 (2005).
60. *Marvel's Jessica Jones,* episode 1–2 "AKA Crush Syndrome" (November 20, 2015).
61. *Daredevil* #189 (1982).
62. Glover (1984); Hendin & Hass, (1991); Henning & Frueh (1997); Hull et al. (2002); Wilson et al. (2006).
63. Hendin & Hass (1991); Wilson et al. (2006).
64. *Daredevil* #8 (1999).
65. *Daredevil vs. the Punisher: Means and Ends* #6 (2005).
66. *Marvel's Jessica Jones,* episode 1–6 "AKA You're a Winner!" (November 20, 2015).
67. Fincham (2000); Martinez-Pilkington (2007); McCullough (2000); Worthington (2003).
68. *Daredevil* #232 (1986); *Daredevil* #1 (1998).
69. Exline et al. (2003); Farhadian & Emmons (2010); Murray-Swank et al. (2007); Spilka & Ladd (2013); Worthington (2003).
70. *Catholic Church* (1995)
71. Hareli & Eisikovits (2006); Weiner (2006).
72. *Daredevil* (2003 motion picture).
73. Coughlan et al. (2017); Frimer (2016); Goethals & Allison (2012); Kinsella et al. (2017).
74. Algoe & Haidt (2009); Aquino et al. (2011); Oliver et al. (2012); Schnall & Roper (2012); Vianello et al. (2010).

CHAPTER 6

NELSON & MURDOCK:
IT'S ALL IN THE FAMILY

LARISA A. GARSKI &
JUSTINE MASTIN

"There are no individuals in the world, only fragments of families."
—psychiatrist/family therapist Carl Whitaker[1]

"I should live in a cave and have no friends. No family. I should care
about no one. Just live in a cave and go out at night to break bones and
teeth. But then I'd probably be even more crazy than I already am."
—Matt Murdock[2]

A child's identity formation begins with his or her core caregiving group, or *family*. The structure of the family has a lifelong impact because it is through the family that the child first learns how to connect, attach, and relate to others. The field of marriage and family therapy has long understood this connection between family and identity, with a number of its practitioners arguing that an individual can only be fully understood within the context of his or her family. Beginning with the loss of his mother as an infant, Matt Murdock has struggled with attachment.[3] Though his early relationships are profound—shaping him into the Daredevil he will become—they are also damaging. Feeling abandoned by mother, father, and sensei,[4] Matt Murdock experiences both the joy and the pain that connection can bring. As an adult, Matt likes to think of himself as having resolved his childhood trauma. But, try as he might, Matt Murdock cannot escape the impact of his early familial experiences.

FAMILY OF ORIGIN: MURDOCK BOYS TO YOUR CORNERS

Rules, roles, and boundaries are essential aspects of family. Whether these are overtly or covertly discussed, they are enforced and reinforced by the power dynamics within the family system.[5] Jack Murdock never explicitly tells his young son, Matt, that their family rule is that the boy must wait late into the night for his father to come home. Jack just comes home each night broken and bleeding and asks his young son to "patch me up."[6] Similarly, Matt's role in the family as his father's *de facto* partner is never explicitly discussed between father and son. Jack treats Matt as his adult friend and the boy does his best to live up to the responsibilities of this role.[7] Rules, roles, and boundaries have a profound impact on all members of the family, but most especially on those at the bottom of the family hierarchy: the children. While adults can often understand and interpret the covert and overt communications that enforce the family's systemic structure, children benefit from explicit instruction. Without clear communication, dysfunctional behavior and maladaptive patterns may develop.

One of the few roles and rules known to be explicitly addressed in the Murdock home is the rule about fighting and the role of the fighter. In all iterations of the Murdock boys, Jack is the fighter and Matt is the scholar: "Don't end up like me. Study hard."[8] Though Matt appreciates his father's love and attention, he struggles under the weight of his father's wishes and demands, longing to find a way to be both a scholar and a fighter.[9] While the emotional boundaries in much of the Murdock house are *diffuse*, or lacking in appropriate structure, the boundary between fighters and scholars is rigid. Marriage and family therapists generally counsel families to move toward flexible boundaries. Neither diffuse nor rigid, *flexible boundaries* allow families to adapt to the inevitable changes that will come their way. Diffuse boundaries often lead to role confusion. *Rigid boundaries* are prone to breaking both themselves and the people enclosed within them.[10]

Diffuse boundaries are characterized by a lack of communication and consistency.[11] These boundaries are more likely when the power dynamic between the parent and the child is out of balance. Marriage and family therapists conceptualize boundary dynamics as existing hierarchically, with the preferred dynamic depicting the parent above the child. When boundaries are diffuse, a parent may begin to act like a child or vice versa. Both the child and the parent may find themselves on the same ladder rung of the hierarchy, thereby fostering a pseudo–partnership. If the child is above the parent on the ladder, this can foster a parentified child dynamic. Role switching and confusion often ensue. With the exception of the boundary separating the fighter, Jack Murdock, from the scholar, Matt, the boundaries between parent and child are more diffuse than is appropriate in the Murdock family hierarchy. Jack is inconsistent in the ways he relates to his son, sometimes forcing him to play the role of partner, at other times a confidant or friend, and at others a child or son.[12]

BOUNDARIES

Just as countries have physical boundaries, we have emotional boundaries between ourselves and others.[13] And in the same way that countries will vet those who enter their country, we vet those who enter our lives. Some countries, such as North Korea, have very rigid (or closed) boundaries and are very hard to enter.[14] This closed system causes them to be quite isolated, neither allowing others to enter their country, nor sharing information about themselves with the outside world. This is not only isolating for the country, but creates a sense of otherness and often fear. Some countries have very diffuse, boundaries, meaning easy to cross without legal restrictions. The ideal boundaries for both countries and people are neither rigid nor diffuse, but rather flexible. Flexible boundaries allow an individual to decide when and how to connect with others in a way that is generally sustainable for all. Matt and his father exhibit diffuse boundaries. After spending time with Stick, Matt begins to adopt rigid boundaries with his family of choice as a way to protect both them and himself from the potential pain of loss or harm. Ultimately, Matt adopts rigid boundaries when engaging with people in his Daredevil persona and more diffuse boundaries as Matt Murdock. If Matt could find a way to move toward flexible boundaries in either one or both of his personas, he could find a way to be both independent and connected to his community.

Particularly in the parent/child dynamic, diffuse boundaries can have damaging consequences. As an adult, Matt struggles with his history of diffuse boundaries and conflicting roles, unintentionally re-creating them in his new relationships with family members of choice. This is perhaps most evident in his relationship with Foggy Nelson, whom he treats as best friend, partner, kid brother, and taskmaster. Eventually, Foggy finds these chaotic roles unsustainable and therefore leaves Matt, sometimes as law partner and sometimes as friend.[15]

Diffuse boundaries can lead to enmeshed relationships between family members. *Enmeshment* is a concept first made popular by Murray Bowen. In his work with schizophrenic families, Bowen found that sometimes the relationship between two family members—often between a parent and a child—could become so close as to be emotionally fused.[16] Enmeshed family members feel each other's emotions and have a difficult time differentiating between their own individual experiences. The result of enmeshment—particularly for children—may be traumatic. Matt's emotionally enmeshed relationship with his father leads him to believe that he is responsible for Jack's death: "It's my fault. It's my fault. I did it. I killed him."[17]

Matt's guilt and shame haunt him as an adult, feeding the conflict between his two lives as Matt Murdock and the Devil of Hell's Kitchen. In terms of family dynamics, *differentiation* is the state in which an individual is able to be both separate from and connected to his or her family of origin.[18] The roles, rules, and boundaries of the family determine the degree of differentiation a child can achieve and the family has a lasting impact on the child's ability to differentiate as an adult. Matt, as Daredevil, struggles to connect with his family of choice because he is breaking the first and most explicit family rule of his family of origin: Don't fight, Matt.[19]

GENOGRAM KEY

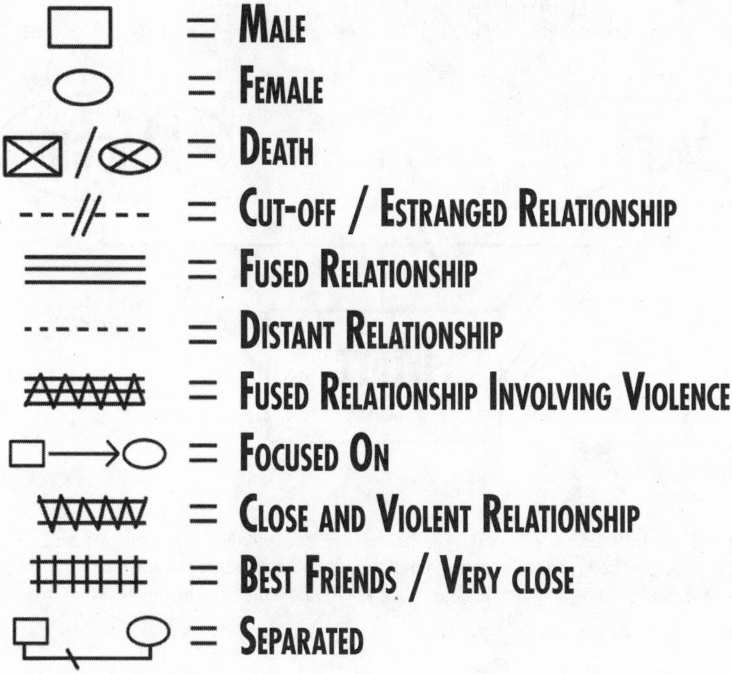

▭ = **MALE**

◯ = **FEMALE**

⊠ / ⊗ = **DEATH**

- - -//- - - = **CUT-OFF / ESTRANGED RELATIONSHIP**

≡ = **FUSED RELATIONSHIP**

- - - - - - = **DISTANT RELATIONSHIP**

△△△△△ = **FUSED RELATIONSHIP INVOLVING VIOLENCE**

▭——▸◯ = **FOCUSED ON**

▽▽▽▽ = **CLOSE AND VIOLENT RELATIONSHIP**

╫╫╫╫ = **BEST FRIENDS / VERY CLOSE**

▭ ◯ = **SEPARATED**

A genogram is a pictorial representation of the family system, along with its roles, rules, and boundaries.[20]

Genogram I: Family of Origin

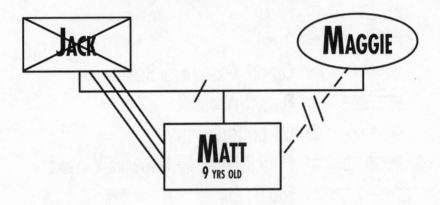

Genogram I: Whereas Matt and his father have a close relationship, Matt and his mother experience emotional cut-off in that they have no contact. Murray Bowen believed that emotional cut-off cost as much energy as emotional fusion.[21]

GENOGRAM II:
FAMILY OF ORIGIN

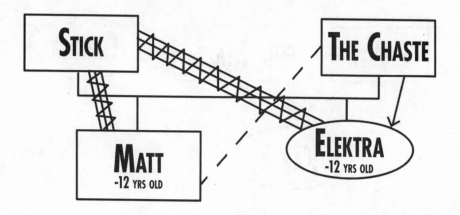

Genogram II: Matt and Elektra both have a close yet violent relationship with Stick at a time when they do not yet know each other.

GENOGRAM III: FAMILY OF CHOICE II

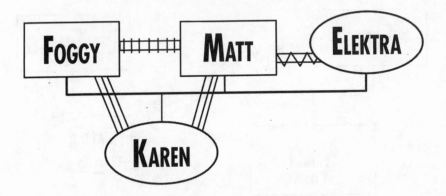

Genogram III: As the founders of Nelson & Murdock, Matt Murdock and Foggy Nelson function as parents of their legal family. When they bring Karen into the firm, they treat her with adoring paternalism and it is only with considerable effort on Karen's part that they eventually recognize her as an equal, instead of as an adult child warranting protection. Matt carries this same struggle into his relationship with Elektra, often treating her paternalistically.

STICK'S DOUBLE BIND

As difficult as a fractured family of origin may be, it becomes the child's norm. Adapting to new circumstances or systems—even when those systems have healthier dynamics—can be challenging. The devil you know is better than the devil you don't. After the murder of his father, the television version of Matt is sent to live at St. Agnes Orphanage. Adrift in grief over the loss of both parents, Matt struggles with his role at the Catholic orphanage, where he is treated like a disabled child. Parentified children often find it difficult to transition back to being treated as "just a child."[22] At the orphanage, Matt's status as disabled discomfits him, while his new role as a child strips him of the purpose he had serving as his father's friend, confidant, and caregiver.

Despite the unconventional and arguably dysfunctional relationship between Matt and his father, Matt's role as pseudo-partner to his father gives him a sense of purpose.[23] His father treats him like a contemporary and Matt rises to meet that challenge. Even after Matt loses his sight, Matt's father does not allow his son to wallow in self-pity. Instead, he encourages him to grow. While this approach might seem harsh, it is in line with later research related to trauma and post-traumatic growth.[24] Just as gaining superpowers can help you cope with the traumatic loss of your sight, thanks to toxic goo exposure, acceptance coping and positive reappraisal coping can help victims understand and grow from their trauma.[25] Jack Murdock pushes his son to face his feelings, accept his loss, and move forward—hallmarks of posttraumatic growth therapy.[26] For the television version of Matt, Jack Murdock's death marks the end of such therapeutic training.

In the comic book incarnation of Matt Murdock, he trains with the blind warrior Stick while his father is still alive. For a brief time, Matt has both a father and a paternal mentorem—one guides him to become a scholar while the other trains him in the art of the fighter.[27] Arguably the happiest time in Matt's young life, this joy is short-lived.[28] Matt suffers the loss of both his father and his sensei simultaneously. By contrast, the television incarnation of Matt Murdock meets his sensei only after Jack Murdock's death[29] and hopes to form a new family of choice with Stick as his pseudo-father and himself as the avenging son. But Stick has other plans.[30] In his tutelage of Matt, Stick regularly deploys what is known as the *double bind*, issuing instructions that contradict each other and yet require direct action from the listener. Matt feels he must fulfill them because he is bound to Stick as his apprentice, but there is no way for him to win. The *double bind*[31] is a highly dysfunctional communication pattern that entraps both the speaker and the listener: "the 'victim'—the person who becomes psychotically unwell—finds him or herself in a communicational matrix, in which messages contradict each other, the contradiction is not able to be [commented] on and the unwell person is not able to leave the field of interaction."[32]

Systemic family therapy would highlight this difference between the explicit and implicit messaging as dysfunctional and potentially harmful if allowed to persist. In therapy, a marriage and family therapist might reflect that Stick's conflicting messages and double bind communication patterns might indicate a contradiction in his own feelings toward Matt. Stick may say that he "need[s] a soldier,"[33] but buying his soldier ice cream and counseling him on his father's death are not the actions of a dispassionate sensei. They are the connections that form the foundation of a parent-child relationship. Confused by Stick's stated meaning, as opposed to his intent, Matt tries to attach to him as if he were not just his sensei but also a surrogate father. The unclear boundaries and conflated roles in Matt's relationship with his earliest caregiver—his father—predispose him for this struggle in future relationships and Stick's dysfunctional communication habits are but a continuation of this pattern. Matt's attachment to both his first and his second fathers results in their loss. For Matt, the lesson seems to be that attachment is dangerous and perhaps best avoided.

As if to emphasize this idea, when the comic book incarnation of Matt first starts dating Elektra, Stick shows up in his life again, for the first time in years, solely to tell his former pupil to stay away from her. This is Matt's first true romantic love, and yet his old mentor identifies her as an enemy, tells the boy, "She's poison," then leaves without any clear explanation for his claim or any care of how this may affect the young man's feelings.[34] Yet, Matt is rarely able to avoid attachment for long. Relating his own self-destructive tendencies to his need to connect to others, Matt muses, "I am my own worst enemy. That's why I could use a friend."[35]

NELSON & MURDOCK: MATT'S FIGHT FOR DIFFERENTIATION

Once individuals enter adulthood, they seek out new supportive groups, or *families of choice*. This phenomenon allows adults to foster community outside of their family system.[36] As an adult, Matt has the power and ability to forge a new path and make a new family. He is no longer a child, caught between a bureaucratic system (Catholicism) and dysfunctional core caregivers (first both his parents, then his father alone, and lastly Stick). Matt struggles to resolve the conflict between the rules of his first two families (*Don't be a fighter*[37] and *Do not attach*)[38] with his core desire to both fight for and connect with his city. What the Devil of Hell's Kitchen truly strives for is differentiation.

Differentiated individuals are those who resolve the conflicts of their family system by choosing which patterns to retain and which to reject while still remaining emotionally attached to their family.[39] As an adult, Matt Murdock oscillates between the extremes of his vigilante persona, Daredevil, who needs nothing and no one, and Matt Murdock, a lawyer attempting to connect with his community and new family of choice. In his comic book life, Matt sometimes pushes the envelope, attempting to kill off or abandon one persona for the other. He even leaves his beloved Hell's Kitchen for a time![40] Arguably, his most extreme attempt to rid himself of the conflict caused by his conflicting roles is when he fakes Matt Murdock's death. Channeling his unattached Daredevil persona, he tells costumed colleagues like Spider-Man that he is a different man who has newly adopted the Daredevil role and, thus, owes them no care, consideration, or allegiance.[41]

Initially, Matt is reticent to connect with others. In college, he treats Foggy as an irritating kid brother, often laughing at his numerous foibles.[42] Post-graduation, Matt and Foggy open a law practice together, signifying Matt's first adult commitment toward building a community where he attaches with others. At first, Matt's second family of choice seems to be solving the problems and healing the wounds of his family of origin and his first chaotic family of choice with surrogate father Stick. In the early days of Nelson & Murdock, Matt strives to fill the role of father or leader while Foggy becomes both his legal and familial partner.[43] While the addition of Karen Page proves complicated, with both Matt and Foggy vying for her affections while condescending to her as though she were a younger sibling, a relative harmony is achieved.[44] Matt keeps his Daredevil persona separate from his life with his new family of choice, creating two selves: one who fights and another who connects. By engaging in a double life, Matt attempts to resolve the conflicting rules and roles of his childhood: Daredevil follows the path laid out for him by Stick while Matt Murdock follows the rules of his family of origin.

At first, living two split lives with distinct dynamics works. Things start to go awry when Matt tries to forge romantic partnerships. The field of marriage and family therapy has long conceptualized committed partnership as one of the most challenging types of attachment because it involves the merging of two or more different family systems.[45] A successful merger requires both parties to have achieved similar levels of differentiation as well as commensurate understanding of each other's and their own family systems. Without such knowledge, the partnership is often doomed to failure. Not only does Matt Murdock struggle with differentiation and the effects of multiple family systems, he lives two distinctly separate lives. Thus, he often finds himself in relationships with women who are best suited to either Matt Murdock (e.g., Karen Page) or Daredevil (e.g., Elektra Natchios)—but rarely to both. Natasha Romanoff, the Black Widow, arguably comes closest to satisfying both sides of his life, but Matt's inability to complete his own differentiation is ultimately the death knell of this relationship.[46] The most consistent relationship of Matt's life is with the city of New York, specifically with Hell's Kitchen. "Don't these people read the papers or watch the news or even trade stories in a seedy bar somewhere?" he muses. "The Kitchen is under my protection."[47] As both Daredevil and Matt Murdock, he attaches to the city in problematic ways, depending on the city to be a constant companion, a child to care for, and a parent to guide him. His struggle is one and the same: How do I connect without losing myself or those I love? Whether Matt can resolve his role confusion and tendency to oscillate between isolation and enmeshment, thereby achieving healthy differentiation, remains to be seen. For now, he remains trapped between two disparate personas, sacrificing himself for those he loves while never allowing himself to fully connect with them. Though Matt Murdock loves his city more than he loves himself,[48] time and again he concludes: "I'm destined to always be—a loner! Where Daredevil walks, he must walk alone."[49]

NOTES

1. Olson et al. (1994), p. 16.
2. *Daredevil* #114 (2009).
3. *Marvel's Daredevil*, episode 2–1, "Cut Man" (April 10, 2015); *Daredevil* #4 (1999).
4. Respectively, mother—abandonment recounted in *Daredevil* #6–7 (2014); father—death in *Daredevil* #1 (1964); sensei, Stick—abandonment in *Daredevil: The Man without Fear* #2 (1993).
5. Minuchin & Fishman (1981/2002).
6. *Marvel's Daredevil*, episodes 1–1, "Into the Ring" (April 10, 2015); 2–1, "Cut Man" (April 10, 2015).
7. *Daredevil: The Man without Fear* #1 (1993).
8. *Daredevil* #1 (1964); *Daredevil: The Man without Fear* #1 (1993); *Marvel's Daredevil*, episode 1–1 "Into the Ring" (April 10, 2015).
9. *Daredevil* #177 (1981).
10. Hooper et al. (2007).
11. Minuchin & Fishman (1981/2002).
12. *Marvel's Daredevil*, episode 1–1 "Into the Ring" (April 10, 2015).
13. Minuchin & Fishman (1981/2002).
14. Kim (2014).
15. *Marvel's Daredevil*, episodes 2–9, "Seven Minutes in Heaven" (March 18, 2016); 2–11, "The Dark at the End of the Tunnel" (March 18, 2016).
16. Brown (1999).
17. *Marvel's Daredevil*, episode 1–7, "Stick" (April 10, 2015).
18. Brown (1999).
19. *Daredevil* #100 (1973).
20. McGoldrick et al. (1999).
21. Bowen (1999).
22. Hooper et al. (2007).
23. Smokowski et al. (1999).
24. Calhoun & Tedeschi (2006, 2013).
25. Van Slyke (2013).
26. Calhoun & Tedeschi (2006, 2013).
27. *Daredevil: The Man without Fear* #1 (1993).
28. *Daredevil: The Man without Fear* #1 (1993); *Daredevil: The Man without Fear* #2 (1993).
29. *Marvel's Daredevil*, episode 1–7, "Stick" (April 10, 2015).
30. *Daredevil: The Man without Fear* #1 (1993).
31. The Palo Alto group discovered the double bind as part of their work on feedback loops within communication systems (Gibney, 2006).
32. Gibney (2006), p. 50.
33. *Marvel's Daredevil*, episode 1–7, "Stick" (April 10, 2015).
34. *Daredevil: The Man without Fear* #3 (1993).
35. *Daredevil* #24 (2017).
36. Braithwaite et al. (2010); Gazso & McDaniel (2015); Voorpostel (2013).
37. *Daredevil* #1 (1964); *Daredevil: The Man without Fear* #1 (1993).
38. *Daredevil: The Man without Fear* #1 (1993).
39. Brown (1999), p. 3.
40. *Daredevil* #87 (1972).
41. *Amazing Spider-Man* #396 (1994).
42. *Daredevil* #1 (1964).

43. *Daredevil* #108 (1974).
44. *Daredevil* #6 (1965).
45. Neil & Kniskern (1982/1989).
46. *Daredevil* #97 (1973), #100 (1973), #108 (1974), #124 (1975).
47. *Daredevil* #1 (1999).
48. *Marvel's The Defenders*, episode 1–8, "The Defenders" (August 18, 2017).
49. *Daredevil* #5 (1964).

CHAPTER 7

THE HEROES AND VILLAINS OF HELL'S KITCHEN

JENNA BUSCH & JANINA SCARLET

"I'm just a guy that got fed up with men like you and I decided to do something about it."
—Daredevil[1]

"The world needs heroes."
—heroism researcher Philip Zimbardo[2]

What causes someone to take a heroic or a villainous action? Most people are capable of heroic actions, yet most do not partake in them.[3] Heroes such as Matt Murdock, who regularly risk their lives to protect others, do not represent the general population. Similarly, some people, such as the assassin Elektra, are capable of villainous acts, even if they are not malicious by nature.[4] Some circumstances can make some people more or less likely to engage in a heroic or a villainous act. Under which circumstances are we more likely to become heroic like Daredevil and when are we likely to commit unkind acts?

THE VILLAINS

"The opposite of a hero is not a villain, it's a bystander."
—heroism speaker Matt Langdon[5]

In his book, *The Lucifer Effect,* Stanford psychologist and heroism researcher, Dr. Philip Zimbardo, asks his readers to consider what makes good people commit evil acts. In his book, Zimbardo suggests that society often might overestimate the role of an individual's personal traits and underestimate the role of the specific situations and circumstances that might have contributed to violence.[6] For example, as a child, one of the prominent Hell's Kitchen villains, Wilson Fisk, is not evil. However, after his father takes him to confront his bully neighbor and forces him to repeatedly kick the bully, Wilson becomes more aggressive, eventually killing his father and many others.[7] This also happens when Karen Page, Murdock's assistant, sells Daredevil's real name to get drugs.[8] A situation like this, in which a person experiences pressure from authority, can lead that individual to take more extreme actions than he or she normally would. Other examples of situations that can lead to villainous behaviors include social learning, conformity and bystander effects, and dehumanization of others.[9]

SOCIAL LEARNING

Individuals can learn to act in a violent and aggressive manner toward others by observing the actions of people around them. For example, children like Wilson Fisk, who are exposed to violent behaviors or films, are more likely to act aggressively immediately after watching the film. Similarly, children who observe adults behaving in a violent way might also mimic this behavior in the future.[10] After Wilson Fisk sees his father beat his mother, he becomes aggressive and later murders his father with a hammer.[11]

OBEDIENCE TO AUTHORITY

Another reason that people might be willing to commit heinous acts is pressure from authority. Many people have a natural inclination to follow authority, as it is part of a common social structure.[12] However, blind obedience to authority can lead to an abandonment of accountability by the individual. For example, when a researcher (Dr. Stanley Milgram) asked his participants to administer an electric shock to another person, approximately 65 percent of the participants not only agreed to shock another individual but agreed to continue administering shocks past the "danger" level and despite the apparent cries of pain and distress by the actor. Unbeknownst to the participants in the study, no actual electricity was being conducted and the person they believed they were administering shocks to were actually actors.[13] Similarly, in *The Defenders*, Alexandra, the leader of an evil organization, the Hand, manipulates Elektra, a trained assassin and Matt's ex-girlfriend. As Alexandra's authority over Elektra grows, Elektra eventually becomes her weapon, the Black Sky, killing many members of the Chaste, an organization to which Matt Murdock and Elektra used to belong.[14]

SOCIAL ROLES

The roles people play can also cause a change in their behavior.[15] In the famous Stanford Prison Experiment, male college students were assigned to role-play as either prisoners or prison guards. In less than one day, the students began acting according to their roles. Specifically, many of the "prisoners" were severely distressed, while many of the "guards" were ruthless and abusive. This experiment had to be cut short due to the severe psychological suffering exhibited by the "prisoners" due to the harsh treatment they received from the "guards."[16] Like the guards in the Stanford Prison Experiment, the police officers in Hell's Kitchen also play a role in being immoral and ruthless to the citizens of New York. For example, when Wilson Fisk is captured, the officers attempt to help him escape in a helicopter.[17]

CONFORMITY AND BYSTANDER EFFECTS

Social roles also play a part in creating a sense of social pressure in the need to conform to social expectations. Specifically, when an individual sees a group of people behaving a particular way, he or she is likely to adopt the behavior and sometimes even the attitudes and beliefs of the group.[18] This might cause an individual to express an opinion different from what he or she believes.[19] Social conformity is seen in Detective Brett Mahoney's behavior. Although he has irrefutable proof of the corruption of the police department, Mahoney outwardly conforms to the actions of the other detectives and pretends that nothing is out of the norm.[20]

Detective Mahoney's behavior also resembles a *bystander effect*. Under some circumstances, such as when surrounded by bystanders, people are less likely to help others than when they are alone.[21] This bystander effect can translate to people failing to intervene when they observe bullying or violence.[22] We see this when Murdock's friend, Glori, is being robbed and no one in the crowded square attempts to help her.[23] Detective Mahoney also displays bystander effects: He is willing to help Foggy and Matt fight the department's corruption when he is alone with them, but when he is with another officer, he does nothing to stop some of the injustices occurring in Hell's Kitchen.[24]

DEHUMANIZATION

Finally, dehumanization effects (seeing other people as less than human) can also lead to someone committing a villainous act.[25] Dehumanization is more likely to occur toward someone who is a member of a different group and is usually accompanied by a feeling of disgust. In plotting to destroy much of Hell's Kitchen, Wilson Fisk explains that he does not see the people of New York City as anything but a group deserving of being destroyed. Instead, he sees them all as evil, filthy, and disgusting, stating that the people of his city do not deserve to live.[26] Because dehumanization allows people to disregard the humanity of certain people, it also allows for less guilt over committing violent acts against them.[27]

THE HEROES

Psychologists traditionally focused on studying villains, but more recently have turned to studying heroes. The word *hero* comes from a Greek word *heros*, which means *"protector."*[28] A heroic act then means a voluntary action in which a person acts to protect another person or group, regardless of the potential adverse physical or social consequences. Matt Murdock fights villains, like human traffickers, despite the potential risk to himself and despite the guilt he feels for attacking others. He frequently goes to confession to ask for forgiveness before or after he must hurt others in order to save the innocent.[29] Hence, heroes are likely to put themselves in physical or emotional danger to right a potential wrong,[30] such as when Elektra leaves Matt to protect him from what is going on with her family.

The notion of heroism is different from compassion and altruism. Whereas heroism implies putting oneself in potential danger in order to protect others, altruism and compassion do not have this requirement. Altruism can include a small

MY AMYGDALA MADE ME DO IT

Both helpful prosocial and villainous psychopathic types of behaviors involve a small almond-shaped part of the brain (the amygdala).[31] The amygdala is the emotion center of the brain, where most emotional events are processed. Emotions, such as fear, anger, and stress, all involve the amygdala.[32] The amygdala also allows us to evaluate threat potential. If a particular threat seems imminent, the amygdala would allow the body to initiate action to prevent the threat from occurring.[33] Daredevil relies not only on his sensory perceptions but also on his emotional responses, such as fear, to alert him when he or someone else may be in danger. For example, when Karen is attacked after sneaking out of his house, Matt's fear senses alert him that he needs to act, prompting him to protect her from her attacker.[34]

act of kindness, such as when Matt offers his wisdom to his young, paralyzed client,[35] which does not necessarily involve a danger to him.[36] Compassion also does not require exposing oneself to danger. Instead, compassion involves empathy (understanding how another person feels) and the desire to help him or her.[37] Claire, a nurse who learns Daredevil's true identity, speaks about the reason she's helping Matt. She says that she understands his desire to help people and talks about all the violence she's seen in the hospital and how the victims cited a masked man who helped them. She feels compassion for her patients, which gives her the strength to help Matt Murdock.[38]

Heroic people are often impulsive, with some individuals, such as members of the military or first responders, being more likely to help others than individuals without a lot of prior training.[39] The considerable risks involved in most heroic actions include physical (death, injury, or pain) and social (rejection, ostracism, loss of status, or loss of finances) threats.[40] Heroes who risk physical harm include service members, emergency responders, and civilians,[41] such as Karen Page, who works for Murdock and his partner, Foggy Nelson. In the television series, Karen risks her life by going to speak to Wilson Fisk's mother in order to get evidence for their case against Fisk.[42] On the other hand, heroes who risk social harm include martyrs, scientists, good Samaritans, and whistle-blowers who risk retaliation in order to right the wrong they witness.[43]

LEADING A HEROIC LIFE

There are many reasons that someone may choose to engage in particular behaviors. Among those reasons are pressure from authority, social learning, and bystander effects. Mob bosses, such as Wilson Fisk and Finn Cooley, are likely to use their authority to force others to perform heinous acts, adopting social roles that require violence and dehumanization of others.[44] On the other hand, heroes like Matt Murdock make a choice to be a hero. Murdock regularly risks his life to help others, despite the risk and cost to himself.[45] Like many first responders, he has extensive training in how to defuse risky situations. He helps others through heroic acts, as well as kind and compassionate gestures. Although heroic actions may be impulsive and may present a physical or a social threat to the individual, these acts may also benefit others.[46]

ARE HEROES HUMBLE?

BY ERIC D. WESSELMANN &
JORDAN P. LABOUFF

Superheroes are often seen as bastions of moral virtue, amplifying personal qualities that we ought to emulate. Daredevil may maintain his secret identity in part to be modest—to avoid the public praise that would compli- cate his mission. However, Daredevil often struggles with other aspects of humility. Humility is a personality trait that goes beyond modestly avoiding recognition. Humble people focus less on themselves and more on the needs of others.[47] They understand and work within their strengths and limitations. Although Daredevil's vigilantism certainly helps others, his motives often reveal his self-focus and lack of awareness of his limits. Daredevil, like his father,[48] puts himself and his companions at risk to pursue what he thinks is right. This strains his partners and relationships, for example, leaving Foggy Nelson to improvise opening statements in *The People v. Frank Castle*.[49]

Daredevil's companions, however, are more humble. Not only are Foggy and Karen focused on other people's needs, they use their unique strengths to help others safely. When Foggy encounters a rapidly escalating situation in the emergency room, he shames the criminals into submis- sion with his rhetorical and legal skills.[50] Similarly, Karen uses her investigative skills to try to redeem the Punisher.[51] Even Stick, Daredevil's teacher, may be considered humble. His focus is beyond himself—preparing for global war.[52] Further, he recognizes his limits and avoids risking himself or his allies unnecessarily.[53] However, his approach is other- wise morally murky, suggesting that humility, although an important social virtue, does not itself make one virtuous.

NOTES

1. *Marvel's Daredevil,* episode 1–6, "Condemned" (April 10, 2015).
2. Quoted by Stafford (2017).
3. Allison & Goethals (2016).
4. Zimbardo (2007).
5. Quoted by Stafford (2017).
6. Zimbardo (2007).
7. *Marvel's Daredevil,* episode 1–8, "Shadows in the Glass" (April 10, 2016).
8. *Daredevil Born Again* (1987).
9. Bandura et al. (1963); Fiske et al. (2004); Milgram (1963); Haney et al. (1973); Latané & Rodin (1969).
10. Bandura et al. (1963).
11. *Marvel's Daredevil,* episode 1–8, "Shadows in the Glass" (April 10, 2016).
12. Milgram (1963).
13. Milgram (1963).
14. *Marvel's The Defenders,* episode 1–1, "The H Word" (August 18, 2017).
15. Zimbardo (2007).
16. Haney et al. (1973).
17. *Marvel's Daredevil,* episode 1–13, "Daredevil: (April 10, 2016).
18. Asch (1955).
19. Asch (1956).
20. *Marvel's Daredevil,* episode 1–1, "Into the Ring" (April 10, 2016).
21. Latané & Rodin (1969); van Bommel et al. (2012).
22. Goldman (2012).
23. *Daredevil Born Again* (1987).
24. *Marvel's Daredevil,* episode 1–1, "Into the Ring" (April 10, 2016).
25. Bandura et al. (1975); Fiske et al. (2004).
26. *Marvel's Daredevil,* episode 1–13, "Daredevil" (April 10, 2016).
27. Fiske et al. (2004); Fiske (2009).
28. Kinsella et al. (2015).
29. *Marvel's Daredevil,* episode 1–1, "Into the Ring" (April 10, 2016); *Daredevil: The Man without Fear* (1994).
30. Buckley (2007); Miller (2016).
31. Franco et al. (2011); Schwartz (2014).
32. Schwartz (2014).
33. Buckley (2007).
34. *Marvel's Daredevil,* episode 1–1, "Into the Ring" (April 10, 2016).
35. *Marvel's The Defenders* episode 1–1, "The H Word" (August 18, 2017).
36. Franco et al. (2011); Israel et al. (2012).
37. Jinpa (2016).
38. *Marvel's Daredevil,* episode 1–2, "Cut Man" (April 10, 2016)
39. Buckley (2007).
40. Franco et al. (2011).
41. Franco et al. (2011).
42. *Marvel's Daredevil,* episode 1–10, "Nelson v. Murdock" (April 10, 2016).
43. Franco et al. (2011).
44. Bandura et al. (1963); Fiske et al. (2004); Milgram (1963); Haney et al. (1973); Latané & Rodin (1969).
45. *Marvel's The Defenders,* episode 1–1, "The H Word" (August 18, 2017).

46. Buckley (2007); Jinpa (2016); Miller (2016).

47. LaBouff et al. (2012); Van Tongeren & Myers (2016).

48. *Daredevil*, episode 1–2 "Cut Man" (April 10, 2015).

49. *Daredevil,* episode 2–7 "Semper Fidelis" (March 18, 2016).

50. *Daredevil*, episode 2–3 "New York's Finest" (March 18, 2016).

51. *Daredevil*, episode 2–12 "The Dark at the End of the Tunnel" (March 18, 2016).

52. *Daredevil*, episode 1–7 "Stick" (April 10, 2015).

53. *Daredevil*, episode 2–13 "A Cold Day in Hell's Kitchen" (March 18, 2016).

III

DETAILS

"The devil's in the details."
—*idiom*

POWERS OF PERCEPTION: WHICH DETAILS?

Detail *(noun)*. 1. A part observed separately from the whole. 2. Persons assigned to a task.
(verb). 1. To report with attention to minutia. 2. To clean meticulously. 3. To assign to a task.

Matt Murdock's ability to detect details that others do not or cannot sense becomes Daredevil's superpower, a power so unusual that even his own allies are often unsure what it is.[1] As far as most know, he might be psychic or he might just be really observant. While he is not the only superhero with super senses, others such as Wolverine tend to be sighted and therefore attend to details differently.[2] Even with a sense of hearing or smell identical to Matt's, a sighted person would notice different things and rely less heavily upon those other senses than he does. Even when they close their eyes, they know they can still open them at any moment and see.

Sensation broadly refers to the processes by which sense organs detect information about a person's external and internal environment, whereas *perception* refers to how the individual receives that input and organizes it. Although a number of modern researchers call it all perception because any measure of what we sense inherently involves finding out what we perceive,[3] much of the earliest research in psychology attempted to identify pure elements of sensation, especially vision and hearing.[4] Those pioneers of psychological science began to build the world of their new field in ways akin to how our minds build the world we perceive: by beginning with whatever details our senses bring us. Matt Murdock builds his perceptual world with different building blocks.

How do his powers really work? Which details does he use that we do not? Which details does he use differently, and what does he do with it all? When we wonder how a blind man makes his way through the world, we might consider that his senses give him different building blocks and therefore construct a different world. He navigates his way through his world, not ours.

—T.L.

NOTES

1. *The Defenders* #1 (2017).
2. Wolverine's enhanced senses are also a side effect of his primary power, the healing factor first revealed in *X-Men* #116 (1978).
3. Goldstein & Brockmole (2017).
4. Stumpf (1883/1890); Wundt (1862/1961).

CHAPTER 8

FOCUS:
WHEN THE BLIND HERO
SEES BETTER

TRAVIS LANGLEY

"Make the most of every sense; glory in all the facets of pleasure and beauty which the world reveals to you through the several means of contact which Nature provides."
—author Helen Keller[1]

"A blind man does not trust any way another man tells him to step! You've got to know the way! Know which path to walk, Matt Murdock!"
—Stick[2]

How often do you close your eyes to fix your attention on other senses, trying to identify a sound or retrieve a memory that has been stirred by a scent? Why does anyone need to do that? It produces no changes on the external stimuli, so what goes on inside us that makes this happen? For many reasons, reducing input from one sense can enhance our perception of another, and that might be why Matt Murdock says, "Sight is overrated."[3]

SEEING CLEARLY

The human eye brings an image into focus when light rays converge on its retina. Despite common misconceptions, a one-eyed individual has some *depth perception* via the relative size of different objects, relative motion, color intensity, texture, and how the eye feels when fixing on one object as opposed to others (*monocular cues*). One-eyed depth perception actually relies on a greater variety of details than the kinds of information (*binocular cues*) that two-eyed depth perception utilizes. By exclusively learning to process the monocular cues, the one-eyed person can become better at noticing and using them than the person with two fully functioning eyes is.[4] The person with no vision at all does not need exposure to radio-active waste to become better at processing completely different cues—such as volume and echo—when judging distance and depth. Why does this happen? When the same sound reaches two different people—one sighted and one blind—why doesn't the sighted individual glean as many of the details that sound can reveal? How does vision interfere with comprehension of sounds, smells, and other sensory cues?

THE DOWNSIDE TO SIGHT
On numerous occasions in the comic book series, the blind superhero worries that if he regains his eyesight, he might lose his special abilities and therefore his edge as Daredevil.[5] He does not want to lose his focus because helping others and "this 'profound sense of justice' of mine is even more important to me" than the chance to see again.[6]

We tend to be a visually oriented species, more easily influenced and manipulated by information presented to us by
visual means. That's why prosecutors like to show brutal crime
scenes to juries and why many judges restrict how much the
prosecutors may show—because the *vividness effect* is preju-
dicial, evoking emotions that can get in the way of logic by
making juries eager to convict someone for such a horrible
crime, regardless of other evidence that may indicate guilt or
innocence.[7] The person who cannot see an unnecessarily prej-
udicial image will not be biased by the sight of it. Because
attorney Matt Murdock remembers what it was like to see and
has spent his life aware of how vision affects others, he knows
how to make use of imagery when necessary.

"Seeing is believing," people say, even though it shouldn't
always be. An *illusion* is a misperception of real sensory information, such as when someone misjudges the distance needed to
throw a ball because the other person is shorter than expected
and therefore appears to be farther away. Optical illusions will
not confuse the man who cannot see them. Conjured images
or holograms will not trick him, either[8] (although an illu-
sionist with the power to affect other senses might fool him
nonetheless).[9] Just as Daredevil is immune to visual illusions
and will not be slowed by blinding lights, he also remains
unhindered when a foe makes the "clever" move of simply
turning out the lights.

One sense may alter our perception of another sense (*sensory
interaction*), such as when smell changes how we perceive flavor
or when watching video shot from a roller-coaster makes
us feel like we're lurching forward even despite sitting still.
Interaction can mean interference. Attention to a sight can
intrude upon interpretation of a feeling, taste, smell, or sound.
It can even throw off our sense of balance because the effect
is not limited to the rest of the traditional five senses. As in
the roller-coaster example, vision can interact with how we

perceive our *kinesthetic, proprioceptive,* and *vestibular senses*—
respectively, our senses of motion, body position, and balance
(the first two of which could be argued to be the same thing).[10]

Vision is limited both horizontally and vertically. Its range
is not 360 degrees in any direction. The *focal point*, where an
image is sharpest at the center (*fovea centralis*) of the retina at
the back of each eye, takes up only a tiny portion of the entire
visual field. Other senses, however, are not so restricted in
their range, and Daredevil takes full advantage of this fact,
both to enhance his performance and to confuse enemies who
do not know he is blind.

THE UPSIDE TO BLINDNESS

Relying on senses other that vision offers certain advantages.
Daredevil's abilities to hear, feel, smell, and even taste details
that other people overlook or simply cannot detect effectively
make Daredevil his own portable crime lab. These enhanced
abilities give him an edge as criminal investigator, crime-
fighter, and courtroom attorney.

Opponents cannot sneak up on Daredevil from behind.
Even though Matt Murdock refers to his hearing giving him
a 360-degree range of perception, that two-dimensional
description fails to convey how great the range of sound-based
perception really is because we live in a three-dimensional
world. Daredevil swings up and down through his city on all
axes—x, y, and z. Admittedly, he enjoys a superhuman form of
radar through his heightened senses and the comic book writers
vary on whether they treat this as an extension of his hearing
or as an extra sense entirely,[11] but blind individuals in real life
can learn to recognize environments through *echolocation*, their
own sort of radar, as chapters 9 and 10 will explain. With this,
some completely blind people do things as seemingly sight-
dependent as riding a bike, and they don't have to look over
their shoulders to see what's coming up from behind.[12] When

"built-in radar tells me where everything is better than eyes,"[13] why let eyes interfere?

Blind individuals gain other auditory advantages as well. They tend to excel at recognizing sounds and retrieving them from *episodic memory* (memory of events).[14]

Anybody with functioning *olfaction* (sense of smell) might notice a strong smell of perfume, aftershave, or body odor from another person, regardless of whether that individual has crossed into our line of sight. Blind individuals, especially those who are born blind or lose eyesight early in life, become much better at distinguishing specific smells.[15] Matt regularly recognizes people by their smell, and not only by those obvious odors. When he meets the nun known as Sister Maggie, one of the first clues to the fact that she is his biological mother is the fact that her scent is similar to his own. Blind individuals without superpowers become better at identifying smell, and *congenitally blind* individuals (those blind from birth) more so.[16] Blind his entire life, Matt's mentor Stick relies on, among other things, naturally superior olfaction. Those born blind use smell more than the sighted do in order to assess environment, recognize settings, and identify other people.[17] One study found that congenitally blind individuals could better identify people's emotions, such as fear and disgust, from their body odors.[18] Matt, having developed as a normally sighted person during his earliest years, would not have gained these benefits to the degree that Stick has if not for his mutagenic enhancement.[19] Some of these effects may be subtle. It's difficult to know because blind individuals' olfaction has not been studied as carefully as most other senses have.[20]

Ability to notice the *pheromones* (airborne hormones) with a sniff may contribute to the list of reasons that Daredevil is normally able to resist the Purple Man's pheromonally based form of mind control.[21] Matt's ability to detect specific details out of sensory chaos around him and the willpower he needs to process it all may also help protect him from such mind control. We may be more easily influenced by others when we're distracted, possibly because distraction reduces the portion of attention available for careful analysis of commands or arguments.[22]

Undistracted by eyesight, Daredevil brings all his other senses into sharp focus. He must. Blindness could help Matt by keeping some *task-irrelevant stimuli* (those cues that do not provide information on target to the task at hand) outside of his awareness. *Cue utilization theory* holds that we each have a limited range of environmental details, *cues*, we can process in any given instant.[23] Although the theory focuses on the role that arousal plays in narrowing the number of cues bombarding our attention, its basic principle has broader implications through the assertion that limiting the number of irrelevant cues entering our attention can focus our attention on the relevant ones. While researchers have disagreed over how and when our nervous system screens irrelevant cues,[24] there is nonetheless considerable agreement that we do need to filter out irrelevant stimuli.

Reducing the number of cognitive or perceptual tasks our minds are working on improves performance overall. We're much worse at multitasking than we like to think. *Meta-analysis* (analysis of other analyses) of findings from many studies showed that trying to multitask interferes with performance on cognitive tasks and makes people more susceptible to persuasion; that is, more likely to change their attitudes without sufficient contemplation.[25] Extensive multitasking impedes the ability to focus attention and to control where one's own attention will turn.[26] Matt Murdock cannot see a touchscreen. Inconvenient as this may be at times,[27] he also does not get lost in the images while impulsively flitting from one tweet or blog post to the next, and this allows him greater *attentional control* than if he still had vision on top of all his super senses.

SEEING WITHOUT SIGHT

Bat-like radar is not the only advantage offered by Matt's remaining senses. Every sense provides a wealth of information that humans tend to miss, things that other species might perceive. Examples and applications of how super senses help a superhero function could fill their own book.

Matt believes that the radioactive material that heightened his remaining senses did so by altering his brain.[28] Physiological changes to his senses inherently mean changes to his nervous system, true, but which part? The mutagen could conceivably produce such effects by altering the sensory nerves themselves, although it would be difficult for it to affect all sensory nerves throughout the body. It is not as though Matt bathed in the material. A change to the *central nervous system* (brain and spinal cord) therefore seems more likely.[29] The next two chapters will explore what those changes might be, how Daredevil's powers might work, and what they have to do with how real people sense and perceive.

NOTES

1. Keller (1933), p. 42.
2. *Daredevil* #254 (1988).
3. *Marvel's The Defenders*, episode 1–04, "Royal Dragon" (August 18, 2017).
4. Adkisson (2006); Rosenfield & Logan (2009).
5. e.g., *Daredevil* #8–9 (1965).
6. *Daredevil* #223 (1985).
7. Bell & Loftus (1985).
8. *Daredevil* #8 (2012).
9. e.g., *Daredevil* #352 (1996).
10. Goldstein & Brockmole (2017).
11. e.g., *Daredevil* #8 (1965), #10 (1965), #41 (2003), #1 (2011). See Hanefalk (2011).
12. Screenocean (2012).
13. *Daredevil* #233 (1985).
14. Kärnekull et al. (2016).
15. Cuevas et al. (2009).
16. Araneda et al. (2016).
17. Beaulieu-Lefebvre et al. (2011).
18. Iversen et al. (2015).
19. Kupers et al. (2011).
20. Araneda et al. (2016); Kärnekull et al. (2016).
21. *Daredevil* #4 (1964).
22. Baron et al. (1973).
23. Easterbrook (1959).
24. Broadbent (1959) vs. Deutsch & Deutsch (1963) or Lavie (1995).
25. Jeong & Hwang (2016).
26. Moisala et al. (2016); Reissland & Manzey (2016).
27. Such as when he cannot see an image on Elektra's phone in *Daredevil* #7 (2016).
28. *Daredevil* #1 (2011).
29. Doidge (2010); Van Ackeren et al. (2017).

CHAPTER 9

HOW THE BLIND SEE

JIM DAVIES

"I guess you have to think of it as more than just five senses. I can't see, not like everyone else, but I can feel. Things like balance and direction. Micro-changes in air density, vibrations, blankets of temperature variations. Mix all that with what I hear, subtle smells. All of the fragments form a sort of impressionistic painting."
—Matt Murdock[1]

"Echolocation is usually attributed to bats and toothed whales, which analyse the echoes of self-generated sounds to navigate and hunt. But blind humans also produce sounds to evaluate their environments; some individuals even have perfected this skill for orientation: By clicking their tongue, objects are ensonified and the reflections can be analysed to create acoustic snapshots of the environment."
—neuroscientists Ludwig Wallmeier, Nikodemus Geßele,
and Lutz Wiegrebe[2]

aredevil is an effective crime-fighter, martial artist, and acrobat, in spite of being completely blind. This apparent paradox is part of what makes him so fascinating: How can he possibly do this?

Like a blind person in the real world, Matt Murdock uses his other senses to great effectiveness to compensate for a lack of vision. When sighted people imagine being blind, the idea of relying on the other senses seems terrifying, suggesting that the blind would have to have their other senses more effective than those in sighted people. Are blind individuals' other senses more effective? Sort of. One study showed that blind people's sense of touch was significantly better than sighted people's. Touch sensitivity declines with age, and researchers found that blind people were, on average, as good as sighted people twenty-three years younger.[3]

What about the other senses? Blind people will often tell you that their sense of smell is more intense than other people's. But it turns out it's not—their ability to identify and detect smells seems to be the same as it is for other people, whether you're testing them with questionnaires or studying their brain responses.[4] The situation is similar with hearing. It's not that blind people have better hearing, in terms of raw sensitivity, but that they get so much more from their hearing because they pay much closer attention to it. In his early years, before his radar sense develops into what we see in modern stories, Matt Murdock becomes very adept at navigating his world simply by listening to sounds around him, often not even needing to employ superhuman sensitivity to do so.[5] The blind are better at knowing where sounds are coming from, for example.[6]

Daredevil's different. The ooze that gave Matt Murdock his powers clearly made his nonvisual senses much more acute. Daredevil can detect lies by listening to heartbeats, and hear police radios from blocks away. He can smell blood sugar rising,[7] and his sense of touch is so sensitive that he can read printed text on paper based on the topology of the ink—but he can't read screens, because what's on them doesn't make any topological deformation.

ECHOLOCATION

Typically the domain of bats and dolphins, echolocation is the use of reflected sound waves to get information about the spatial organization of the environment. You might experience a minor kind of echolocation when you close your eyes and repeat a word over and over again while you slowly bring the palm of your hand toward your face; the sound quality changes as things get closer. Sighted people can also tell the rough size of a room by the sounds in it,[8] and you can find a stud by knocking on the wall at different places.

But some blind people take this to another level entirely. They generate clicking sounds and then use the echoes to identify the position, size, shape, distance and texture of the objects and surfaces around them.[9] The physics and psychology of sound put some limits on this skill, however. Sound travels at about 300 meters per second, and the time it takes for sound to come back to you indicates how far away it is. That's pretty fast. It's so fast that if you're trying to use echolocation for something less than 2 meters away from you, you can't consciously tell the sound from its echo. But people are able to use echolocation at these distances anyway, meaning that some unconscious part of the brain can detect sound differences as small as 0.3 milliseconds![10] Normal human hearing also has the limitation that it can't detect sounds with frequencies above about 20 kHz. The physics of this means that humans can't use echolocation for things smaller than about 2 cm. Bats can hear sounds up to 200 kHz, which is why they are able to use sound to find mosquitoes.[11] We don't know how small an object Daredevil can detect exactly, as the

THE DAREDEVIL AND NOAH WEBSTER: COMPENSATIONS

TRAVIS LANGLEY

"Blindness is part of his personality. Part of his motivation is not simply altruism; he's overcompensating."
—comic book writer/artist Frank Miller[15]

COMPENSATION

Making up for feeling inferior in one area of life by optimizing strengths and advantages in another can be good and healthy.[16] In college, Foggy Nelson might compensate for his lack of athletic prowess by majoring in prelaw in order to pursue a high-status career suited to his talents. Even without exposure to radioactive waste, Stick compensates for being blind since birth by learning to use his other senses far better than other people, even most blind people, do.[17]

explanation sometimes changes. In his first story, he describes it as a tingling sensation when he nears objects, similar to Spider-Man's spider-sense.[12] Over time, he compares it to a bat's sonar, and his comic describes it as a process of emitting low-frequency waves inaudible to humans without his heightened sense of hearing, and then listening to how those sound waves bounce back.[13] Most comics, however, and the television series *Marvel's*

UNDERCOMPENSATION

Failing to compensate in healthy ways can make people needy and afraid, demanding that others help them as they lack courage to try doing things for themselves. Stick cautions against this when he tells young Matt, "A blind man does not trust any way another man tells him to step! You've got to know the way!"[18]

OVERCOMPENSATION

Instead of achieving a balance in life, an individual might go too far, expending excessive time, attention, or resources in order to feel safe, secure, or self-assured. Narcissistic overcompensators may strive for power or dominance over others. While the choice to become superhero or supervillain at all may seem a bit like egotistical overcompensation, the villains are the ones who exploit, steal, overpower, and try to take over the world.

Not willing to settle for becoming strong and successful to overcome having been an impoverished, "unpopular, blubbery child," Wilson Fisk becomes the Kingpin of Crime.[19] No matter how he damages key relationships or how many times superheroes, authorities, gangsters, and a few frustrated family members take him down,[20] Fisk keeps pushing himself to dominate. Even if he could lose a lot of his weight, he would not. He wants to be an imposing presence.

Daredevil, indicate that his "radar" is created by combining the information gleaned from his heightened senses. In particular, he is paying attention to how sound and air bounce off objects around him from other sources, rather than creating any kind of low-frequency sound himself.[14] With enhanced hearing, perhaps through cochlear implants, maybe someday people will develop bat-like abilities of echolocation.

But even without enhancement, some blind people can do some pretty amazing things. Ben Underwood, for example, was a blind boy who able to play foosball, ride a bike, play video games, and score baskets in basketball by using sound. What he could do was truly astounding, as online videos demonstrate. Long-term echolocators like Ben move their heads to help them gather spatial information about their environment, to help get 3-D information, a little like binocular vision.[21] Interestingly, they also start to recruit for echolocation brain areas normally used for vision (*cross-modal neuroplasticity*),[22] which puts an interesting twist on the very idea of blindness—they are getting spatial information normally taken in by the eyes, and using the same brain areas as the eyes, to perform similar functions as eyes. Even sighted people can learn to do this, but because most people have their vision systems intact, they don't bother to learn.[23] Sensory deprivation in one sense, even if it's temporary, can make one pay more attention to and, as a result, sometimes have better discrimination with, other senses. Just wearing blindfolds for a few minutes, for example, allowed people in an experiment to be able to identify more layers of harmony in musical notes. Visual deprivation also seems to make people better at picking out sound in a noisy environment—something often called the *cocktail party effect*, named after the phenomenon that occurs when you hear your own name when someone says it at a party.[24]

In many stories and the television series, while Daredevil most certainly uses echoes to understand his environment, he rarely uses sounds he himself generates for that purpose. He seems to use what's called "passive echolocation": using the echoes of sounds generated elsewhere in the environment. There are exceptions. In the *Daredevil* film (2003), he knocks his baton on a surface to get a sense of the layout of a subway station.

This reliance on sound, in some versions of Daredevil, can cause a genuine disability in the presence of too much noise: Loud sounds can sometimes render his powers useless, as when a train goes by, flooding his echolocation with too much noise.[25] Indeed, Daredevil's enemies often use sound to "blind" him. In the made-for-TV movie, *The Trial of the Incredible Hulk*, the Kingpin uses blaring sound to render Daredevil's echolocation useless.[26] In the comics, we've seen that rain, especially a heavy downpour, can interfere with Daredevil's perceptions: The sounds of the drops hitting so many surfaces around him cause interference and the physical sensation of them against his body causes a distraction he describes as "a pepper-fire of needles and razors."[27]

Other versions show Daredevil using something akin to radar, rather than sonar. *Daredevil* comic book writer Mark Wald and his artists work hard (and effectively) to give the reader an idea of what our hero's perceptual world is like. Murdock gets a clear, three-dimensional perception of the surfaces in his environment by interpreting echoes of a radar-like signal he sends out, described as "probing, high-frequency waves."[28] This comic cleverly shows the world from his point of view with the drawings of fuchsia contour lines over the environment, much like the way the *Daredevil* motion picture uses blue shapes.

The cover of this comic book is particularly interesting, showing all surfaces of Hell's Kitchen written in words describing what they sound like: Birds' surfaces say "flap" and a fan's surface says "whoosh," for example. This radar perception also gets disrupted with a jamming signal by his enemies, through the use of antiradar chaff: filling the air with bits of debris to hide radar detection of more important objects, a technique that was also used in World War II to keep aircraft from being detected by the enemy.[29]

In all cases, however, there are things that Daredevil cannot see, such as color, whether a smooth surface is a mirror or just glass, or anything on a screen. Basically, any properties that *require* the perception of reflected light, as opposed to 3-D shapes, are invisible to Daredevil.

"Radar sense feels like walking through the room and touching
everything at once . . . My brain has developed a language of its own
to interpret physical things. It's gotten so that words like 'rectangular'
or 'yellow' or even 'slim' or 'fat' are not the sort of terms I tend to
think in anymore."
—Matt Murdock[30]

SPATIAL VERSUS VISUAL

To better understand Daredevil's perceptual world requires
understanding a subtle distinction that sighted people don't
naturally think about: the difference between visual and spatial
information. When sighted people see a scene, what we're
consciously experiencing feels like a complete, integrated
sensory package. But, in spite of how it feels, different parts
of the brain are working on processing different parts of the
scene. For example, the human visual system can be roughly
broken into "what" and "where" pathways.

The "what" pathway is visual. It runs along the bottom of
your brain, and deals with things like color and shape in two
dimensions. This is the information that Daredevil doesn't
have. By contrast, the "where" pathway is spatial. It processes
the locations of objects in three-dimensional space around you,
and runs along the top of the brain.

One of the reasons we know that these are separate pathways is that if the visual pathway gets damaged, we lose some
information and not others. The titular character from Oliver
Sacks's fascinating book *The Man Who Mistook His Wife for a
Hat* knows where things are, but has no idea *what* they are,
causing him, in some instances, to try to pick up his wife by
the head, because he can't tell the difference between her and
his hat. Similarly, if you lose your "where" pathway, you can
get into the intriguing situation where you know what's in

front of you, and what color is in front of you, but have no idea where it is.[31]

This is hard to understand, so I'll give you an exercise that might help: Imagine a woman standing in front of you, wherever you happen to be right now, reading this. Imagine her with a red dress (if you can't do this, don't worry, it's pretty common—5 percent of people get nothing like a visual image when they try to do this). Now imagine her walking behind you. But don't change the point of view of your imagination— that is, don't pull the camera back, so that you and the woman are both in the image. Just look ahead, imagining, to the best of your ability, that she's behind you.

If you're like most people I try this with, the character of the imagination changes when she's behind you. For me, she loses any vivid sense of color and other visual properties. It's not that I *see* her behind me, I just kind of *know* that she's there. What's happening is that your imagined woman is going from a visual and spatial representation in your mind to a completely spatial one.

Another difference is that strictly visual information comes from the eyes only. But spatial information comes from many senses,[32] and this is part of why Daredevil's understanding of the world around him is so rich. Murdock's spatial sense is incredible, and it's three-dimensional, which allows him to do things like dodge attacks coming from behind him.

As we've seen, sound can be used to distinguish where surfaces are. Touching, with your hand or with a cane, also provides information. Even smell is used by some animals to get a 3-D understanding of space. Snakes, for example, use their forked tongue to detect different smell intensities. If the right side of the tongue gets more mouse smell on it than the left, it knows that the mouse is to the right of the snake (when the tongue is pulled into the mouth, it rubs against olfactory sensors there—this is why snakes flick their tongues). Daredevil seems to use smell to some extent—in *The Defenders*, he knows which server is holding a pork dish as opposed to a shrimp dish, presumably because of smell intensity differences in a Chinese restaurant.[33] We've been told that with time, he can identify people by their scents and—while his olfactory sense is not as sharp as Wolverine's—he can track that person from fifty feet away in a crowd.[34]

And, of course, the eyes also provide spatial information, if the eyes are intact. But the point is that the sense of space is a multisensory experience, which is how blind people understand the layout of their house and neighborhood without the use of their eyes. Because of Daredevil's reliance on, and careful attention to, his spatial awareness, he has a richer 3-D representation than sighted people enjoy. In a combat situation, where you're surrounded by enemies, this can be a distinct advantage.

WHAT DOES DAREDEVIL ACTUALLY SEE?

Blind people get asked "What do you actually see?" all the time.[35] The intuitive answer is that they see a vast, undifferentiated blackness. But for people blind since birth, they don't see blackness—they see nothing.[36] This might be hard to imagine, but suppose you could talk to loggerhead turtles, who can sense which way is north. A baffled turtle finds out that you can't sense the Earth's magnetic field and asks you, "Well, then, what do you sense when you change direction?" Your answer wouldn't be the magnetic equivalent of black— your answer would be that you sense nothing at all. The turtle might have trouble understanding your answer, just as you might have trouble understanding that blind people see nothing *instead of darkness*. "Nothing" is also what you see out of the back of your head: Spread your arms out until your fingertips are no longer visible. Now, what is the color of the space your hands now occupy? It's not black or white. It just *isn't*.

But what about Daredevil? Like other blind people, we can presume that Daredevil's visual cortex has been recruited by other senses to help with spatial understanding.[37] We also know that people often don't know which senses they are using when they get meaning from the world. Perhaps, because the visual cortex is being used, albeit by other senses, we can say that the superhuman Daredevil is, in a manner of speaking, having a visual experience. Different comics have shown Daredevil's perception of his surroundings as a 3-D map of blue shapes or white shapes or textured, vibrating pink shapes.[38] In the television show, we get one view of what Daredevil's perceptual experience might be like. Claire asks him what he sees and he says it's a "world on fire."[39] Visually, we see shapes but no colors, stylized as though everything were made of burning embers.

Blind people in real life have rich sensory experiences, and the ways they compensate for blindness are various and clever. Some blind people are visual artists, and even photographers.[40] (Repeat, *some*! Never assume any specific individual can perform such feats.) The amazing abilities of blind people in the real world show that you don't need superpowers to live your life without your eyes—but if you're going to beat up criminals in Hell's Kitchen, it probably helps.[41]

NOTES

1. *Marvel's Daredevil*, episode 1–5, "World on Fire" (April 10, 2015).
2. Wallmeier et al. (2013).
3. Goldreich & Kanics (2003).
4. Schwenn et al. (2002).
5. *Daredevil* #164 (1980).
6. Gougoux et al. (2005).
7. *Daredevil* #1–6 (2011).
8. Teng et al. (2016). It often bothers me, when I'm watching animation, that the sound character of the voices are not appropriate for the environment their cartoon versions are in. Whether the character is outside in the wind, or in a small room, often the voices just sound like they're in a sound studio.
9. These clicks tend to be about 10 milliseconds long, and spectrally broad. The most effective clicks are palatal—made by moving the tongue backward and downwards from the top of the mouth, just behind the teeth (Thaler et al., 2011).
10. Kellogg (1962).
11. Stoffregen & Pittenger (1995).
12. *Daredevil* #1 (1964); #164 (1980).
13. *Daredevil* #167 (1980)
14. *Daredevil* #177 (1981).
15. Interviewed by Sanderson (1982), p. 18.
16. Adler (1907/1917); Vaughn (1926).
16. *Daredevil: The Man without Fear* #1 (1993).
18. *Daredevil* #254 (1988).
19. *Daredevil* #300 (1992).
20. e.g., *Web of Spider-Man* #30 (1987).
21. Rosenblum et al. (2000).
22. Thaler et al. (2011).
23. Wallmeier et al. (2013).
24. Pagé et al. (2016).
25. Foster & Johnson (2003).
26. *The Trial of the Incredible Hulk* (1989 television movie).
27. *Daredevil* #15 (2012).
28. *Daredevil* #1–6 (2011); *Daredevil* #167 (1980).
29. Jones (1978), p. 39.
30. *Daredevil* #1 (2011).
31. Levine et al. (1985).
32. Halpern & Collaer (2005).
33. Marvel's *The Defenders*, episode 1–4, "Royal Dragon" (August 18, 2017).
34. *Marvel Universe Handbook* (2004).
35. Tommy Edison (2013), a blind man, reports that he gets asked this a lot.
36. Davies (2014).
37. Merabet & Pascual-Leone (2009).
38. *Daredevil* #1 (2011).
39. *Marvel's Daredevil,* episode 1–5, "World on Fire" (April 10, 2015.
40. Gallagher (2015).
41. That said, a blind judo champion successfully took down his mugger (*Daily Mail*, 2007).

CHAPTER 10

DAREDEVIL'S SUPER-INTEGRATED SENSORY SYSTEM

CRAIG POHLMAN

"He that is strucken blind cannot forget the precious treasure
of his eyesight lost."
—playwright William Shakespeare[1]

"You got opened up to senses everybody's got, but don't use."
—Stick[2]

When radioactive material strikes young Matt Murdock in the face, his eyes sustain significant trauma.[3] Significantly, his brain appears to be altered.[4] How and why this cognitive rewiring occurs is the stuff of comic books and science fiction; after all, every fan knows that exposure to radiation can be a boon for attaining superpowers. Nevertheless, real science offers clues about how Murdock acquires amped-up senses of hearing, smell, taste, and touch. Specifically, studies on neuroplasticity, synesthesia, and echolocation help explain how Daredevil's brain might work. Data from his remaining senses, along with his radar sense, must be integrated to give him something even more formidable than sight: a cognitive system that provides detailed sensory coverage of his environment.

MATT'S BRAIN

The brain is very adaptable; it can heal and recover even when damaged by injury or disease. This adaptability is known as *neuroplasticity*.[5] The fields of psychology and neuroscience long held that abilities are localized in parts of the brain and that damage to specific parts causes permanent loss of function. Later research showed that functionality can be regained or even shift to other areas of the brain.[6] Obviously, Matt's eyes are damaged. Less clear is whether his optic nerves and visual cortex also are affected. But something must happen to his cortex to account for the boosted functioning of his remaining senses.

CROSS-MODAL ENHANCEMENT AND BLINDSIGHT

When one sensory modality is damaged, science suggests that others compensate (*cross-modal enhancement*). It has been suggested, though, that an exception to this type of neuroplasticity is the negative effect that loss of smell has on perception of taste. When your nose is stuffed up, it sure *seems* like it's harder to taste food. However, one study exposed this notion as a myth, finding that taste perception was unaffected by olfactory dysfunction when other effects (such as age) were controlled.[7] Blind individuals have often been shown to possess enhanced nonvisual perceptual abilities. One example of such cross-modal enhancement that closely relates to Matt involves forms of auditory processing. Blind listeners were found to be superior to sighted individuals at accurately selecting target voices from test arrays.[8] Also, blind study participants displayed localization abilities that were superior to those of sighted control participants when attending to sounds in peripheral auditory space.[9] Thus, setting aside the potential effects of radiation on his nervous system, Matt's auditory system would get a boost just from his loss of sight.

What might be happening in Matt's cerebral cortex? Early-blind research participants (those who have lost eyesight early in life) were found to be superior at sound localization displayed activation in two areas of the brain's *occipital* (visual) cortex. The more accurate a person was at localizing, the higher the degree of cortical activation.[10] So not only could Matt get better at localizing sound than people who can see, he would be able to do so by utilizing portions of his brain typically devoted to visual processing; the more his occipital cortex was used for auditory processing, the higher his accuracy is. It is probably significant that Matt sustains his injury as a young boy, as visual deprivation from an early age can lead to more cross-modal enhancement. For one thing, practice effects can mount over time. Blind persons get practice navigating their environments with auditory cues. Researchers have concluded, though, that individual differences in cross-modal enhancement probably have a lot to do with innate factors not related to practice[11] (or radiation exposure, perhaps).

Matt's trauma and recovery seem analogous to a particular sort of cross-modal neuroplasticity known as *blindsight*, which refers to the residual visual abilities of patients with primary visual cortex lesions.[12] Blindsight is characterized by the ability to localize a visual target without actually seeing it. This ability actually is controlled by residual portions of the visual cortex.[13] Blindsight shows that perceptions from various modalities (hearing, smelling, etc.) and distinct cortical regions

SENSORY DEPRIVATION
AND MINDFULNESS

Matt's enhanced sensory system gives him numerous advantages for reconnaissance and combat. It comes with risk, however, when the magnitude of his perceptions goes beyond what he can control. When he is struck with a second dose of radiation in adulthood,[14] his senses are further amplified to dysfunctional extremes. The effects come in waves when the faintest aromas overwhelm him and he hears whispers as thunder.[15]

Matt contracts, in essence, a rare but real condition called *hyperacusis*, which is an abnormally strong reaction in auditory pathways when someone is exposed to moderate-level sound.[16] His symptoms become so severe that he sequesters himself in a sensory deprivation chamber. He pleads to Stick, the man who long ago taught him to master his abilities, to let him stay in the chamber indefinitely to escape the pain

can be integrated through neural pathways. Put simply, different parts of the brain talk to each other to create a unified depiction of the environment. This relates to Matt's fascinating superpower: Even though his brain does not receive visual data, it still formulates pictures that are based on nonvisual data. He is seeing what is not really in front of him, akin to virtual reality. However, because our nonvisual senses operate *omnidirectionally* (in every direction) as opposed to *unidirectionally* (in one direction) the way vision operates, his composited visual layout is not restricted to what is in front of him.

brought by his senses gone amok. Stick is known for his tough-love approach to mentoring. Accordingly, he taunts Matt and orders him to leave the tank.[17] Interestingly, Stick is following a real-life protocol for treating hyperacusis. Those with the condition actually need rich sound environments. They need to abandon any ear protection (muffs, plugs, etc.) because it causes an increase in the sensitivity of the auditory system as a result of decreased input.[18]

In addition to being a drill sergeant of sorts, Stick is Matt's spiritual adviser. He coaches Matt to push aside competing sensory input, however amplified, and center his perception. That kind of control is akin to meditation. Mindfulness-based stress reduction (MBSR) is a program that incorporates meditation and body awareness to alleviate harmful effects of negative emotions. Neuroimaging has revealed that MBSR training affects areas of the brain related to attention, introspection, and emotional processing.[19] So whether it's due to radiation exposure, neuroplasticity, MBSR, or whatever, Matt's brain just keeps on changing.

SYNESTHESIA

With *synesthesia*, stimuli from one sensory modality induce perceptions in another sensory modality in ways that can vary from person to person (or synesthete to synesthete in this case).[20] For instance, a taste might generate a perceived sound. One specific form involves reading digits and consequently experiencing vivid color.[21] Similarly, some individuals experience sensations of color when reading printed letters.[22] For some people with synesthesia, smells can reliably and automatically induce experiences in other sensory modalities.

In olfactory-visual synesthesia, people experience smells as images.[23] This gives credence to the notion that Matt could convert nonvisual input into a cognitive visual display.

Research has found in some people generalized and continuously distributed individual differences in the capacity to represent sounds as colors.[24] The oxymoronic term *auditory imagery* captures the phenomenon of "visualizing" what is heard in consistent and patterned ways (such as a pitch or timbre always generating a certain image). Not only does auditory imagery preserve many structural and temporal properties of auditory information, it involves many of the same brain areas as auditory perception.[25]

Synesthesia seems to represent one way that typical development can unfold by magnifying connections that are present in early life but get pruned or inhibited during development. These connections persist in muted form in all adults but are unrestrained in those with synesthesia.[26] For Matt, the connections may have been unleashed by the radioactive material. As important as his hypersenses is the hyperconnectivity of his brain. Just as those with synesthesia convert sensory data to other sensory modalities (utilizing cross-purposed cortical regions), Matt's brain converts nonvisual input to a visual perception (likely making ample use of his occipital cortex). However, there is another component to his cognitive system that, when integrated with nonvisual sensory input, takes his perception to a whole other level.

ECHOLOCATION

Radiation robs Matt of his sight, amplifies his other senses, and apparently boosts his brain's connectivity to allow integration of various sensory input. In addition, the radiation gives him a radar sense that allows him to detect surrounding objects and people. Again, science fiction and superhero literature take liberties with how radiation could affect the human nervous system. However, because radar involves the transmission and reception of radio waves, it makes more sense that Matt's hyped auditory sense enables him to develop sonar. Further, the technology used by ships and submarines mimics an ability found in nature (including in some humans).

Echolocation is the transmission and reception of sound waves; echoes are cognitively processed to locate objects and track movements. The bottlenose dolphin is one species that can discriminate between objects on the basis of the echoes reflected by the objects. Experiments have shown that human listeners can perform as well as or better than dolphins at discriminating objects quickly by using salient combinations of echo features.[27] In other research, blindfolded subjects could learn to locate a target by talking to it; for many subjects their training generated a sensory perception that was not auditory but tactile or visual.[28] So humans can emit sounds, process returning echoes, and integrate a visual layout of surroundings. Although a radar sense like Matt's is rare, maybe it isn't really super.

Again, the integration of input is critical to what Matt can do regarding echolocation. As with cross-modal enhancement and synesthesia, cortical connections are key. A study looked at blind echolocation experts (including individuals who lost sight early and later in life). When they processed click echoes, their brain regions typically devoted to vision were activated (rather than auditory regions).[29] The human brain shows remarkable adaptability and resilience even without a boost from radiation exposure.

PULLING IT ALL TOGETHER

There's that saying about the folly of describing red to a blind man. The converse applies to the sensory system of Daredevil. How could Matt describe the cognitive picture of his environment? How does he see with his radar/sonar? What images are conjured by smells, tastes, and tactile input? He might have a fighting chance given that he has had several years of sight to inform his explanations. Those years might even influence how he visualizes sensory input (mental sonar screen, perhaps?).

As has been mentioned, Matt's sonar, hearing, and smell are omnidirectional and far-ranging. His taste and tactile senses also are acute but are confined to his person. Input from his extended environment likely lights up his occipital cortex, and so he may visualize something. The omnidirectionality is what is really hard to comprehend. His abilities seem like cognitive virtual reality, but that comparison does not seem to apply because turning one's head changes what is perceived by the technology.

Perhaps Matt's brain constructs a three-dimensional model from the myriad of sensory input. This model is probably in color, though what the colors represent is an open question (as in synesthesia). Integrating all this dynamic input and perception would put enormous strain on his active working memory, which is the ability to mentally suspend information while using it in some fashion[30] (a common application of active working memory is solving a mental math problem, and juggling all of Matt's sensory input is one hugely complicated equation).

Somehow Matt would need to navigate this mental landscape. Even with advanced active working memory, he would be hard-pressed to focus on everything simultaneously. Maybe he moves his focus around this landscape like a drone, zeroing in on specific input. This would be akin to the contrast of central vision and peripheral vision. For example, he could use a heartbeat to signal the presence of someone a quarter mile away and identify him by his aftershave but then quickly shift to the padding of paws next to him and visualize a stray cat with his sonar and then zoom down the street when he feels the vibrations from an oncoming truck.

Radiation blinding Matt Murdock and amplifying his other senses is only part of the story. His real superpower is an altered brain. His cortex is hyperconnected, even making use of regions that processed sight before his accident. He combines sensory inputs to form mental manifestations of people, objects, buildings, vehicles, weather conditions, and so on. His eyes don't see anything, but his mind perceives everything.

NOTES

1. *Romeo and Juliet*, Act I, Scene I (circa 1597).
2. *Daredevil* #188 (1982)
3. *Daredevil* #1 (1964).
4. Pelletier (n.d.).
5. Doidge (2016).
6. Tokuhama-Espinosa (2010).
7. Stinton et al. (2010).
8. Bull et al. (1983).
9. Röder et al. (1999).
10. Gougoux et al. (2005).
11. Gougoux et al. (2005).
12. Danckert & Culham (2010).
13. Celesia (2010).
14. *Daredevil* #185 (1982).
15. *Daredevil* #186 (1982).
16. Jastreboff & Jastreboff (2000).
17. *Daredevil* #188 (1982).
18. Jastreboff & Jastreboff (2000).
19. Hatchard et al. (2017).
20. Spector & Maurer (2013).
21. Teichmann et al. (2017).
22. Arnold et al. (2012).
23. Stevenson & Tomiczek (2007).
24. Rader & Tellegen (1987).
25. Hubbard (2010).
26. Spector & Maurer (2013).
27. DeLong et al. (2007).
28. Taylor (1966).
29. Thaler et al. (2011).
30. Pohlman (2008).

IV

OTHERS

"Hell is other people."
—philosopher/playwright Jean-Paul Sartre,
No Exit (1944 play)

UNTO OTHERS

Other *(noun)*. 1. Someone else. 2. Someone perceived as different, alien, strange.
(verb). 1. To exclude. 2. To treat someone else as different, alien, strange.
(adjective). 1. Additional. 2. Different or distinct.

We are all caged inside our own skulls. No person can ever fully know someone else or truly confirm that everyone else is real. At some point in the first year of life, an infant begins to distinguish people and things in terms of what is or is not familiar, and so begin the degrees of otherness. Distinctions of "us" versus "them" will grow.[1] Discovering some levels of life's complexities will teach the child to categorize, although this relationship between complexity and categorization may follow a curve as the maturing individual breaks those categories down. Life is too complicated not to categorize people and things, and yet, contradictory as it may seem, life is too complicated to limit individuals according to the categories into which they fall.[2] We learn the concepts of *us* and *them*, and then we might also learn to see beyond them.[3]

Matt Murdock is not simply a blind man. He is not simply a lawyer. No one is. Every aspect of a person that puts him or her in a different category from oneself can heighten the sense of otherness. Perceived disability or stigma can foster a perception of otherness.[4] Because he is accustomed to being seen as a blind man when Matt Murdock, tactical advantages might not be the only reason Daredevil keeps his blindness secret. Because Matt Murdock's superhero colleagues usually do not know such things about him, that information would not necessarily heighten their sense of otherness about him, and yet he knows these things regarding himself.[5] He may "other" himself and create distance if he feels he does not fit in, which may be why he is not much of a team player. Sometimes people alienate themselves from others, and those others might not like that.[6] A person can strongly want social connections while paradoxically avoiding them or pushing them away.[7]

His mentor Stick tells Matt that attachment to others is weakness. Matt does not accept this as true because he values attachments even though he limits those attachments in both quantity and quality. A person can need people without needing a lot of them and without needing psychological intimacy. That person still needs others, though.

—T.L.

NOTES

1. Mortlock (2015).
2. Piaget (1954).
3. Govrin (2016).
4. Lalvani (2015).
5. Spider-Man in *Daredevil* #9 (2016), Luke Cage in *The Defenders* #7 (2017), and others have confronted Daredevil about his lack of self-disclosure.
6. Koritar (2017).
7. Lampe (2015).

CHAPTER 11

MOTHER SUPERIOR, FEELING INFERIOR: POST-PARTUM DEPRESSION AND THE MOTHER HE DIDN'T KNOW

REBECCA M. LANGLEY

"Is this what you want, Matthew? Answers to questions I haven't allowed myself to think about in almost thirty years?"
—Sister Maggie (Margaret Grace Murdock)[1]

"I couldn't shake the feeling of doom and gloom that pervaded each moment. I was afraid of myself and felt threatened by the dangerous thoughts running so calmly through my head. They all felt too real. When would I wake up from this bad dream?"
—author/actress Brooke Shields on her own post-partum depression[2]

A 1986 story introduced Matt Murdock's mother as a nun, Sister Maggie, 22 years after Daredevil's debut,[3] and yet no explanation for why she'd abandoned her husband and infant son would be provided until the 2014 story in which she finally describes having suffered post-partum depression so severe that she'd feared she posed a danger to herself or those she loved.[4] A combination of physical and emotional factors after delivering a child (*post-partum*) or during the weeks before or time after giving birth (*perinatal*) can indeed produce depression or in some cases psychosis. Beliefs about how mothers are "supposed" to feel, including expectations imposed by others and by the new parents themselves, and feelings that may include guilt can make these problems hard to acknowledge before they worsen and still difficult to discuss long afterward. Almost 30 years passed in real time, nearly the same as had passed within the fiction on the sliding scale of time that keeps superheroes from turning geriatric, before any writer addressed the issue and Maggie finally let herself talk about it with her son.[5]

DARKNESS

"I am depressed. . . ." "I have cancer. . . ."

We so often define ourselves and others suffering from mental illnesses in ways in which we never define physical ones. No one says, "I am cancer," but many people speak of their mental health maladies as though they were their defining characteristics. A person going through chemotherapy may be leading a life defined by the illness, but most of those patients do not feel as though the illness is the only thing in their lives once the treatment is completed. Instead, it is a part of each individual's experience as a person with an illness that is treatable and in many cases curable.[6] The shadow of the illness may follow them, but it does not often plunge them into a darkness they feel will never cease.[7] Is it by coincidence that writers depict both the blind superhero and his mother as experiencing darkness within their mental states?[8]

MOTHER AND SISTER

Matt Murdock's relationship with his mother is virtually nonexistent throughout his childhood and into adulthood. Even after Daredevil connects with the nun known as Sister Maggie and quickly identifies her as his mother, their relationship is not one of mother and son. Despite the friction it may cause between people, sticking to an obvious lie may induce less stress than would the frightening prospect of having to discuss the truth, and it can help the individual avoid thinking about unpleasant truths internally as well.[9] Although she takes on a role of nursing her son physically and emotionally, Sister Maggie does not admit to being his mother for quite some time. More than a few mothers have taken on sisterly roles in their children's lives rather than discuss the truth about their biological links.[10]

After Matt rescues her and urges her to open up at last, she finally discusses how she had, many years before, abandoned her husband and son because of debilitating post-partum depression (PPD). The backstory of Maggie Murdock is not discussed with much detail in the series until the *Original Sin* issues of *Daredevil* in 2014.[11] Within those few issues, the history of Matt's mother and her departure from his life are described and clear up some big questions about how and why his mother was not part of Matt's childhood.[12]

Matt Murdock's mother, Maggie, becomes a nun for most of her adult life and devotes her life to the church shortly after Matt's birth. When she finally divulges details to her son, Maggie discusses her past fears of hurting herself or her baby in what appears to be a case of perinatal depression bordering on psychosis. In her last-ditch effort to protect him, she leaves the baby in his father's care and joins a convent. She effectively banishes herself from her son's life, leaving him with his own later struggles with depression that culminate in relationship and intimacy issues, anger at his father whom he sees as having driven her away, and a thorough misinterpretation of what actually caused his mother to leave them.[13]

One of the most difficult issues regarding the treatment of depression in all its forms is the inability of people with depression to see that there is indeed light at the end of the tunnel of darkness that they are experiencing so strongly. Depression, by its very nature, entails experiencing powerful and relentless feelings of hopelessness, helplessness, and worthlessness.[14]

Post-partum depression has a different and potentially more powerful impact, as if major depressive disorder were not severe enough on its own. People so often expect new mothers to be happy if not outright ecstatic over the birth of their children. It is culturally frowned upon to feel nothing or even animosity toward your own infant. Women experiencing PPD often hide their feelings and become even more guilt-ridden and miserable because of the judgment they may fear from others if they admit their feelings. The fear of judgment is unfortunately justified considering how our treatment of women with PPD often results in court orders to limit a mother's contact with her child when actual danger is very rarely an issue. The sensationalized coverage of women who suffer from post-partum psychosis and commit horrific crimes against their children overrides commonsense and standards of care in far too many cases.

The reality is that at least an estimated 70 to 80 percent of women have what is almost jokingly called the "baby blues," which generally resolves on its own by the third week after delivery. Around 10 percent develop debilitating depressive symptoms during pregnancy (called *antenatal depression*) or shortly after childbirth (called *peripartum depression*) that can prevent normal bonding with the child and in the most severe cases actually cause the mother to have a psychotic break in which she can lose touch with reality and hurt herself or her child. This does not resolve on its own and can last for months or even years after childbirth.[15]

Further complicating the diagnosis and treatment of PPD is the tremendous shame and guilt that often accompany it. Women who are recovering from childbirth and the tremendous physiological changes impacting everything from estrogen levels to sleep patterns often think that they are not experiencing anything out of the ordinary when they are experiencing severe depressive symptoms.[16]

At the time when Maggie Murdock experiences her PPD, the average person in real life would have been unfamiliar with the difference between baby blues and PPD. The dividing line between normal and abnormal post–partum recovery was not well known, especially to a layperson, and the information was not readily available without tremendous effort and was likely to be well out of reach of a new mother struggling with PPD.

Comic book story timelines being what they are, it is hard to determine exactly when Matt Murdock was born. However, it is clear that he could *not* have been born when depression and its treatments were being advertised on television and print ads for antidepressant medications were on the pages of virtually every magazine aimed at women of childbearing age. Screenings for PPD were not in place as a standard of care for expectant mothers until fairly recently, and the stigma that persists regarding mental disorders was significantly greater than it is today.

One of the main treatments for depression is a class of medications called antidepressants. In 1961, three years before the first issue of *Daredevil*, the drug amitriptyline was released, and since it has sedation as a common side effect and is passed through to the infant via breast milk, it was not used in nursing mothers very often. The class of drugs of which amitriptyline is a part is called *tricyclic antidepressants*, and those medications were largely overtaken in the late 1980s by the *selective serotonin reuptake inhibitors* (SSRIs). The SSRIs and similar drugs have fewer side effects than the tricyclics but similar efficacy, and so they are prescribed much more commonly for all forms of depression, not just PPD.[17]

Fluoxetine, much better known by its brand name, Prozac, was not available for the treatment of depression until 1987, and it was part of the new wave of antidepressants that were touted as signaling the end of depression. Of course, as with all drugs touted as panaceas, it was soon proved to be limited in its usefulness. It acts on the neurotransmitter serotonin, which affects mood regulation. This in turn is theorized to lift mood in a depressed individual without many of the more negative side effects of the tricyclics, such as drowsiness. It and its cohorts are generally safe to use when a woman is nursing and do not have sedating effects, thereby making them the first line of medication treatment against PPD along with therapy and psychosocial support.

The DSM-5 changed the designation of post-partum depression to *major depressive disorder with peripartum onset*: "This specifier can be applied to the current or, if full criteria are not currently met for a major depressive episode, most recent episode of major depression if onset of mood symptoms occurs during pregnancy or in the 4 weeks following delivery."[18]

Specifiers in the DSM-5 are used extensively in the diagnosis of mood disorders. The specifiers describe the current or most recent episode, which indicates whether the symptoms are ongoing or new and how the patient may be having differences from other persons in the way the illness is manifesting in spite of similar symptoms. In the case of major depressive disorder with peripartum onset as the specifier, it tells the clinician and other health care personnel that the depression likely either was caused by or had some impactful relationship with the woman's pregnancy and that the standard of care will need to be modified to best care for the patient and minimize the effect on her ability to mother her child.[19]

The description of major depressive disorder with peripartum onset further discusses how mood can be impacted even before delivery, and it stands to reason that having a difficult pregnancy and/or delivery may heighten the chances of having a depressive episode. Numerous sources cite a roughly 50 percent incidence of post-partum depression that begins during pregnancy.[20]

It is also reported that many women with PPD can also experience tremendous anxiety symptoms well beyond those understandable concerns about the demands of caring for an infant. Having a baby can be overwhelming even under ideal circumstances, and society places expectations that are often highly idealistic and unrealistic on the experience of dealing with a newborn child.[21] When Maggie finally talks to her son Matt about the circumstances surrounding her abandonment of her family, she speaks of her regret and how she failed him. He discusses having defended women with "perinatal issues" whom he clearly sees as being without fault, and he mentions how 10 percent of women struggle with them. The legal repercussions of post-partum or perinatal depression are in flux, changing as lawmakers' understanding of them evolve and varying from state to state.[22] Matt is essentially right about the frequency, though, because several studies suggest that the number is at least 10 percent and could be up to 20 percent.[23]

When Maggie talks of having failed Matt, his personal view is loud and clear in his response: "Oh, failing. Right. You mean by pulling yourself up out of a suicidal depression by faith and sheer force of will to become a force for good on this planet? We should all fail so tragically."

Matt's own struggles with depression and intimacy may well provide him with a glimmer of insight into his mother's struggle. Maggie's disturbing thoughts and act of running away from her family are possibly also indicative of a post-partum psychosis that is not common among PPD sufferers but often plays a part in infanticide cases among new mothers.[24] Her recognition that she is in a state of mind so abnormal that Matt's father has to stop her from hurting Matt prompts her decision to leave. Not all women with post-partum psychosis recognize the potential danger they are putting themselves and their children in, sometimes leading to tragic results.[25]

Women who have a prior history of mental illness have increased risk for the development of PPD and related disorders. When a woman has a history of depressive or bipolar disorders, the risk is greater, and it is even greater if there is a history of PPD in earlier pregnancies. "Once a woman has had a postpartum episode with psychotic features, the risk of recurrence with each subsequent delivery is between 30 and 50%."[26]

"It is very real and has quietly devastated the lives of many people. . . .
I hate to think about the women who endure this kind of depression for
long periods of time without knowing that there is help available."
—author/actress Brooke Shields on her own postpartum depression[27]

"The wounds are still raw."
—Sister Maggie (Margaret Grace Murdock)[28]

DELIVERY

Having a child can be mentally taxing on even the most capable of women, and for those who may be already struggling, the physical changes can influence the psychological state in striking ways. The hormonal changes that take place during pregnancy and then delivery are an onslaught of physical changes required to grow and then feed a new baby. Many of those hormonal changes can have a positive impact, such as the release of oxytocin and endorphins that prompt feelings of love and connection. The flip side of this is that other hormones,

THE DAREDEVIL'S OWN DEPRESSION

I. RUNNING IN THE FAMILY

TRAVIS LANGLEY

Depressive tendencies can run in the family.[29] Numerous genes are known to raise the odds of developing depression for different reasons and in various ways,[30] although the genes alone do not control whether that latent potential turns into manifestation. If they did, 100 percent of all people with causal genes would suffer mood disorders. Life stresses, hormonal fluctuations, and other factors both psychological and physiological play roles in determining who will be most at risk.[31] Although neither Matt Murdock nor his mother spends all of life in a depressed state, both have undergone bouts of depression[32] and considered or attempted suicide.[33] Despite being known as the "common cold of mental illness"[34] because it's diagnosed more often than any other specific mental disorder, major depression—a condition severe enough to qualify as pathological—is not something the majority of people experience. A person can feel terrible and extremely down in the dumps without qualifying for a diagnosis. No matter how badly a person may feel, a mood state common to most people is by definition not abnormal. Abnormal depression lasts longer, feels worse, has more symptoms, and more harshly detracts from the ability to function in life.[35] In considering himself to be "quite the expert in self-destructive despair,"[36] Daredevil acknowledges that his depressive symptoms have been *maladaptive*, meaning that they interfere with the individual's ability to function or adapt to life.

such as estrogen, increase to reach gargantuan proportions. A
woman will release more estrogen during one pregnancy than
during the rest of her nonpregnant life. This is not usually a
problematic issue, but in some women this hormonal change
can have a significant behavioral impact.[37]

The societal stigma of having a mental illness only increases
during pregnancy, as the woman not only has the demands
of motherhood being placed upon her, but if she is not up to
the demands, especially if the cause is mental illness, there is
often the underlying threat of the child being removed from

THE DAREDEVIL'S
OWN DEPRESSION

II. DROWNING IN DESPAIR

TRAVIS LANGLEY

When the Purple Children's combined power immerses
Daredevil in a wave of negativity—submerging him in pain,
grief, rage, loneliness, and despair—he cannot fight it. "I try
to," he thinks. "I've been trying to. I thought I could, but it's
impossible. I thought I could. I'm not strong enough. Happy
Matt is just an act. That's all it ever was, and I just can't pull it
off anymore."[39] He lies in a fetal pile, feeling as though he
cannot breathe, move, or do anything. While most people will
never experience a superpowered attack, numerous external
forces (such as certain medications, sunlight levels, allergens[40])
can induce depression-like symptoms in some.

Whether a depressive state is brief or enduring, singular or
recurring, a person in that state can feel so miserable that the

the home before treatment of the mother is pursued. Women may be told they should not have children if they suffer from mental illnesses that are highly responsive to treatment in ways that are never discussed with physical illnesses.[38] At any possible time Maggie would have been pregnant with Matt, these were real issues that plagued standard prenatal care practices. The guilt and shame about her having failed her son would feel overwhelming, and the turmoil that churned unbidden within her leaves him without a mother and with a father racked over the loss of the woman he loves.

gloom hangs on when that person is recalling better times and can shade those recollections. The depressed individual lost in emotional darkness may not correctly recall what better states were like.[41] "Happy Matt" could be an act, an attempt to put on a happy face until it feels real or just to avoid thinking and talking about the depression, in which case Purple-dominated Matt accurately admits this to himself, but it's also possible that Matt has been much happier at times but just can't recall them when drowning in despair. "Depression is like a living thing. It exists by feeding on your darkest moods, and it is always hungry," as Matt describes it to himself. "At its worst, you are numb, you are drained, you are immobilized."[42]

His observation that "I haven't felt this way in a long time" acknowledges that he has previously felt this way when not under the Purple Children's power. In the state they induce, he cannot summon the energy to stand up and stop their father, the Purple Man, from trying to kill him. Those suffering the darkest depression lack even the motivation to do things that would protect them to get them to a better place.[43]

If you or someone you know is experiencing what you think might be post-partum depression, encourage that person to seek assistance. Consider these and other available sources:

* Postpartum Support International (postpartum.net)
* Mental Health America (mnha.org)
* National Institute of Mental Health (nimh.nih.gov)

NOTES

1. *Daredevil* #4 (1999).
2. Shields (2006), p. 72.
3. Respectively, *Daredevil* #229 (1986); *Daredevil* #1 (1964).
4. *Daredevil* #7 (2014).
5. *Daredevil* #7 (2014).
6. Panno (2004).
7. Laurent & Ablow (2012).
8. *Daredevil* #10 (2014) addresses Matt's depressive tendencies.
9. Burton (2012); Goleman (1996).
10. Examples of those led to believe their mothers were simply their older sisters include individuals as diverse as actor Jack Nicholson (Biography, n.d.) and serial killer Ted Bundy (Michaud & Aynesworth, 1983/1999).
11. *Daredevil* #6–7 (2014)
12. *Original Sin* #2 (2014).
13. *Daredevil* #6 (2014).
14. American Psychiatric Association (2013).
15. Stewart & Vigod (2016).
16. e.g., Shields (2006).
17. Malone et al. (2014).
18. American Psychiatric Association (2013), p. 186.
19. American Psychiatric Association (2013).
20. American Psychiatric Association (2013); Woo & Keatinge (2016).
21. Puryear (2007).
22. Rhodes & Segre (2014).
23. Centers for Disease Control & Prevention (2008); Down et al. (2013); Miller et al. (2013).
24. Susman (1996).
25. Gold et al. (2012); Pope et al. (2013).
26. American Psychiatric Association (2013), p. 187.
27. Shields (2006), p. 217.
28. *Daredevil* #7 (2014).
29. e.g., Belzeaux et al. (2014); Huo et al. (2016); Watters et al. (2013); Zimmerman et al. (2006).
30. Mossakowska-Mójcik et al. (2018).
31. Eberhart et al. (2011); Patten (2013).

32. *Daredevil* #7 (2014); 9–10 (2014).
33. e.g., *Daredevil* #348 (1996)—Matt; *Daredevil* #7 (2014)—Maggie.
34. e.g., Lorenzo-Luaces (2015).
35. American Psychiatric Association (2013).
36. *Daredevil* #4 (2014).
37. Henry & Sherwin (2012); Nelson & Kriegsfeld (2017).
38. Puryear (2007).
39. *Daredevil* #9 (2014).
40. Medications: Krousel-Wood et al. (2010); Thakrar & Robinson (2009). Sunlight: Knippenberg et al. (2014); Xu et al. (2016). Allergens: Kovacs et al. (2003); Trikojat et al. (2017).
41. Marchetti et al. (2018).
42. *Daredevil* #10 (2014).
43. American Psychiatric Association (2013).

CHAPTER 12

ELEKTRA: PORTRAIT OF THE ASSASSIN AS A YOUNG WOMAN

LARISA A. GARSKI
& JENNIFER L. YEN

"Life doesn't make any sense without interdependence.
We need each other, and the sooner we learn that, the better for us all."
—author Joan Erikson[1]

"I am Elektra Natchios. Not even the stars are safe in the sky."
—Elektra[2]

*H*ow does a person develop a sense of self? Psychologists, psychoanalysts, and psychotherapists have puzzled over this question of identity for generations. Today, we understand identity as a developmental process that begins at birth and ends in death. But for superheroes and supervillains, identity development is never quite so simple. For a woman as enigmatic as the deadly Elektra Natchios, the social and emotional growth of identity development can require literal resurrection.[3]

Throughout her life, Elektra's personality is judged by others—Matt Murdock, Stick, the Chaste, the Hand's Jonin,[4] the Black Widow—to be too aggressive, too violent, too demanding, and too "full of pain and hate."[5] Yet, despite the assertions of both the Chaste of the Hand, Elektra does not emerge from her mother's dead womb fully formed as evil incarnate. Human growth and development—the process of identity formation—is never so simple. Often described in terms established by Erik Erikson's psychosocial development model, identity formation progresses through a series of eight stages, enabling the individual to face challenges and develop a greater understanding of themselves and their world.[6] In each stage her identity has the opportunity to either grow or to stagnate.[7] Elektra's personality seems to defy conventional models: While she clearly has problematic elements of her identity, she is anything but stagnant. Ever the ninja, Elektra fights both stagnation and growth, lovers and old friends all in an effort to become wholly herself.

ERIKSON'S EIGHT-STAGE MODEL

According to Erikson's model, identity growth occurs at each developmental stage due to a trial or struggle. Understanding these stages provides a window into how humans form and sustain attachments to others.[8] If the personality successfully grows, it gains a core virtue or ability such as purpose, will, or love.[9] But what happens when a child is unable to face the challenges of a given developmental stage? Are they trapped in a state of arrested development or—worse yet—doomed to a pathological or warped personality? Erikson argued that it is possible for someone to return to previously failed or incomplete stages and with the right supports—ideally a combination of supportive attachment figures and a competent psychotherapist—resolve past conflicts.[10] This allows the individual to return to age appropriate developmental stages newly equipped to progress. In both of her lives, the television adaptation of *Daredevil* and her various comic book iterations, Elektra has battled for independent identity.[11] Yet at every developmental stage, Elektra meets with barriers and obstacles. Throughout her comic book and television lives, Stick warns, "[Elektra is] on her way to the worst side,"[12] almost as if she were a doomed villain, constantly giving in to her baser impulses. Yet Erikson's model stresses the importance of core caregivers, attachment figures, teachers, guides, and community to foster healthy identity growth. If Elektra is truly the evil that Stick alleges,[13] is she alone to blame?

In order to understand all of Elektra's complexities, we may begin at the first stage—the birth of her identity. Though much of the television version of Elektra's core personality traits and history remain faithful to the comic books, there are some distinct deviations. While in her comic book life Elektra is the beloved only daughter of a wealthy Greek diplomat, in her television life she is an orphan of Asian descent, adopted by the Chaste and trained to be a warrior until she is expelled at the age of twelve. While she has a violently combative relationship with Stick in her comic book life, in the television series her relationship with Stick is loving and nurturing throughout her childhood, twisting into malice only in adulthood. Perhaps most importantly, in the television iteration Elektra is the embodiment of the enigmatic Black Sky, a powerful weapon of the Hand.[14] While the secret of her origin is kept from her, it still affects her development and causes multiple attachment wounds.

ELEKTRA: THE FORMATION OF AN ASSASSIN

The stages of development analyze three facets of identity: *the ego identity,* or self; *personal identity,* or those personal traits that differentiate people from each other; and *social/cultural identity,* or the myriad social roles people play.[15] All three are vital to development. In both her comic book and television lives, Elektra faces challenges and overcomes them at almost every turn.

STAGE 1: TRUST VERSUS MISTRUST (0–1.5 YEARS)

In this first stage, the individual grapples with trust, learning when and how to turn towards connection i.e. attachment with others. The *crisis,* or developmental challenge, of the first stage is the struggle between trust and mistrust as the infant learns how to securely attach. Elektra comes to her struggle with identity development early. Before she is born, her mother is shot—murdered for aberrant sexual desires,[16] a trait her daughter will later be accused of possessing.[17] Elektra is removed from her dead mother's womb. Her father explains: "The doctor's tests proved you were mine after all, little amber."[18] This early maternal loss is a catastrophic blow to her emotional growth. As Elektra herself observes: "I ought to remember death. I've always been on such intimate terms with it. I was born of death. My mother was killed before I could know her. They managed to save me. Brought me to life from a dead womb. I'm still uncertain whether I should be grateful."[19]

Can a child learn to attach without her mother? It is rarely just the rupture itself but rather the rupture followed by the failure to reconnect that creates attachment injury.[20] Though maternal attachment is important, it is the child's opportunity to securely attach with *core caregivers* or parental figures regardless of gender that is key. While attachment is formed in this stage, the implications are life-long. Elektra tries repeatedly to seek out secure attachment figures—her father, Stick, the Chaste, the Hand—and her attempts for a reciprocal and trusting relationship are met by trauma and rejection.[21] In her television life, Elektra gets a second chance at both attachment and mothering when she is reborn under the nurturing care of Alexandra, leader of the Hand.[22] Though initially reticent, Elektra seems to blossom under the loving care of her new mother who gently coos: "My child, you are everything."[23]

STAGE 2: AUTONOMY VERSUS SHAME (1.5–3 YEARS)

During this stage, a child's developmental task is to learn how to control their physical self or body as well as their physical surroundings. Again, feedback from core caregivers is key as shaming messages connected to activities such as toilet training can cause the young child to doubt herself, priming her for self-esteem struggles in her future. In her television life, Elektra's awareness of her body and graceful movements as a pre-adolescent demonstrates successful completion of the physical tasks of stage two. The Chaste provides the perfect setting for limit testing and forming independence. However, instead of "self-control without a loss of self-esteem," it results in Elektra developing too much of the latter and not enough of the former.[24]

Overindulged children may also struggle if their core caregivers attempt to do everything for them, robbing them of opportunities to engage with the challenges of autonomy. This is a problem that Elektra clearly avoids in her television life as an orphan whose only parental figure is the emotionally challenged Stick.[25] In Elektra's comic book childhood, her father is often depicted as doting and overprotective, constantly surrounding her with bodyguards.[26] In spite of this Elektra avoids the potential pitfalls of this stage and emerges with her self-esteem intact, gaining the virtue of a strong will.

STAGE 3: INITIATIVE VERSUS GUILT (3-5 YEARS)

At this stage, the child grows in her awareness of her core caregivers and attempts to imitate them through peer play.[27] Historically, an emphasis was placed on the importance of the child having the opportunity to observe and mimic their parental figure of the same gender. Ironically, in both her comic book and television life, Elektra may have benefited from her mother's absence. Surrounded by men, she imitates their strength, courage, and virility as positive attributes. The men of the Chaste, as repeatedly shown in the comic, tell Elektra she must shed her feelings and emotional attachments if she intends to be a true warrior.[28] Under the Chaste, any student navigating this stage works it out not in play, but in combat. As an adult, Elektra regularly demonstrates an ability to take initiative though she struggles for a sense of purpose.[29] Her inability to embody the core virtue of this stage would indicate that she did not fully resolve the crisis of stage three. Perhaps this is due to the absence of a maternal figure. But it may also be due to the sexual trauma perpetrated by her father.[30]

STAGE 4: INDUSTRY VERSUS INFERIORITY (5-12 YEARS)

For Elektra, this stage is marked by her successful training as a ninja.[31] Children who are prevented from successful struggle due to helicopter parents, poor instructors, and/or lack of support may flounder. Though Elektra's ninja training is challenging, her competent and supportive instructors help her to achieve mastery. In her comic book life, Elektra is trained to become an industrious killing machine. Elektra's estimation of her own abilities falters in her teenage years under the tutelage of both Stick and the Chaste. Still, during this stage Elektra excels and, arguably, becomes overly confident in her abilities.[32] She suffers a similar fate in her television life. The Chaste's training program is a breeding ground for both jealousy and competition.[33] Her natural aptitude both isolates her

ELECTRA AND ELEKTRA: A COMPLEX KILLER EITHER WAY

TRAVIS LANGLEY

The Electra of Greek mythology is a lethal lady. To avenge her father, King Agamemnon, she plots her mother Clytemnestra's death and persuades her brother Orestes to act as the assassin.[34] Unlike other murderous figures in Greek tragedies, Electra goes unpunished. Psychiatrist Carl Jung named the Electra complex after her when he proposed a female counterpart to Sigmund Freud's famous Oedipus complex.[35] Freud thought that, at least unconsciously, boys aged three to six grow attracted to their mothers and therefore fear their fathers as rivals. Jung suggested that girls that age might experience a similar attraction to their fathers and animosity toward their mothers, though Freud disagreed.[36]

When writer/artist Frank Miller created Elektra Natchios,[37] did he name this Greek assassin for the mythological figure or for

and inflates her ego. It is also a patriarchal system,[43] and *gender microaggressions* appear with her sparring partners in the form of microassaults and microinsults. Both accepted and rejected for her aptitude and work ethic, Elektra struggles and is never fully able to resolve the conflicts of this developmental milestone.

STAGE 5: IDENTITY VERSUS ROLE CONFUSION (12–18 YEARS)

Despite her evident talent in her comic book life, teenage Elektra is rejected from her training by Stick and the Chaste because of her emotional conflict and darker nature.[44] Television Elektra the psychological complex? Although she does not plot to kill her mother, Elektra is born out of her mother's death, saved from the womb as her mom dies in a terrorist attack (which Elektra's older brother, Orestez, orchestrates).[38] Some 20 years later, the death of her doting father drives Elektra into a life of murder.[39] Elektra goes from training to fight evil to committing assassination for hire to admitting that she's addicted to violence.[40]

"This particular character was designed around her name," Miller has said. "The name Elektra has come to represent an entire psychological phenomenon. She was a young woman who had her sexual interest centered on her father, and just as she was transferring this to another man, her father is killed."[41] In a dreamlike, noncanonical tale authored by Miller, Elektra renames her parents in her head after the mythical Agamemnon and Clytemnestra. In this account, the grown Elektra vaguely recalls her father sexually abusing her when she was five, something she has learned is a false memory (*pseudomemory*) that is based on her own desire for intimacy, although she still wonders about that.[42]

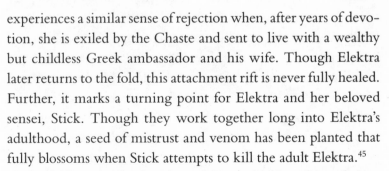

experiences a similar sense of rejection when, after years of devotion, she is exiled by the Chaste and sent to live with a wealthy but childless Greek ambassador and his wife. Though Elektra later returns to the fold, this attachment rift is never fully healed. Further, it marks a turning point for Elektra and her beloved sensei, Stick. Though they work together long into Elektra's adulthood, a seed of mistrust and venom has been planted that fully blossoms when Stick attempts to kill the adult Elektra.[45]

This fifth stage of Erikson's model is marked by role confusion, a conflict that Elektra struggles with both here and throughout her life. Is she a diplomat's daughter or a trained assassin? Is she a member of the Chaste or the Hand's greatest weapon, the Black Sky? Is she Matt Murdock's true love or his greatest enemy? Awash in contradiction, Elektra never fully resolves the identity struggle of this stage. But she also never gives up the fight, returning to this internal place of conflict throughout her adulthood.

STAGE 6: INTIMACY VERSUS ISOLATION (18-40)

As is typical, the unresolved conflicts of Elektra's previous identity stages follow her to stage six. When Elektra loses her father at age nineteen,[46] this trauma pushes her toward the role of assassin that is not in total alignment with her core self. Because Elektra does not resolve the identity fluidity at the appropriate stage, the trauma of losing her father damages the teenager, stunting her growth and pushing her toward a role that is not in full alignment with her personality.

In the sixth stage, the individual learns how to love and engage intimately with others. Resolving the crisis between intimacy and isolation results in the individual's ability to both give and receive romantic love. The danger of this stage is giving in to isolation. Throughout her lives—both comic book and television—Elektra struggles with intimacy. Due to the trauma of her beloved father's death,[47] comic book Elektra is unable to successfully complete this stage. She flees broken-hearted from Matt Murdock, vowing to never love again and later criticizes herself for opening herself to love and hope with him, concluding "That was hubris."[48] In her television life, she suffers a similar fate as she is unable to resolve the isolating demands of the Chaste with the desire for attachment she feels towards Matt.[49] But Elektra is tenacious and, as she does with stages five and three, she continues to return to this stage in repeated attempts to reconnect with Matt and heal this conflict. Elektra's circumstances cripple her at every turn, but she never fully gives in to pathology, i.e., her blood-thirsty impulses.[50]

In her television life, Elektra tentatively seeks out emotionally corrective experiences, first with Stick and then with Matt. Despite their emotional conflicts, Matt's decision to both love and accept her—even as Black Sky—provides an emotionally corrective experience that allows her to heal parts of her attachment wounding.[51] Once she is revived at the command of the Hand, it is his love that brings her memories back just before they are trapped in an explosion.[52] Similarly, when the Hand resurrects her in the comic book canon, it is his love that ensures she returns with her mind and free will intact rather than as a slave.[53]

STAGE 7: GENERATIVITY VERSUS STAGNATION (40–65) AND STAGE 8: EGO INTEGRITY VS. DESPAIR (65+)

These later stages focus on the identity evolution of middle and old age with the seventh stage focusing on adding to the world via either children or good works and the final stage preparing the individual to face death. Elektra has yet to reach these final stages—in part because she is regularly killed and resurrected during stage six.[54] But her attempts to form her own version of the Chaste (comic book life) or the Hand (television life) speak to a desire to both create and add to the world. "My reward—our reward—will be aiming our darker impulses toward more affirmative goals"[55] Despite her joy in engaging with her violent desires, Elektra does not act without conscience—her own assassin's creed: "I will allow them an opportunity to accept the truth. We have no reason to spill each other's blood. If I had wronged them, I would simply kill them all."[56]

Powerful, driven, and violent, Elektra has struggled throughout her life to define her identity on her own terms. Either failed or abused by the parental figures and organizations charged with her care, Elektra's identity forms not just via her own joy in killing but through the traumas, attachment injuries, and failed training of those charged with her care and protection. When Elektra reaches adulthood, she is finally empowered to take control of her own growth and development. At times, she falters.[57] But at others she rises.[58] Elektra is compelling precisely because her fight for identity has never been easy or clean. Though she may be a killer, she need not be a maniacal one. "It is the nature of my existence to be hunted by those I've wronged. To kill them brings me no joy, though I do it swiftly."[59] After all her struggles, Elektra's self is an honorable assassin.

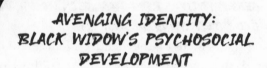

AVENGING IDENTITY: BLACK WIDOW'S PSYCHOSOCIAL DEVELOPMENT

For the other significant femme fatale romance in Matt Murdock's comic book life, Natasha Romanoff (the Black Widow), identity development is not quite so adversarial. Natasha is a product of the Red Room, a Russian program that trains young women to become the deadly assassins of the Black Widow program.[61] Like Elektra, her assassin's journey is marked by trauma beginning with the death of her mother during Russia's bitter war.[62] However, Natasha's ability to cope and securely attach with her adult rescuer, Ivan, indicates that her early attachment experiences are positive.[63] Secure attachment during the early stages is a strong indicator for increased resiliency later in life[64] and Natasha clearly benefits from spending her early years, stages one-three, in an intact attachment system. Unlike Elektra and Stick, Natasha and Ivan

Whether in comic book lore or television canon, Elektra Natchios battles the opposing forces of the self: light and dark, love and hate, aggression and compassion. She is neither alone in this struggle nor is she entirely to blame.[60] Throughout her identity development, Elektra is failed by the parents, mentors, and communities charged with supporting and guiding her growth. Given the circumstances, it seems inevitable that of the three dimensions of her identity—personal, ego, and social/cultural—the first is the most developed. Both ego identity and social/cultural identity require greater external guides

maintain a positive and secure attachment well into Natasha's adulthood.[65] Natasha's emotionally corrective experience with Ivan allows her to heal the wounding experiences of traumatic loss and move on to stage four.[66] Both girls experience success during their third stage of development, resolving the crisis of this stage to achieve the virtue of competence. But adolescence knocks them off the same course. Though both suffer at the hands of corrupt organizations—the Chaste and the Red Room respectively—only Natasha is embraced by her organization. The Soviet command value Natasha's skills and abilities, inviting her into their spy family. While this doesn't entirely prevent Natasha's struggle with role confusion it shields her from the rejection experienced by her counterpart, Elektra, laying groundwork for the healing and growth that will come later. Provided with opportunities Elektra never had, Natasha's history of acceptance and predominantly positive attachment following the loss of her family of origin enables her to heal her pathology and eventually fully complete her ego growth.

and supports to complete the maturation process. As an adult, Elektra reveals her strength by literally rising from the dead and overcoming those who attempt to erase what little identity she has left. Perhaps the key to unlocking her adult transformation lies in relinquishing her life as a renegade ronin assassin. Only then may she be free to pursue the life of a true samurai, one with a clan capable of accepting and nurturing her complex identity.

NOTES

1. Goelman (1988). Joan Erickson was the wife of Erik Erikson and she worked with her husband to edit, revise, and reformulate his psychosocial model of development.
2. *Dark Reign: Elektra* #5 (2009).
3. *The Elektra Saga* #4 (1984).
4. *The Elektra Saga* #1 (1984).
5. *The Elektra Saga* #1 (1984).
6. Erikson (1950/2012).
7. Erikson (1950/2012).
8. Ainsworth et al. (1970).
9. Stages 2, 3, & 6 respectively
10. Fleming (2004) & Erikson (1950/2012).
11. *Elektra Root of Evil* #1 (1995).
12. *Daredevil: The Man Without Fear* #3 (1993)
13. *The Elektra Saga* #1 (1984), *Daredevil: The Man Without Fear* #3 (1993), *Elektra Root of Evil* #2 (1995), *Marvel's Daredevil*, episode 2–10, "The Man in the Box" (18 March, 2016), & *Marvel's Daredevil*, episode 2–11 "The Dark at the End of the Tunnel" (18 March, 2016).
14. *Marvel's Daredevil*, episode 2–12, "The Dark at the End of the Tunnel" (18 March, 2016).
15. Fleming (2004).
16. *Elektra Assassin* #1 (1986), *Elektra Root of Evil* #4 (1995).
17. *Elektra Root of Evil* #2 (1995).
18. *Elektra Root of Evil* #4 (1995).
19. *Elektra* #35 (2004).
20. Sroufe et al. (2011).
21. *The Elektra Saga* #1 (1984).
22. *Marvel's The Defenders*, episode 1–3 "Worst Behavior" (18 August 2017).
23. *Marvel's The Defenders*, episode 1–3 "Worst Behavior" (18 August 2017).
24. Gross (1992).
25. *Marvel's Daredevil*, episode 2–12, "The Dark at the End of the Tunnel" (18 March, 2016).
26. *Daredevil* #168 (1981).
27. Sokol (2009).
28. *Elektra Assassin* #1 (1986).
29. *Elektra Root of Evil* #1 (1995).
30. *Elektra Assassin* #1 (1986).

31. *Elektra Assassin* #1 (1986) & *Elektra Root of Evil* #2 (1995).

32. *Elektra Root of Evil* #2 (1995).

33. Nadal et al. (2013).

34. Electra appears as the central figure in numerous plays, beginning with *Electra* by Euripides and *Electra* by Sophocles, c. 410. Which play came first is unknown.

35. Freud (1909/1955); Jung (1913).

36. Freud (1920/2001).

37. *Daredevil* #168 (1981).

38. *Elektra: Assassin* #1 (1986); *Elektra: Root of Evil* #2 (1995).

39. *Daredevil* #190 (1983). However, *Daredevil: The Man without Fear* #3 suggests that it's the other way around, that her murderous path leads to her father's death because voices in her head (*auditory hallucinations*) decide he must die for her to be free.

40. *Elektra* #18 (2003).

41. Interviewed by Sanderson (1982), p. 27.

42. *Elektra: Assassin* #1 (1986).

43. Episode 2–12, "The Dark at the End of the Tunnel" (18 March, 2016).

44. *Elektra: Assassin* #1 (1986) & *Elektra Root of Evil* #1 (1995), *Elektra Root of Evil* #2 (1995), & *The Elektra Saga* #1 (1984).

45. *Marvel's Daredevil*, episode 2–10, "The Man in the Box" (18 March, 2016) & *Marvel's Daredevil*, episode 2–11 "The Dark at the End of the Tunnel" (18 March, 2016).

46. *Daredevil* #168 (1981).

47. *Daredevil* #168 (1981).

48. *Elektra* #35 (2004).

49. *Marvel's Daredevil*, episode 2–8, "Guilty as Sin" (18 March, 2016).

50. *Dark Reign: Elektra* #5 (2009).

51. Episode 2–13, "A Cold Day in Hell's Kitchen" (18 March, 2016).

52. *The Defenders.* Episode 1–8. "The Defenders" (8 August, 2017).

53. *Daredevil* #190 (1983).

54. *The Elektra Saga* #3 (1984), *The Elektra Saga* #4 (1984), *Dark Reign: Elektra* #3 (2009), & *Dark Reign: Elektra* #5 (2009)

55. *Elektra Root of Evil* #2 (1995).

56. *Dark Reign: Elektra* #5 (2009).

57. *The Elektra Saga* #2 (1984), *Dark Reign: Elektra* #5 (2009).

58. *Elektra Root of Evil* #4 (1995).

59. *Dark Reign: Elektra* #5 (2009)

60. *Elektra* #18 (2003

61. *Black Widow* #4 (2005) & *Black Widow* #5 (2005).

62. *Daredevil* #88 (1972).

63. Sroufe (2011) & Solomon (2003).

64. Sroufe (2011).

65. *Daredevil* #188 (1982).

66. *Daredevil* #88 (1972).

CHAPTER 13

THE PATH TO PUNISHER: HOW MOTIVATIONS MAKE THE MAN

COLT J. BLUNT

*"[M]en ought either to be well treated or crushed, because they can
avenge themselves of lighter injuries, of more serious ones they cannot;
therefore the injury that is to be done to a man ought to be of such a kind
that one does not stand in fear of revenge."*
—author, philosopher, and politician Niccolò Machiavelli[1]

*"They'll blame it all on Vietnam. And they'll be right. And they'll
be wrong. I know what the world needs now. Same thing it's needed
all along. I walk off the Brooklyn rooftop and into the future: A future
full of screams and bullets, and bad men dying in the ancient dark.
And I show the world a face not made by God."*
—Frank Castle[2]

*I*f Daredevil is the man without fear, the Punisher is the man
who causes fear. Both forged from tragedy, Matt Murdock
and Frank Castle ostensibly have a lot in common. They have
overcome trauma that would discourage most. They are both
vigilantes. They even often find themselves operating in the

same geographic area against the same foes. Yet in the ways that matter, Matt Murdock and Frank Castle could not be more different. Whereas Murdock refuses to kill his adversaries and upholds the principle of justice, Castle exists to punish his enemies and rarely lets them live. What sets the Punisher apart from Daredevil is much more than a difference in their origin stories. At their very core, Castle and Murdock are cast from different molds, with glaringly different personality compositions, vocations, and morals.

Continuity is a fluid concept in comics. Series are often rebooted and rebranded multiple times during the course of a character's history, with different writers all taking their own approach to a character's life, presentation, and focus. However, though characters are often refreshed to more closely mesh with the current times, their origins often remain the same or at least very similar. Matt Murdock is universally known as the blind lawyer who takes up the mantle of Daredevil to get justice for the death of his father.[3] Likewise, it would be easy to conclude that Frank Castle has made the choice to become the Punisher when his wife and children are gunned down by the Mafia.[4] However, closer inspection suggests that the ground is actually laid years earlier; the death of Frank's family merely put a name to the force that had been inside him all along.

PERSONALITY'S ROLE IN THE BIRTH OF THE PUNISHER

Frank Castle's beliefs regarding punishment begin well before the death of his family. As a student in the seminary on his way to becoming a Catholic priest, Frank begins to question why God lets bad things to happen to good people as well as why the people responsible for those acts are allowed to escape punishment. Frank acknowledges that he wishes to see the perpetrators of evil dead. This line of thinking leads him to consider how he might more directly affect the world, ultimately resulting in his withdrawal from the seminary and enlistment in the Marines.[5] This line of thinking also highlights a trait not often seen in the folks we root for in comics: Frank Castle is a bit of a psychopath.

Frank Castle is simply wired differently from most people. Personality plays a large role in who we are as people, and, like many things psychological, is affected by both *nature* (our biology) and *nurture* (our environment and experiences).[6] Frank's personality structure is notable for traits commonly associated with *psychopathy*, a personality construct often seen in criminal populations. Though not a formally recognized diagnosis, psychopathy is a highly researched personality construct first made popular by psychiatrist Hervey Cleckley in his book *The Mask of Sanity*.[7] Based on his work with patients in secure institutions, Cleckley described a personality profile involving superficial charm, unreliability, untruthfulness, lack of remorse, antisocial behavior, lack of emotion, egocentrism, poor insight, lack of plans, and an impersonal sex life. The book was named after the "mask" worn by psychopaths that hides their pathology. Psychologist Robert Hare developed the Psychopathy Checklist (PCL) and later the Psychopathy Checklist-Revised (PCL-R) as a measure for assessing psychopathy. Though still based largely on Cleckley's original model, the PCL-R was expanded significantly on the basis of Hare's research and experience. The PCL-R looks at both personality and behavioral characteristics and ultimately splits items out into four different facets:

* The *Interpersonal* facet involves personality characteristics that center on exploiting and manipulating others. Matt Murdock and Frank Castle have a bit in common with regard to this facet, as neither is a

con man and both tend to be fairly straightforward about their intentions.

* The *Affective* facet addresses the subject's emotional response, especially with regard to negative actions toward others. Whereas Matt Murdock is an empathetic lawyer with strong sense of morality, Frank Castle does not experience remorse or guilt from the actions he takes. In fact, the Punisher doesn't seem to experience much of anything. Even his disposition toward those he considers allies is cold and pragmatic.

* The *Lifestyle* facet describes the individual's general behavior and ability to plan. Both Frank and Matt live fairly responsible lives until they turn to vigilantism. The difference is that Matt continues to hold down gainful employment and fulfill his responsibilities, whereas Frank never holds an honest job again, instead relying on the money he is able to take from his victims to fund his war. Frank still differs from a true psychopath in this regard, though, as he doesn't rely on the support of others and engages in planned behavior.

* The *Antisocial* facet specifically evaluates their history of criminal and rule-breaking behavior. Both Matt and Frank engage in their fair share of violence, though the Punisher takes his antisocial behavior to the extreme. Matt Murdock doesn't shy away from coming to blows with his adversaries yet invariably stops short of killing. Castle engages in assaults, murders, arson, extortion, and robberies.

Matt Murdock doesn't really present with any concrete signs of psychopathy, instead being a fairly upstanding citizen who abhors killing. Frank Castle is a different story. He lacks the emotions and conscience inherent to most people. But to say his actions are uncontrolled would be inaccurate; rather, the

Punisher's cold, calculated demeanor even translates to his most brutal acts. Though he may be no Ted Bundy, those on the barrel end of the Punisher would hardly count themselves as lucky.

Research has taught us that the brain structure and chemistry of psychopaths can differ significantly from those of the average human. *Meta-analysis* (comparison of the results of multiple studies—an analysis of other analyses) has shown that psychopaths often show evidence of a lack of development of structures in the *prefrontal cortex*, the area of the brain most associated with personality and *executive functioning* (the ability to adapt and make decisions).[8] The prefrontal cortex is believed to be responsible for feelings of guilt and remorse, with those evidencing underdevelopment experiencing a reduced capacity for such emotions.[9] Though we may not have imaging of the Punisher's brain to know for sure, it certainly wouldn't be surprising to find out Frank was born that way. However, just because someone lacks remorse doesn't mean that person will become a killer. That may be where nurture comes in.

BECOMING A KILLER

Castle's disposition may allow for antisocial acts, but it's not until he joins the Marines that he gets the training he needs to actually kill. Frank excels in the Marines, where he is programmed to see his adversaries as something less than human. This can be a difficult transition for the average soldier as humans rarely desire to kill other humans. Indeed, the percentage of American soldiers actually firing at the enemy only surpassed 50 percent with the Korean War and reached as high as 95 percent in Vietnam; this difference is largely attributed to improvements in programming soldiers to ignore their nature.[10] Beyond this, the goal of basic training is to make soldiers effective and efficient at killing. Frank Castle's nature makes it largely unnecessary to try to convince him not to feel bad about his actions; as has been mentioned, his very personality, if not his entire brain structure, already has left him with a bit of a hole where the average person has a fully developed conscience. If anything, his initial indoctrination in the military gives him agency to do what he feels he was put on Earth to do: punish the wicked. This also leaves him open to soak up all the combat training offered to him, at which he excels.

After completing Infantry School, Castle graduates from Special Forces training and is deployed to Vietnam for three tours, serving on a Special Forces fire team for two of them.[11] And unlike most people deployed to Vietnam, many of whom were drafted, Frank relishes war and never wants it to end. War slakes his thirst for violence and allows him to act out in a way that is brutal yet socially acceptable. He excels at killing and doesn't stop with the Vietcong. Frank lures a commanding officer into the sights of a Vietcong sniper and kills one of his own men, punishing them both for their transgressions.[12] During his third tour, when he is assigned to Valley Forge, he becomes the sole survivor of an assault by the Vietcong. The very maladaptive personality traits that give him permission to kill also steel him against the horrors of being on the wrong side of a massacre. As he watches his men die around him one by one, as his M60 runs dry, as every weapon he picks up is emptied until all he is left with is a twisted club of metal and plastic that had once been an M16 to defend his bullet-riddled body, Frank Castle embraces his role in life, vowing, whether to himself or to some sinister unseen presence, to wage an unending war.[13] As Frank is united with his family back home, we see that he wears the very mask that Hervey Cleckley described. But it is a mask he does not wear for long.

THE ENDLESS WAR

A heaping dose of *survivor guilt*[14] would be expected for someone who has experienced what Frank sees at Valley Forge. Indeed, many veterans experience *posttraumatic stress disorder* (PTSD) that is due not only to the danger they've seen but also to the people they've lost and the lives they've taken. Research has consistently shown that the taking of a life is one of the most traumatic experiences a person can have.[15] Yet Frank Castle experiences none of this. Likely owing to his personality structure more than to his training, Frank is seemingly inoculated against the guilt and anxiety that often plagues soldiers returning from war.

The Punisher, a persona that has arguably existed within Frank Castle his entire life, finally unveils itself to the world after he and his family are gunned down after witnessing a mob hit.[16] They are unfortunate victims of circumstance, simply being in the wrong place at the wrong time. But Frank survives, a common theme in his arc. Though ostensibly it appears that the loss of Frank's family causes him to become the Punisher, it can be argued that this tragedy merely gives him the excuse to wage the endless war he has always wanted. A character called Microchip, once the Punisher's ally, accuses Castle of as much at the end of their relationship.[17]

The Punisher fills a different role in the cycle of justice than what we typically see in comics. Heroes usually represent honor, integrity, fairness, and mercy. Consider Daredevil, the alias of blind lawyer Matt Murdock. Murdock operates in a manner that sees the villain brought to justice, using both his legal training and his martial skills to put bad guys in the right hands to see them behind bars. Daredevil doesn't kill because Matt Murdock doesn't see himself as the absolute arbiter of guilt and certainly doesn't see himself as executioner. Spider-Man has a similar aversion to killing, often tying criminals up in a nice bow for the police. As is blatantly obvious in his chosen identity, Frank Castle sees himself as falling farther down the line in the criminal justice system and is all too eager to judge and punish those whom he sees as guilty. He has deemed the justice system ineffective and does what he feels the system is too weak to do itself.

The Punisher's victims typically include criminals, mercenaries, and corrupt officials. Though he typically sticks to those associated with organized crime, he's not against going after larger targets when the situation presents. After the Superhuman Registration Act passes, the Punisher finds himself at odds with a deputized Stilt-Man, whom he kills.[18] Later, at Stilt-Man's memorial service, Castle poisons a number of Stilt-Man's supervillain friends before blowing up the site of the service.[19] He even kills Microchip, the closest thing to a friend and ally in Castle's war, for smuggling narcotics and weapons to fund a CIA black ops program.[20] The Punisher has a code, but it's not necessarily one of honor. Rather, Castle tends to dispense punishment indiscriminately, without consideration of the targets, their motivations, or extenuating circumstances.

WHY DO FANS ROOT FOR THE PUNISHER?

The Punisher is a murderer. His kills are premeditated, and he experiences no remorse. He doesn't kill in self-defense, instead using his military training and tactical brain to be as efficient as possible. Though he's not above engaging in a direct firefight, Frank Castle is more likely to ambush his prey to push the odds in his favor. The Punisher isn't even a hero when first introduced to the Marvel universe, instead serving as an antagonist to Spider-Man.[21] However, the readers loved him, and he evolved from a minor villain to an antihero who has starred in multiple comic book titles, movies, and TV series. With so many positive forces in the comic book world, why do people cheer for a mass murderer?

A Freudian would say that the Punisher in many ways represents our *id*, the part of our psyche that Freud said serves our more basal drives, including aggression.[22] Thus, the Punisher does what our more bestial selves might like to do when we see injustice in the world. Every time we see a violent criminal or exploiter of the weak walk free and wish there was something we could do, wish we could see the transgressor punished, we are lending credence to the actions of Frank Castle. The Punisher allows us to indulge this desire, as well as tap into our dark sides, in a safe manner. Unlike more traditional serial killers such as Jeffrey Dahmer and Ted Bundy, the Punisher targets those who are undeniably bad. There's no mistaking those on the receiving end of the Punisher's ire for innocent victims, and thus we don't have to feel bad when they die. The Punisher works best when he represents the justice we wish existed in the world. That's not to say that the Punisher and Daredevil cannot be simultaneously enjoyed by the same stand in for the *superego*, a higher-order process of the psyche that represents our conscience and drives our understanding of right and wrong. The debate between the Punisher and Daredevil over what is right might represent the id and superego's struggle to dominate the *ego*, the main portion of what we think of as ourselves.

Perhaps it is fitting that Freud most closely associated the superego with the father, the person most responsible for instilling the values held by Matt Murdock.[23] Both the Punisher and Daredevil represent aspects of ourselves that strive to be heard and that can be said to keep each other in check. Thus, not only is it understandable to root for a character like the Punisher, you could even argue it's healthy. Just make sure you're not rooting only for him.

HIDING IN PLAIN SIGHT

There's no denying that Frank Castle is a tragic character, though his tragedy began decades before the death of his family. Born as a man without conscience, Frank Castle conceals the spark that is the Punisher within him throughout his life. In a way, the Punisher is his true self while Frank Castle is simply the mask he wears to blend in. Honed like a combat knife through the trials of Special Forces training and three tours in Vietnam, Frank Castle cultivates the skills to become one of the most effective killing machines the world has ever seen. Yet he initially directs his violence toward the Vietcong, only occasionally taking the lives of those on his own side who get

SI VIS PACEM, PARA BELLUM

If you want peace, prepare for war. This Latin adage, as well as a number of variants, has been uttered multiple times by philosophers and tacticians across history. It also happens to be a phrase favored by Frank Castle that he uses in both comics[24] and film.[25] To Frank Castle, there can be no peace, no tranquility, without a body count. And only after every last potential bad guy is dead might Castle find peace, which means his is truly a war without end. It is also of note that the most common handgun cartridge in the world (and one which Frank Castle has been using since he first appeared in the Marvel universe), the 9x19mm, is also dubbed the *Parabellum*.

into his way. This all changes after the war is over, when his family is killed. At this moment, the pool of potential enemies increases exponentially, with criminals at all levels liable to find their way into the Punisher's crosshairs. Castle's psychopathic tendencies allow him to kill without concern or conscience, especially as he finally has the excuse necessary to wage his endless war. In stark contrast to Daredevil, the Punisher represents our more basal instincts, balancing our desire for fairness and justice with that for punishment. The Punisher is bound to keep killing until his body finally fails him, as there is no doubt he will continue to find opponents worthy of his ire. However, this is no curse to Frank Castle but rather a guarantee that he will ever be a tool in need of use.

NOTES

1. Machiavelli (1532/2017), location 101.
2. *The Punisher: The Tyger* #1 (2000). 3. *Daredevil* #1 (1964).
4. *Marvel Preview* #2 (1975).
5. *The Punisher: Intruder* (1989).
6. Pervin (1996).
7. Cleckley (1941/1976).
8. Yang & Rain (2009).
9. Anderson et al. (1999).
10. Grossman (2009).
11. *The Punisher: Born* #1 (2003).
12. *The Punisher: Born* #1 (2003).
13. *The Punisher: Born* #4 (2003).
14. Brockner et al. (1986); Opp & Samson (1989); Shapiro (2014).
15. Violanti & Aron (1994).
16. *Marvel Preview* #2 (1974).
17. *The Punisher MAX* #6 (2004).
18. *Punisher War Journal* #1 (2006).
19. *Punisher War Journal* #4 (2007).
20. *The Punisher MAX* #6 (2004).
21. *The Amazing Spider-Man* #129 (1974).
22. Freud (1923/1990).
23. Freud (1923/1990).
24. *Punisher Year One* #4 (1995).
25. *The Punisher MAX* #6 (2004).

CHAPTER 14

MAKING RELATIONSHIPS WORK

M A R A   W O O D   &
J E F F R E Y   H E N D E R S O N

*"I think beneath your noble, quiet exterior lies the heart of a man who
feels betrayed by women. Think about it: You were abandoned by
your mother at such a young age, and then when you get involved with
women, they scar you terribly."*
—Natalia "Natasha" Romanova, the Black Widow[1]

*"It is evident, however, that attachment behaviour is in no way
confined to children."*
—John Bowlby[2]

Exposure to adverse effects in childhood significantly
increases risk to physical and mental health in adulthood.[3] Adverse effects that directly affect the primary attachment figure, such as a parent, characterize the type and quality
of relationships that people have as they transition from childhood to adulthood.[4] Matt Murdock has a history of trauma that

impacts the quality of relationships he has as an adult. Through the years, he has had many relationships, both platonic and romantic, that have ended badly for the other party, mostly as a result of the host of extraordinary factors that defined his upbringing. In a sense, Matt Murdock is fated to become Daredevil—a man split between his moral, dutiful, and aspirational better self and a vengeful, violent devil whose need to serve his worst impulses is hardwired into him.

Although the definition of a healthy relationship is somewhat subjective, there are a number of elements that are present, such as shared trust, personal disclosures, and investment in each other's ideas.[5] Unfortunately, for the important people in his life, his upbringing makes having normal, healthy relationships almost impossible for Matt Murdock.

GROWING UP IN HELL'S KITCHEN

The type and quality of interaction between parents and child establishes the pattern of attachment that the child carries into adulthood.[6] Depending on the responsiveness of the primary caregiver (usually the mother), the child can be classified as securely attached or insecurely attached. Children who develop an insecure attachment to their primary caregiver can experience lasting negative effects on self-esteem and sociability.[7] In a very real way, almost everything during Matt Murdock's formative years is characterized by extreme highs and lows. A pattern of overstimulation and a lack of normal, healthy balance in his young life is established very early.

His youth is defined by secrecy, high drama, and violence.[8] Even before his fateful accident, Matt's life is difficult. After his mother abandons him as a child, he is raised by his father, a journeyman boxer who also worked as a "collector" for the mob. It is a vocation the elder Murdock is deeply ashamed of but feels he has to continue because of the threats made against his only child by the mobsters he works for. "Battlin'" Jack Murdock, although loving and supportive, remains beholden to the violent practices of the world he is part of. Childhood trauma, abuse, and neglect can contribute to depressive and even psychotic symptomatology.[9] Between his mother leaving him and his father's violent example, Matt grows up with an anxious-preoccupied pattern of adult attachment. Individuals with a history of multiple forms of abuse (neglect, sexual, physical, emotional, etc.) over several developmental periods are more likely to exhibit a preoccupied state of mind during adulthood.[10] There is essentially a preoccupation with specific relationships in Matt's life, especially with his primary attachment figure, Jack Murdock. People with anxious-preoccupied attachment patterns desperately work to maintain their attachment and exhibit anxiety at the separation and loss of that attachment figure.[11]

After the accident that leaves him sightless, Matt becomes, quite literally, biologically predisposed to *overstimulation*, which will influence his developing personality into adulthood. Overstimulation is often linked with stress, which in turn affects the cortical development of children.[12] Stick trained Matt and helps him control his "radar sense," but that relationship is also abnormal and unhealthy. Matt is a dedicated and diligent pupil but becomes more and more entrenched in a world of normalized violence and secrecy as a result of Stick's intense training methods. Violence in childhood impacts posttraumatic stress and depressive symptomatology whether the child is removed from the violent environment or not.

All these factors become polarized after the death of Matt's father. The terrible incident lights a fuse in Matt that has been just under the surface the whole time, and it culminates in the young Murdock meting out violent, vigilante justice to everyone involved in the murder of his father. But it is Matt who pays the ultimate price because exposure to violence can lead to depression, lowered self-esteem, and social isolation.[13] *Adverse childhood experiences* (ACEs) are linked to a number of adult outcomes, both physically and psychologically.[14] In Matt's case, the impact of a single-parent household with repeated violence exposure increases adult symptomatology of depression, suicidality, and impaired work performance.[15]

Unlike many of his more emotionally stable and healthy superhero counterparts, Matt's alter ego Daredevil serves as a type of release valve, a way to unleash all the anger, frustration, and violence he has to suppress in his normal, day-to-day life, and that release is as essential to Matt Murdock as breathing. The *catharsis* theory of aggression posits that engaging in aggressive activities reduces the likelihood of future aggression actions.[16] This theory also extends to viewing aggressive actions, particularly those found in the media. Even though evidence does not consistently confirm the effectiveness of catharsis, people may seek it.[17] Matt's aggression actions as a superhero toward those who would cause harm to citizens may be the cathartic release he needs to ensure a more "normalized" life as a lawyer.

In light of all these factors, it would seem almost inevitable that Matt Murdock's adult life, as well as his relationships, would be defined by secrecy, drama, and violence. This is not exactly a recipe for healthy, beneficial relationships.

TWO OF A KIND

It's no mystery why Elektra Natchios casts such a long shadow over the story of Matt Murdock/Daredevil. After all, they are, according to her, "two of a kind." They become each other's first loves, sharing a bond that runs deeper and is more profound than either of them realize in their youth. Both of their childhoods are defined by tragedy, and their respective adult lives are defined by secrecy and violence. They are perfect for each other in all the wrong ways.

Elektra is literally born into tragedy: In one version of Elektra's background, her mother Christina gives birth to Elektra with her dying breath after being mortally wounded in an assassination attempt.[18] As a result, Elektra is raised alone by her father, who is later assassinated as well. Fueled by a raging thirst for vengeance, she uses her considerable resources to travel the world, devoting herself completely to training as an assassin. Eventually, she even trains with Stick, the hard-as-nails instructor who has previously trained Matt Murdock. Elektra's adverse childhood exposure parallels Matt's, with the loss of one parental figure, the strained relationship with the remaining figure, the death of the other parent, and the intense exposure to violence.

Many years later, she returns to New York (and to Matt's life), but the qualities that have been simmering under the surface in her youth—the rage, the impulsiveness, and the violence—are all exaggerated. Those qualities are now front and center, dictating Elektra's actions and defining her life in a much more powerful way than ever before. She returns a stone-cold killer, but Matt can still perceive (or convinces himself that he still can) the young girl he fell in love with years before.

Throughout Daredevil's history in comics, film, and TV, Matt keeps trying to save his beloved Elektra.[19] Matt, with elements of an anxious–preoccupied attachment style, is more likely to have a positive view of others and a negative view of himself.[20] Additionally, the relationships he establishes are characterized by fear of abandonment, hypervigilance, and jealousy.[21] Ultimately, no amount of faith and intervention from Matt will save Elektra from her own destructiveness.

TOXIC BROMANCE

Social interaction for adults with a history of insecure attachments can be difficult. Social anxiety and depression are linked to insecure attachment, affecting the quality of friendships a person forms in his or her lifetime.[22] Despite Matt's history of poor attachment to caregiver figures as a child, he develops a lasting friendship with Foggy Nelson. The two superficially seem to be opposites of each other: Matt is tall, confident, handsome, and charming, whereas Foggy is short, a bit out of shape, and insecure. Matt seems to have an effortless time with women, whereas Foggy is unsure and awkward; it is the "bad boy" versus the "nice guy" dynamic playing out over and over again.

The relationship between the two is almost familial, and despite their differences, they love each other and ultimately need each other. Foggy feeds off of Matt's confidence and bravado, inspired by his friend's ability to overcome his "handicap," whereas Matt needs Foggy's honesty and generosity. Foggy is essentially Matt's moral compass, at times almost single-handedly keeping Matt out of the dark places that consume Elektra.

Even Foggy's career path is based on his trust in Matt; he gives up a hefty salary and cushy job at a corporate law firm to partner with his friend in a fledgling "bottom of the ladder" law firm. That trust is shaken to the core when Foggy finally finds out about Matt's secret life as a masked vigilante.[23] Despite his anger and disappointment in his friend, he stands by Matt— albeit reluctantly—and tries helps him navigate out of the dark.

ACE IN THE HOLE

As demonstrated by those among the insecurely attached children who eventually manage to have successful relationships, this does not mean Matt Murdock can never fill those holes in himself, but it will be much harder. Even with secure attachment in childhood, relationships are difficult. Insecure attachment resulting from adverse childhood experiences has a lasting impact on the romantic and platonic relationships an adult forms. When one of the people in a relationship is struggling with untreated emotional problems, psychological traumas and/or personality disorders, it becomes exponentially harder to cultivate anything resembling a normal or healthy relationship. Matt, like other adults with a history of insecure attachment, would have to commit to fully understanding the impact of his childhood on his interactions with others in order to develop normal, healthy relationships.

BARRISTERS OF A FEATHER

TRAVIS LANGLEY

The *complementary hypothesis* supposes that for a relationship (whether romantic, friendly, familial, or other) to succeed, each person in the relationship should supply what is missing in the other. This would suit the old adage that "opposites attract," but even if differences draw attention, research overwhelmingly finds the reverse to be true. One of the greatest predictors of success in a relationship is instead *similarity*. As a competing adage suggests, "birds of a feather flock together." This applies to similarity in a wide array of qualities in terms of attitudes, behavior, economic level, appearance, and intelligence.[24] Matt and Foggy share enough common interests and values that they both become lawyers who are motivated to help others, but their differences—especially their differences over Matt's lifestyle—keep driving them apart.[25]

"It's kinda spooky, actually, but if there's a stunning woman with questionable character in the room, Matt Murdock's gonna find her and Foggy Nelson is gonna suffer."

—Foggy Nelson[26]

NOTES

1. *Daredevil* #8 (1999).
2. Bowlby (1988), p. 2.
3. Felitti et al. (1998).
4. Eng et al. (2001).
5. Boyes (2013).
6. Bretherton (1992).
7. Eng et al. (2001).
8. *Daredevil* #1 (1964); *Daredevil* #164 (1980); *Daredevil* #1 (2011).
9. Van Dam et al. (2015).
10. Raby et al. (2017).
11. Blatt & Levy (2003).
12. Lindroos et al. (1984).
13. Barboza & Dominguez (2017).
14. Merrick et al. (2017).
15. Merrick et al. (2017).
16. Bresin & Gordon (2013).
17. Bushman & Whitaker (2010); Denzer & Förster (2012).
18. e.g., *Daredevil* #190 (1983).
19. *Elektra: Assassin* #1 (1986).
20. Eng et al. (2001).
21. Eng et al. (2001).
22. Eng et al. (2001).
23. Botwin et al. (1997); Buss (1985); Kandel (1978).
24. *Daredevil* #48 (1969), among many examples.
25. *Daredevil* #347 (1995); #348 (1996).
26. Marvel's Daredevil episode 1–1, "Into the Ring" (April 10, 2015).

ROLL CALL: ABOUT THOSE OTHERS

TRAVIS LANGLEY

Franklin "Foggy" Nelson, Karen Page, and Jack Murdock all first appeared along with Matt Murdock in *Daredevil #1* (1964). Other characters discussed in this section made their debuts in stories cited below.

Margaret Grace Murdock, a.k.a. Sister Maggie: *Daredevil #229* (1986)

Elektra Natchios: *Daredevil #168* (1981)

Stick: *Daredevil #176* (1981)

Natasha Romanoff, born Natalia Romanova, a.k.a. the Black Widow: *Tales of Suspense #52* (1964)
> Natasha is the informal version of the name Natalia, like calling Margaret "Maggie," and Romanoff is an anglicized version of her Russian surname Romanova.

Milla Donovan (who becomes Matt's wife, then ex-wife): *Daredevil #41* (2003)

Frank Castle, a.k.a. the Punisher: *The Amazing Spider-Man #129* (1974)

AND DAREDEVIL'S FELLOW DEFENDERS

Luke Cage, born Carl Lucas, a.k.a. Power Man: *Luke Cage, Hero for Hire #1* (1972)

Danny Rand, a.k.a. Iron Fist: *Marvel Premiere #15* (1974)

Jessica Campbell Jones, a.k.a. Jewel, Power Woman, Knightress: *Alias #1* (2001)
> An unnamed high school student in *The Amazing Spider-Man #4* (1963) has been retroactively identified as Jessica within comic book continuity.

V

BARGAINS

"The Devil shall have his bargain . . ."
—playwright William Shakespeare,
Henry IV, Part 1 (circa 1597)

STRIKING BARGAINS

Bargain *(noun)*. 1. A deal made regarding give and take between parties. 2. An advantageous acquisition.
(verb). 1. To negotiate. 2. To anticipate.

As a child, Matt Murdock strikes a bargain with his father, essentially a no-striking bargain: He will not fight. He will devote himself to his education so that he might make something better of himself instead of becoming a boxer or ruffian like his father. As an adult, though, he becomes both the lawyer who works with his brains and the superhero who works with his fists, both keeping and breaking his bargain with his long-departed father.[1]

Lawyers make bargains all the time. Courtroom lawyers strike plea bargains; contract lawyers negotiate terms; mergers and acquisitions lawyers structure deals for the sales of companies.[2] Some serve the spirit of the law, the intent behind the wording of the agreement or rule, while others seek loopholes,[3] ways to twist words to create opportunities never intended, and still others cheat by deliberately creating loopholes or slipping in terms not previously agreed on or even discussed.[4] People who make deals with devils supposedly face long, confusing, tricky contracts that inevitably cause their deals to backfire on them.

Deal makers and deal breakers carry motives aplenty. Either can be selfish, selfless, or some mixture thereof. Some of them do so in order to pursue power for its own sake no matter how they hurt or inconvenience others.[5] Some have nobler or at least more considerate motives. Much as the challenge motivates lawyer Murdock when he speaks eloquently on behalf of the innocent and helps them navigate their way through a sea of sharks, his determination to make things right for others motivates him more. Whereas heroes help others find security or freedom, villains rob others of both, especially the freedom to make their own choices and deals in life.[6] An extreme example is one of Daredevil's oldest foes, Killgrave the Purple Man, who lacks the patience and confidence to request and negotiate as he simply robs others of their ability to bargain.[7]

Dealing with devils is an ancient theme, possibly woven into the fabric of the collective unconscious.[8] We often feel we're dealing with devils or angels when, in fact, human beings are more complex with a bit of both somewhere in all of us. We may need to deal with the darkest parts of ourselves before we can work toward achieving any happiness in the light.

—T. L.

NOTES

1. *Daredevil* #191 (1983).
2. Feinman (2014); Ventura (2005).
3. "The lawyer in you always finding a loophole for your selfish self." Mephisto in *Daredevil* #266 (1989).
4. Memon et al. (2003).
5. McClelland (1975).
6. Fromm (1964).
7. *Daredevil* #4 (1964); *Alias* #25 (2003).
8. Jung (1956/1976; 1959/1973).

CHAPTER 15

WHAT LURKS IN SHADOW: JUNG'S NOTION OF THE DEVIL AND EVIL IN DAREDEVIL

LAURA VECCHIOLLA

"If ever you have the rare opportunity to speak with the devil, then do not forget to confront him in all seriousness. He is your devil after all."

—psychiatrist Carl Jung[1]

"The Devil is full of tricks."[2]

—Foggy Nelson

The problem of evil and the question of the devil's existence are dilemmas that have been contemplated by philosophers and vigilantes alike. For Matt Murdock, the influence of the devil and his evils is evident yet illusory. Long before the days of donning his horned mask and billy club, young Matthew spends his days in churches and schools that foster in him a deep respect for and belief in Catholic ideology. As a young boy, Matt knew the devil and knew him well. He sensed the devil's presence in the cruelty of bullies in the schoolyard and in the callousness of the men who killed his father. Such familiarity with the devil and all his evil established in Matt's mind clear and unquestionable parameters for what is right and what is wrong. Despite the clear compartmentalization within Murdock's worldview, we still find our main character frequently questioning the demarcations of sin and virtue. At his very core, Matt is a hero conflicted, torn between his duty as a good Catholic boy and his obligation as a forceful vigilante. Matt may have supernatural powers, but what arguably makes him such a good character is the very human dilemma of a man split in two: a savior and a devil. What draws audiences to the character of Matt Murdock goes beyond his "radar sense"; it is his very human and very relatable experience of ambivalence and his struggles with his inner demons that have led Daredevil to become one of the most popular and fascinating characters in the Marvel Comics universe. Matt's experience with incongruity and his struggles with "the devils inside" signify a profound psychological phenomenon that can be best explained by the work of Swiss psychiatrist Carl Jung and his notion of the Shadow archetype.

THE PSYCHOLOGICAL DEVIL

Religious imagery and undercurrents of theological debates are so present in the Daredevil narrative that the devil may as well be considered a chief character. In Daredevil's world, the devil manifests as many different people, places, and events. The devil is Wilson Fisk as he systematically obliterates Murdock's finances, friendships, and identity to leave behind a shell of a man who once was Daredevil.[3] The devil is the influx of heroin that corrupts Hell's Kitchen and eventually and debases Karen Page.[4] The devil is the Hand and their preternatural magic that threatens all that Murdock swears to protect. Yet as a psychological concept, "the devil" is really only one thing: the symbolic representation of the archetype Shadow in our unconscious.

Jung paid special interest to concepts such as evil and the devil over the course of his career. However, Jung made it clear that he was not interested in the philosophical or theological understandings of the devil. Rather, he took a practical approach to the dilemma of evil and the devil. He wanted to know the psychological significance of those themes. The devil, for Jung, served a necessary psychological function. As a variant of the Shadow archetype, the devil is a clear and recognizable representation of the dangerous aspects of the "unrecognized dark half" of one's personality.[5]

JUNG'S MODEL OF THE PSYCHE

All the traits and characteristics that are labeled as part of our identity, in Jung's theory, constitute what he termed the ego. The ego is, simply put, the center of our consciousness. The ego deals with all matters of identity development and maintenance, reality testing, and decision-making and discernment.[6] A person's ego emerges early in development. As a child grows in psychological maturity, he or she learns what behaviors, thoughts, and feelings feel "right," and those judgments subsequently are shifted to the ego. Early experiences shape Matt's burgeoning ego. Two men in young Murdock's life facilitate the development of Matt's identity: Matt's father, Jack, and his trainer, Stick. From his father, Matt learns the importance of redemption, of determination and the notion that "sometimes even if you get knocked down you can still win."[7] Stick teaches Matt the clear-cut purpose and discipline that he takes with him into law school and all his future endeavors.

The ego also serves as a mediator in the interactions between the conscious and the unconscious.[8] There lies in the unconscious an unknown counterpart, or the opposite, for all that is conscious in the ego. The unconscious consists of all the contents of one's identity that are out of awareness. Jung further splits the unconscious into two types: the personal and the collective. For Jung, the *personal unconscious* holds one's unique repository of unwanted information: elements of an individual identity that are forgotten, repressed, or ignored.[9] The contents of the personal unconscious lie at the threshold of our consciousness and have the potential to become part of consciousness at any given time. Beyond the personal unconscious, Jung described the *collective unconscious*. The collective unconscious is a receptacle that consists of infinite amounts of psychic material shared by all of humankind.[10] The contents that make up the collective unconscious encompass all human characteristics, or what Jung termed *archetypes*. Archetypes are the images, figures, and symbols organized around recurrent themes in the human experience. Themes such as light and dark and angels and devils are all archetypal and reside within the collective unconscious. In the Daredevil universe, the eternal conflict between the Hand and the Chaste symbolizes the immemorial theme of good versus evil that inhabits all of humanity's unconscious. Murdock understands how the devil himself lives within us, occupying our personal and collective unconscious in the form of the *Shadow archetype*. He warns, "Be careful of the Murdock boys. They got the devil in 'em."[11]

THE SHADOW ARCHETYPE

The ego does not exist without opposition. There are unknown, severed aspects of the personality kept hidden in the darkness. Jung names this component of the psyche the Shadow.[12] The Shadow is composed of all the unconscious aspects of an individual's personality that the conscious ego has scorned and detached from. Jung associated the Shadow with all the rejected or "dark" contents of an individual's personality. All that a person cannot admit or accept about himself or herself— inferiorities or forbidden wishes—constitutes the Shadow archetype. It is the "dumping ground for all those characteristics of our personality that we disown."[13]

In Jung's theory, "the devil" is just as real a phenomenon as it is for Matt Murdock. It is as real as the nagging demon inside Matt that tempts him to beat a man with no mercy, the "cold part of him" that "takes over" as pursues the criminals of Hell's Kitchen.[14] Jung recognized the devil's sway on humankind and took it very seriously as a threat to the survival of the human race.[15] However, the "devil" as Jung knew him was not an external, autonomous force that lay outside the ego but rather the most fiercely denied contents of one's Shadow. Jung contested that in denying aspects of oneself, one is "simply feeding the devils."[16]

The devil lives and labors within the shadows of the unconscious, which in Jung's theory means that the devil is at play on two levels: the personal Shadow and the collective Shadow. For Jung, the shadow of the individual harbors personal devils: demons of incongruence and denial. In the collective unconscious lives a larger devil, the shadow of humankind that brings forth undeniable evils.

FORMING THE SHADOW

As Matt grew up, he too began to place ideas and values in classifications of good and evil. A pivotal moment in Daredevil's Shadow origin comes to us in Frank Miller's *Man without Fear*. Young Matt runs home to proudly tell his father that he finally bested one of his playground bullies in a fight only to have his father angrily strike him across the face as punishment. It occurred to Matt that "Dad was wrong" and that the only the way to stop bad people is to "study the rules . . . study the Law."[17] The development of our personal Shadow parallels that of our developing ego.[18] As a child makes decisions about what he or she wishes to include as part of an identity, unavoidable choices of what to disown are being made as well. The rejected aspects of our identity are cast into the darkness of the Shadow archetype and renounced. Throughout our development, parts of the personality are judged by us as "good" and "evil" and then shifted to our conscious or unconscious. This is a necessary process as we decide who we are and what belongs to our personality. Young Matt's resolution to study the rules is a moment in his development that prefigures his path to becoming a lawyer, but it also demonstrates the evaluation and splitting of values that ultimately shape both our ego and our Shadow. This example reveals how ideas first are judged as "acceptable" or "not acceptable" and then allied to or disconnected from the ego, subsequently shaping the Shadow.

The more a person forbids certain aspects of his or her personality or the more intense the denial remains, the "denser" the Shadow becomes. Those with rigid or dogmatic beliefs often have the blackest of Shadows, seemingly impenetrable by the light of consciousness.[19] However, regardless of the density of the Shadow, according to Jung's theory, all unconscious material has a desire to be seen and acknowledged by the ego. According to Jung, the more an individual denies his or her Shadow, the more it will seek out one's attention. All that is refused or seemingly disowned does not magically disappear; it stays deep within the psyche and waits for opportunity to express itself.[20]

CONFRONTING THE SHADOW

Jung proposed that when one is so deeply in denial of his or her Shadow contents, there are recognizable "symptoms." The Shadow wants to be seen in order to be reintegrated in a healthy and balanced way.[21] But if the Shadow is buried in the unconscious, how can it be seen? Jung argues that the most common means by which Shadow content makes itself known is projection. *Shadow projection* is an automatic process by which the contents of one's own unconscious are perceived to be in others. "Unless we do conscious work on it, the Shadow is almost always projected, that is, it is neatly laid on someone or something else so we do not have to take responsibility for it."[22] A priest, Father Lantom, explains the phenomenon of projection when he tells Murdock, "Another man's evil does not make you good. Men have used the atrocities of their enemies to justify their own throughout history."[23] Matt's Shadow side is easily realized when he becomes stuck in his rigid and dogmatic ego ideals and is seen condemning the values or choices of others. An example of Shadow projection is impeccably laid out in a long, morally laden conversation between Daredevil and the Punisher on a rooftop. Daredevil makes it known that he is deeply offended by the Punisher's choice to kill. He judges Frank Castle for killing those whom only God can judge. The ability and the desire to kill are deeply hidden in Matt's Shadow side, so he can only see these Shadow characteristics in others whom he judges. But Frank reminds him of the nature of Shadow projection by saying, "You know the one thing that you just can't see? You know you're one bad day away from being me."[24]

But for those who are willing to complete the arduous and frightening work of confronting the Shadow directly, it is possible to see one's own devils without needing to cast the shadow onto others. This is what is often referred to as "Shadow work," and it involves making a conscious effort to identify, acknowledge, and accept the dark and undesirable parts of one's own identity. Jung attested that actively confronting and knowing one's Shadow is a great and brave undertaking consisting of "considerable moral effort."[25] The initiation into Shadow work can begin with simply asking oneself difficult questions and completing an ardent moral inventory. This type of Shadow work is not beyond the practices of Matt Murdock. Daredevil is seen at the bedside of a paralyzed Bullseye holding a gun to his head, beckoning Bullseye to play a game of Russian roulette. He is desperate for vindication after Bullseye has murdered Elektra. While pulling the trigger back and forth, Daredevil

A FEVER INSIDE: ANN NOCENTI ON TYPHOID MARY

Travis Langley

Dissociative identity disorder, the modern diagnostic term for *multiple personality disorder*,[27] is so unusual that mental health professionals do not agree whether it even exists. Because we all are full of contradictions, presenting different faces in different situations, a bit of multiplicity is normal and therefore not mental illness.

Daredevil writer Ann Nocenti introduced Typhoid Mary, a pyrokinetic assassin who fights Daredevil and romances Matt Murdock.[28] The character Mary Walker is a mutant with multiple personality, one whose *alter* personality Typhoid is especially likely to emerge when men mistreat her. Historically, "Typhoid Mary" was originally a nickname given to a real woman named Mary Mallon, a symptom-free carrier of the pathogen for typhoid fever.[29] Did Nocenti name her supervillain after Mallon's obliviousness to her own problem or perhaps for the way she spread fire, so to speak, by causing others to burn with deadly fever?

questions his own role in the bloodshed when he asks himself, "Am I fighting violence, or teaching it?"[26] In the end his gun has no bullets and Daredevil admits they are "stuck with each other." Nonetheless, this example exhibits Daredevil's direct confrontation with the devil inside, the devil that savors his ties to violence and rationalizes tormenting and nearly killing his enemy.

Q: Did you do research on multiple personality when you were creating Typhoid Mary?

Nocenti: Yes, I did a lot of research on that. It was coming out in three different places as I recall, but memory is suspect: (1) I worked in asylums; (2) I was curious about different people I encountered that seems to have bipolar disorder; and (3) I was interested in how women seemed to fall into a certain number of categories in comics. I wanted to present all the different stereotypes in one character. Some of it comes from existential thoughts: "What am I? Why did I behave that way at that point in my life?" I wanted to create a complex female character. Research I did included interviewing *not* people with multiple personality—because I think that's quite rare—but some with what would now be called bipolar.

Q: Why did you call her Typhoid Mary?

Nocenti: Because so many other names had already been used. There are parallels because she was a plague spreader and she was in denial about it. Maybe that was in my subconscious, but I really don't remember it meaning anything.

Murdock's real confrontation comes in the form of a dream-like sequence. While training with Stick, he is struck across the face and rendered unconscious, and his mind sinks to a deeper place. There, he is confronted by his father in a boxing ring, who condemns his vigilante lifestyle. His father then transforms into a towering and evil beast. "I'm your own private devil, lawyer man," the beast says, "I'm the part of you that hates."[30] This dreamlike confrontation is the perfect representation of Shadow work: an occurrence of looking one's "private devil" in the face and choosing to stay in the ring.

INTEGRATING THE SHADOW

When the Shadow no longer can be denied, and contact has been made, Jung upheld the necessity of integrating Shadow contents into the totality of the personality. This was a step in what Jung considered to be each person's ultimate psychological goal: *individuation*,[31] development into a mentally whole individual. As Jung saw it, the process requires that the contents of the unconscious be brought into conscious awareness, thus allowing for balance and wholeness in the individual. Individuation occurs when the ego allows for a cooperative dialogue between the conscious and the unconscious. There is a Shadow side of Daredevil that yearns to kill—to be the judge, jury, and executioner. This side of him is largely cut off from his awareness, as evidenced by his righteous lectures to the Punisher on the sin of murder and the virtue of redemption.[32] Yet in Murdock's conversations with the priest Father Lantom, he can entertain a dialogue that might have occurred between his Shadow and his ego. Matt can contemplate his ambivalence toward taking a life, acknowledging that deep in himself this is what part of him wants to do.[33]

Ultimately Shadow integration involves recognizing the disservice in splitting personality aspects. Those who can truly integrate their Shadow contents into their conscious awareness comprehend the value of uniting good and evil so that they may be reconciled.

Jung states that individuation can occur only when there is a tension of opposites. Only through enduring this tension can one experience the relief of reconciliation. There are clues that Matt is attempting to reconcile his opposites by integrating his Shadow. He asks Father Lantom, "How do you know the angels and the devil inside me aren't the same thing?"[34] Matt is beginning to see that he must honor both his angels and his devils—his ego and his Shadow—to survive the streets of Hell's Kitchen.

THE DEVIL AND THE SAVIOR

Matt Murdock is indeed is a hero at odds with himself, wavering between angel and devil, lawyer and vigilante, redemption and condemnation. Yet perhaps his ambivalence and incongruence are not a sign of a hero conflicted but rather illustrative of the experience of conflict and confusion one can experience when engulfed in deep and revealing Shadow work. Murdock is a character both tormented and liberated by his Shadow side. We see that for all the good that he aims to accomplish, he is still capable of embracing the devil within. While he is tumbling across the rooftops and alleyways of Hell's Kitchen, we see a final example of Shadow integration in the simple act of accepting a once unacceptable name: "Daredevil. Echoing from the schoolyard, from the bullies' taunts. Daredevil. He hated that name. He wanted to shove it down their throats. And now he wears it like a badge."[35]

NOTES

1. Jung (1973), p. 261.
2. *Daredevil #5* (2014).
3. *Daredevil #228* (1986).
4. *Daredevil #228* (1986).
5. Jung (1953/1966).
6. Jung (1953/1966).
7. *Marvel's Daredevil*, episode 1–2, "Cut Man" (April 10, 2015).
8. Jung (1956/1976).
9. Jung (1953/1966).
10. Jung (1953/1966).
11. *Marvel's Daredevil*, episode 1–1, "Into the Ring" (April 10, 2015).
12. Jung (1959/1978).
13. Johnson (1991), p. ix.
14. *Daredevil #1* (1993)
15. Stein (1996), p. 1.
16. Jung (1995), p. 53.
17. *Daredevil #1* (1993)
18. Jung (1956/1976).
19. Johnson (1991).
20. Johnson (1991).
21. Stein (1996).
22. Johnson (1991), p. 31.
23. *Marvel's Daredevil*, episode 1–9, "Speak of the Devil" (April 10, 2015).
24. *Marvel's Daredevil*, episode 2–3, "New York's Finest" (March 18, 2016).
25. Jung (1959/1978), p. 14.
26. *Daredevil #191* (1981).
27. American Psychiatric Association (2013).
28. *Daredevil #254–263* (1988–1989).
29. Bourdain (2001); Keane (2013).
30. Daredevil #177 (1981).
31. Jung (1956/1976).
32. *Marvel's Daredevil*, episode 2–3, "New York's Finest" (March 18, 2016).
33. *Marvel's Daredevil*, episode 1–9, "Speak of the Devil" (April 10, 2015).
34. *Marvel's Daredevil*, episode 1–11, "Path of Righteousness" (April 10, 2015).
35. *Daredevil #5* (1994).

CHAPTER 16

WHY BEING BLIND TO THE DEVIL INSIDE STUNTS EMOTIONAL GROWTH

WILLIAM SHARP

"What we learn about the child and the adult through psychoanalysis [is]
that every child. . . goes through an immeasurable degree of suffering."
—psychoanalyst Melanie Klein[1]

"Smart don't come out of books, kid. Smart is making the right decision
at the right time. You gonna dig deep and find out what it takes?"
—Stick to nine-year-old Matt[2]

aredevil is the good guy; Wilson Fist, New York's Kingpin of Crime, is the bad guy. Foggy and Karen Page are good guys, too; Fisk's employees James Wesley and Bullseye are bad guys, too. Frank Castle, the Punisher, is. . . . well, now it's getting complicated! When one is growing up, things appear simple. Good and bad have clear lines. Matt Murdock knows what he has to do and believes he has truth and justice on his side. Wilson Fisk deals in the shadows and is out only for his own self-interest (although both the TV show and the comics have multiple incidents in which he believes he is acting for his wife or will change his course on the basis of her wishes).[3] As we accompany Daredevil on his adventures, it becomes apparent that things are not always as simple as he (and we) want them to be. Daredevil is a vigilante and by definition goes above and "breaks" the law. Kingpin certainly has a temper but wants to make Hell's Kitchen great again.[4] Could the ends ever justify the means?

Part of growing up involves learning that the lines between good and bad are often blurred. This is part of social and emotional development. The first person to write about this from a *psychoanalytic* viewpoint (a.k.a. *psychodynamic*, essentially the Freudian perspective that unconscious drives guide our actions and personality development) was psychoanalyst Melanie Klein, who read Freud's work and used her observations of children to come up with a model of the mind. According to her theory, called object relations theory, we start experiencing objects as good or bad—and only that. As we mature, we eventually see that one object may be both good *and* bad. For Kleinians, that is progress. Progress however, is not automatic and often is nonlinear. We have a new insight about a person that may be mature, but then we can regress again to black-and-white thinking. She called this "growing" and moving between the paranoid–schizoid position and the depressive position.

What might an assessment of Matt Murdock/Daredevil's personality show about his social and emotional development along object relations lines? As he sometimes is depicted, Matt is in the paranoid–schizoid position. In the comics, one of the reasons he adopts a costumed identity is to circumvent his childhood promise to his father that he will not resort to fighting and violence: Daredevil is not the one who made the promise, he argues to himself, and so Matt Murdock is not breaking any promises.[5] Lawyer Matt must realize that this legalistic argument doesn't fulfill the spirit of the promise, but it's good enough to justify defying his father's wishes. Years later, his refusal to process his feelings leads to a break from reality as he assumes several identities at once, each with a different personality and wearing a different Daredevil costume.[6] His growing pains and struggles come from the fact that he unconsciously views the world in terms of good and bad and works hard to avoid the depressive position.[7] Why?

We have infantile wishes to have the perfect parent, which becomes the wish for a perfect partner, the perfect life, and the perfect world. Inherent in that is a belief that we too are also "all good." It is hard to accept that we too are both good and bad; hence, that position is called the depressive position. The alternative to moving to the depressive position however, staying in the paranoid-schizoid position, leads to anger, resentment, and destructive actions such as splitting and suffering. The only way to a mature position (Klein's depressive position) is to choose to confront our own devils inside.

DEVELOPMENT: SPLITTING OUR WAY TO MATURATION

Matt Murdock and the rest of us start our lives in a state of oceanic oneness. We begin in an ocean of amniotic fluid without a real sense of self or other. Slowly we realize that there are other people with their own motives. Some of those motives are obvious, and others are more unconscious and hidden. Mirroring this, Daredevil has often had to team up with people he's not sure he can trust or who may fight evil but have motives and methods that go against his morality, such as the Punisher, who acts like a man of honor at times but will try to follow his own mission at all costs.[8] Our experiences with our first objects in the world lay down a "blueprint" of sorts for all future relationships. When our primary caregiver (our "mom" for short) responds to our cry, she is good mom. When we cry in our crib, it isn't the good mom who ignores us (how could it be?); it is the other, "bad" mom's shift. We love the good mom. We hate the bad mom. Never the two shall meet. This is the paranoid-schizoid position. Typically (one hopes), in development, we come to see that it is actually the same "mom" who sometimes gets it right and sometimes gets it wrong. We are able to both love and hate her safely. However, we lose a little of our optimism, coming to what Klein calls the depressive position. It is mature but sad as we now realize that "happily ever after" is only in fairy tales. Sometimes people are good, and sometimes they are bad. Even after she redeems herself and goes from assassin to antihero, Elektra is a person whose methods, motivations, and inner darkness will always push Matt away even while he acknowledges his feelings for her and the times when she fights against evil.[9]

One day Matt Murdock can see; the next day he can't. One day his senses are within normal limits; the next day he has a form of echolocation and radar that any bat would envy. His physical development takes a leap, but it seems Daredevil's social and emotional development is arrested. He has to undergo a lot of suffering to learn that the solution to Hell's Kitchen isn't as simple as "getting rid of the bad guys." Matt has to go from "seeing" the world in terms of only good and bad to eventually coming to recognize that most things come in shades of gray. Fisk's right-hand man, Wesley, says it clearly: "Growing to love something is really simply forgetting slowly what you dislike about it."[10] Stick, nine-year-old Matt Murdock's teacher, says, "Big world, not all of it flowers and sunshine."[11] Matt has tremendous agility and physical balance, but we see that his simple plan to fix Hell's Kitchen is constantly thwarted and he is thrown off balance emotionally when "good doesn't always triumph." He suffers emotionally in relationships, trying to fit people into neat categories of good and bad, which people do not match all the time. Karen Page is a murderer, Foggy has a series of relationships that often fail and concern Matt, and of course Matt's relationship with Elektra—you can see again that staying in the depressive position can be, well . . . depressing. Probably even enough to want to hang up your superhero costume (at least for a while) and give up.

HEALTHY SOCIAL AND EMOTIONAL DEVELOPMENT: A RABBIT IN A SNOWSTORM

> *"A man who has not passed through the inferno of his passions has never overcome them."*
> —analytic psychiatrist Carl Jung[12]

> *"Of right and wrong, good and evil. Sometimes the delineation between the two is a sharp line. Sometimes it's a blur."*
> —Matt Murdock[13]

What is health? Perhaps a mature person knows what she or he wants, knows how to get it, and gets it.[14] Matt Murdock knows what he wants: a safe Hell's Kitchen. He believes he knows how to get it: by cleaning up the streets as the vigilante Daredevil. However, he is thwarted and stuck in the paranoid-schizoid position. Even after attending law school, where he must have taken ethics classes and learned that even criminals deserve a defense, he often seems to act simply on the belief that there is good or bad in all. Matt Murdock just doesn't seem to know how to get what he wants. This is where his social and emotional growth is stunted.

Psychoanalysts view health and maturity as being free to have all feelings and to act appropriately in one's best interests.[15] Matt has to learn that Hell's Kitchen is more complex than just the good and the bad. Much of Daredevil's career involves Matt desperately trying to do the right thing. We root for him because we want him to be right—a simple solution to a problem. We see, however, that his morals and oath continually make his ultimate goal impossible. The bad guy always gets away. In fact, in some ways, the villain seems to be learning more and becoming more powerful, as we see in Wilson Fisk, the Kingpin, who eventually comes out of the shadows of the mobster life to rise to a spotlight of political power.

Standing in an art gallery, Fisk looks at a painting of a rabbit in a snowstorm[16] and feels "alone." This moment in the story timeline however is significant symbolically for all the characters. Wesley attempts to retain the law firm of Murdock and Nelson and get them to defend a shady individual. Foggy sees zeroes on a check and wants to say yes; Matt wants to say no. After meeting with Healy and getting interested in how he can use him to find out about the mysterious supervillain of the shadows, he wants to take the case (and money), whereas Foggy has had second thoughts and wants to turn it down. After defending Healy and protecting him, Daredevil gets the name "Wilson Fisk," which triggers Healy to take his own life when Daredevil won't kill him. Daredevil's blindness is an interesting metaphor. We will "see" that in addition to Daredevil being blind, the series has numerous references to seeing and not wanting to see, and Healy's impaling of his face, specifically his eye, emphasizes that social and emotional development isn't easy as we fight hard to not see what is right in front of us. Daredevil can't see but does make out people and objects. He can hear heartbeats and tell if someone is lying, but this doesn't equate with knowing the truth. In all these ways, Matt is blind to the shades of gray in the world, keeping him in Klein's paranoid-schizoid position.

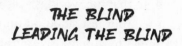

THE BLIND
LEADING THE BLIND

The blind in Greek mythology often are people of importance. They are portrayed as sages and intellects. They often possess better metaphorical "sight" than those around them. Both Sophocles and Euripides include a blind prophet known as Tiresias in their stories. Tiresias was the person who warned Oedipus's father, King Laius, that he would be killed by his own son. Because Laius tempted that fate, he helped the prediction come true. Sigmund Freud used the Oedipus story to create the classic psychoanalytic triangle of the Oedipus Complex. This theory states that every boy wants to kill his father and possess his mother. Oedipus, driven by guilt, eventually blinds himself when he finds out that he has killed his father and taken his mother as a wife.

Seeing or being blind to what we see is a task to work through in the process of social and emotional development. Matt Murdock tries to lead others to accept what he thinks to be true. It doesn't work for him. Matt is a blind person who is more like the Oedipus character. Psychoanalysis is about opening one's eyes to live a fuller and more examined life. It is something that Matt Murdock and Daredevil could benefit from.

Giving closing arguments at a trial, Matt says of good and evil that "the delineation between the two isn't a sharp line. Sometimes it's a blur,"[17] yet Daredevil acts most of the time as if he thinks it's a sharp line. When will Matt believe his own closing arguments? When will Matt finally learn and stop acting on the belief that people are all good and instead take a lesson from the Kingpin that the world is very complicated and things need to discussed, not just acted on impulsively?

Is it necessary to move to a depressive position? If we look at the characters of Daredevil, the Marvel universe seems to answer that with a resounding "yes." When we only see the world in black and white, we get stuck like Matt and sometimes die as a result. Consider Ben Urich, who tries to point out some of Matt's blind spots. Daredevil is pushing for Ben to write about Wilson Fisk, saying that Fisk is in the shadows and nobody knows who he is, which is dangerous. Ben says, "Said the man in the mask,"[18] pointing to Matt's blindness to his own personal devil side.

GETTING THE HELP NEEDED TO GROW

Being stuck leads us down paths we have already traveled. We don't see ourselves repeating the same behavior again and again. This is the essence of Freud's repetition compulsion— that which we resist, persists. Also stuck in such a compulsion, the Punisher is sometimes "good" and sometimes "bad" but is not able to take any middle ground or see shades of gray. As a result, he falls repeatedly into Kingpin's plans and carries out things that ultimately do not get him the peace he is clearly seeking. The only character who seems to survive without a deeper sense of the world and others is Foggy Nelson, Matt's partner in the law firm.

Compare Matt's suffering to that of other characters who struggle but also seem to grow in the context of this show. These characters are in Klein's depressive position. Karen Page, who has become Matt and Foggy's office administrator, kills Wilson Fisk's right-hand man, Wesley, because she fears that Fisk will find out she visited Fisk's mother.[19]

Those who learn to accept *all* their feelings—especially those we don't want to see in ourselves—survive and become more mature and complex individuals. They suffer but seem to be better people for it. They are open to the risks of connection, friendship, and love.[20] Matt just seems to keep getting himself (almost) killed. Luckily, murder and aiding and abetting criminals aren't the only way to mature. Having feelings doesn't mean you have to act on them, and that is where therapy and a good psychoanalyst can help! Maybe superhero stories need to find a psychoanalyst character who can provide 50-minute sessions to these vigilantes.

Father Lantom is the closest to a therapeutic character we see in Daredevil. Matt goes to confession, and Lantom becomes his social and emotional tutor. He tries to help Matt see the shades of gray. He wants Matt to see that the "devil" does walk among people in many forms and is not just one all-evil being. "Few things are absolute, Matthew. Even Lucifer was once an angel. It's why judgment and vengeance . . . are best left to God. . . . There is a *wide* gulf between inaction and murder, Matthew. Another man's evil *does not* make you good. Men have used the atrocities of their enemies to justify their own throughout history. So the question you have to ask yourself is: are you struggling with the fact that you don't want to kill this man but have to? Or that you don't have to kill him but *want* to?"[21]

Is growing up all suffering? The depressive state is basically being able to see the world and those who populate it in terms of complex and subtle shades of gray. As odd as it seems, though, when we accept the suffering, we can experience pleasure. The opposite is also true. The more we try to avoid suffering, the more we become stuck with nothing but suffering. Freud said we can engage in a full life with daydreams and creativity. He wrote that a person can "throw off the too heavy burden imposed on him by life and win the high yield of pleasure afforded by humor."[22] This may help us actually understand why Foggy has survived so long. A serious but also humorous sidekick to Matt Murdock, Foggy shows good insight and provides another chance for Matt to see the devil in himself when he says, "You don't get to create danger, and then protect us from that danger. That's not heroic. That's insane."[23]

WHY DO WE FOLLOW STORIES SHOWS LIKE DAREDEVIL?

"I see from the uniform you've taken the Devil's name to heart."
—Madame Gao[24]

". . . our actual enjoyment of an imaginative work proceeds from a liberation of tension in our minds."
—psychoanalyst Sigmund Freud[25]

Freud wrote that we enjoy creative works and daydreams because they help us release tension caused by the frustration of not getting what we want.[26] It is the very fact that these stories of struggles between good and evil hark back to our own days in the paranoid-schizoid position (or perhaps our current position) that they are enjoyable. We want to think that Daredevil is right. If he just does the right thing, he can save Hell's Kitchen and make it safe for all the good citizens. Even we sometimes feel that if we just did the right things, our parents might have given us everything. In reality, no one can give us everything. No one is all right or all good all the time. Extremists on both sides during an election often want to think their candidate is all good and the other is all bad, but that kind of splitting leads to a very divided nation, a nation in a paranoid-schizoid position. It is much harder to stay in the depressive position.[27]

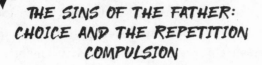

THE SINS OF THE FATHER: CHOICE AND THE REPETITION COMPULSION

Matt cannot get out from under his father's shadow. His father, a boxer, doesn't want his son to become a fighter. Being something other than what we have lived and experienced is tough. By day, he fights in the courtroom as a lawyer, often defending the poor. By night, he is Daredevil, fighter and defender of Hell's Kitchen. In fact, they both have become fighters. Does Matt realize that? Freud identified the *repetition compulsion*, a condition in which we are often stuck enacting the same choices, repeating behaviors, and ending up with the same results. Are there other choices for him? Yes, but can Matt/Daredevil see the other choices? This is the psychoanalytic question. Self-awareness is one side effect of psychoanalysis. Developing insight means gaining the freedom to choose. The examined life has been promoted by people from the time of Socrates. It is a standard in many eastern mindfulness approaches. So what might Matt Murdock have done if he ever realized that he ended up fighting like his father? Might he have chosen a different path? Possibly, but sometimes even when we see alternative choices, we do that with which we are most comfortable. Even Wilson Fisk tells Vanessa he got away from Hell's Kitchen when he was sent to the country and later returned: "Yes. Time and distance, they afford a certain clarity. I realized that this city was a part of me, that it was in my blood."[28] Thus, once we break the repetition compulsion, we may still end up doing the same things, but now at least we are doing it with our eyes open.

For Daredevil's sake, he must learn the subtleties of the balance of power in Hell's Kitchen. Perhaps together with other characters from parts of Manhattan (Jessica Jones, Luke Cage, and Iron Fist) Matt Murdock can grow and remain more in the depressive position. One hopes Matt can come to see he is a Punisher, Kingpin, and a devil. This is what I believe he resists seeing. If he can learn this, he may finally know what he wants, know how to get it, and finally get it. He can spend more of his time in the depressive position.

NOTES

1. Klein (2002), p. 173.
2. *Marvel's Daredevil*, episode 1–7, "Stick" (April 10, 2015).
3. *Amazing Spider-Man* #197 (1979).
4. *Marvel's Daredevil* episode 1–8, "Shadows in the Glass" (April 10, 2015); *Daredevil* #595 (2017).
5. *Daredevil* #1 (1964).
6. *Daredevil* #347 (1995).
7. *Daredevil* #10 (2014).
8. *Daredevil* #11 (2012).
9. *Daredevil* #325 (1994).
10. *Marvel's Daredevil*, episode 1–11, "The Path of the Righteous" (April 10, 2015).
11. *Marvel's Daredevil*, episode 1–7, "Stick" (April 10, 2015).
12. Jung (1989), p. 277.
13. *Marvel's Daredevil*, episode 1–3, "Rabbit in a Snowstorm" (April 10, 2015).
14. Clevans (1983).
15. Clevans (1983), p. 133.
16. *Marvel's Daredevil*, episode 1–3, "Rabbit in a Snowstorm" (April 10, 2015).
17. *Marvel's Daredevil*, episode 1–3, "Rabbit in a Snowstorm" (April 10, 2015).
18. *Marvel's Daredevil*, episode 1–8, "Shadow in the Glass" (April 10, 2015).
19. *Marvel's Daredevil*, episode 1–11, "The Path of the Righteous" (April 10, 2015).
20. *Marvel's Daredevil*, episode 1-2, "Cut Man" (April 10, 2015).
21. *Marvel's Daredevil*, episode 1-9, "Speak the Devil" (April 10, 2015).
22. Freud (1908/1948), p. 177.
23. *Marvel's Daredevil*, episode 2–9, "Seven Minutes in Heaven" (March 18, 2016).
24. *Marvel's Daredevil*, episode 2–11, ".380" (March 18, 2016).
25. Freud (1908), p. 153.
26. Spotnitz (1995), p. 21.
27. *Marvel's Daredevil*, episode 1–8, "Shadows in the Glass" (April 10, 2015).
28. *Marvel's Daredevil*, episode 1–4, "In the Blood" (April 10, 2015).

CHAPTER 17

WHOSE MIND IS IT ANYWAY? DEFENDING CONSCIOUS WILL IN A PURPLE MAN'S WORLD

J. SCOTT JORDAN

"In my mind I can't tell the difference between what he made me do or say and what I do or say on my own."
—Jessica Jones[1]

"Our sense of being a conscious agent comes at a cost of being technically wrong all the time."
—social psychologist Daniel M. Wegner[2]

"My first act of free will shall be to believe in free will."
—functional psychologist William James[3]

"**I**f you say 'it's complicated,' I will punch you in the face!"[4] Karen Page tells a stammering Foggy Nelson as he tries to avoid explaining his recent falling out with Matt Murdock. We all feel Karen's frustration when we try to understand someone else's behavior. How can it be so complicated when our own behavior seems so straightforward? You decided to read this chapter. You opened the book and started reading. It was simple.

This *feeling* we have that our thoughts cause our actions is precisely how people described the experience of being controlled by one of Daredevil's earlier enemies, Killgrave the Purple Man.[5] Daredevil's ability and sheer willpower usually grant him immunity to Killgrave's mind control power, but most others are not so fortunate. When Jessica Jones attempts to prove the innocence of Hope, a young woman who shoots her parents while under Killgrave's mind control, Hope describes Killgrave's influence this way: "All I could feel was this need. He said, 'Wish her a happy birthday,' and that was suddenly the only thing I wanted to say."[6] Cognitive scientists refer to the feeling of freedom as *conscious will*.[7] It's *conscious* because we are *aware* of having a thought, and it's *will* because the thought reflects something we want.

Despite our belief in the power of conscious will, many researchers claim it is an illusion.[8] After a winning roll of the dice for example, gamblers sometimes *feel* they are able to *will* the dice to roll a particular way.[9] When Luke Cage tries to convince Jessica Jones that she is not responsible for anything she did will under the influence of Killgrave's mind control, she says that "it doesn't *feel* any different than when you think it *yourself*. Not only does it feel the same, it actually feels *better* because the thought—the *command*—is pure."[10] In short, Jessica Jones *feels* that her thoughts caused bad things to happen to other people, when in fact Killgrave is responsible for having put those thoughts into her head.

THE PROSECUTION:
CONSCIOUS WILL IS AN ILLUSION

So which is it? Do we have conscious will or not? According to the theory of *apparent mental causation*,[11] we do not. Conscious will is an illusion because research indicates that our feeling of being in control can be systematically manipulated. Let's review the evidence.

PROSECUTION EXHIBIT ONE: PRIMACY

"I'm not seeking penance for what I've done, Father. I'm seeking forgiveness . . . for what I'm about to do," says Matt Murdock. "That's not how this works," responds Father Lantom.[12] Although Matt's preemptive search for forgiveness is used for dramatic effect in the script, the point Father Lantom makes is consistent with the way we experience conscious will. Specifically, we feel that our thoughts cause our actions when the thought has *primacy* over the action (i.e., when the thought comes first).

Regardless of our belief in primacy, however, research clearly indicates that our brains are preparing our actions *before* we think we are going to do them. Researchers discovered this curious fact by asking people to voluntarily produce a simple behavior such as flexing their wrists whenever they "chose" to do so. Electrical recordings from their scalps revealed that their brains were preparing the behavior roughly one second before it occurred.[13] In another experiment, participants watched a quickly moving arm on a clock while making voluntary finger taps and reported the position the arm was in at the moment they decided to tap. Although the brain was preparing the finger tap a full second before it happened, the participants were not aware that they were going to tap until roughly one-fifth of a second (200 milliseconds) before the action occurred.[14] In short, the brain knew what the person was going to do before the person did it. From these data, many psychologists argue that thoughts don't cause our actions. As a result, they claim our feeling of conscious will is an illusion.

PROSECUTION EXHIBIT TWO: CONSISTENCY

People who use long sticks or poles hanging from their waist to search for water (dowsers) often feel they are not making the stick move up and down when in fact they are.[15] This occurs because the handles of the stick move left and right, causing the stick to move up and down. Because the hand movements to the left and right are not *consistent* with the up and down movements of the stick, dowsers don't feel they caused the stick movements. We have a stronger feeling that our thoughts caused our actions when the thought and the action are *consistent* with each other.[16]

The Purple Man suffers from consistency issues on many occasions, particularly when his attempts at mind control fail. When Kingpin meets Killgrave for the first time, he insults him for using his mind control powers for nothing more than petty crimes, or at least what Kingpin considers *petty* crimes. The insulted Killgrave attempts to leave, and Kingpin fires a warning shot with his Obliterator Cane. Infuriated, Killgrave commands Kingpin to "take that cane, point it at your own head, and blow your brains out." Kingpin immediately points the cane at his own head, as if under Killgrave's power. He then slowly looks up at Killgrave, smiles wickedly, and says, "No. I give the orders, now."[17]

This interaction wonderfully illustrates the notion of *consistency*. First, while Kingpin has the rifle pointed at his head, Killgrave *feels* as if his thoughts have *caused* Kingpin's actions because Killgrave's thoughts (i.e., "blow your brains out") are consistent with what appears to be happening. Second, when Kingpin then flashes Killgrave a wicked smile and says, "No," Killgrave loses his feeling of control over Kingpin—"You resisted my will! In all my life, only one other could disobey me"—because his thoughts and the resulting actions are no longer consistent.

PROSECUTION EXHIBIT THREE: EXCLUSIVITY

When a group spells a word on a Ouija board, individual group members do not feel they caused the planchet to move. This is the case because there are too many other reasons for why it moved, specifically, the other group members. We have a stronger feeling that our thoughts cause our actions when our thoughts seem to be the only possible cause.[18]

The Punisher expresses remarkable insight on the issue of exclusivity while attempting to persuade Daredevil to shoot a member of the mob. Daredevil refuses and judges the Punisher harshly for his habitual killing of criminals. The Punisher scoffs and says, "You go home at night, right? Take that mask off, maybe you think . . . it wasn't you who did those things, maybe it was somebody else."[19] The Punisher is claiming that by wearing a mask as he dispenses violence, Daredevil is actually increasing the number of *selves*—Daredevil or Matt Murdock—who could have willed the use of violence. As a result, the feeling of owning the action, of being responsible for the violence, actually *decreases* because it has two possible causes: either Daredevil or Matt Murdock.

THE PROSECUTION'S CONCLUDING REMARKS

There it is. Because of primacy, consistency, and exclusivity, we can state without hesitation and beyond a shadow of a doubt that conscious will is an illusion. As a result, not one of us is ultimately responsible for his or her actions.

THE DEFENSE: WE ARE WORLDS WITHIN A WORLD

During one of Matt's initial immersions in the-ways-of-the-world-according-to-Stick, the crotchety, blind old Samurai buys the boy an ice cream, sits with him on a park bench, and

THE COSTS OF WEARING THE MASK

By Leandra Parris

When heroes put on a mask, it is often to safeguard their identity. Yet the mask also can represent the heavy burden placed on heroes. It is a physical symbol of the barrier between one life and another. Often, the dissonance between these two halves of a self can lead to psychological difficulty. Specifically, research has shown that when people feel they have two separate versions of themselves, the forced juxtaposition can lead to symptoms related to depression.[20] When those halves are forced to look at each other and evaluate what the sum of their parts represents, the resulting cacophony of ideals can be unbearable. In the case of Murdock, these ideals are those of (1) not killing anyone and (2) protecting lives regardless of other costs. Murdock will not kill someone and actively avoids situations in which death would be the necessary choice. Yet there are times when protecting others puts those close to him at risk. The consequence of his inability to kill and permanently stop a multiple murderer such as Bullseye is sometimes the death of those he would protect.[21] Unlike some other heroes, Murdock faces this reality with a kind of awareness that can be soul crushing and inescapable.

challenges him with the following: "Whole world around you, Matty, and it is friggin' huge. And all you need . . . are the guts to let it in."[22] Much later in Matt's life, Father Lantom challenges him as well, somewhat more gently than Stick and with quite a bit more patience, to be sure. Nonetheless, the challenge is real. "One person is not just one person," says Father Lantom during the funeral for a recently deceased criminal. "In each of us, there is a world, webbing out, reaching others."[23]

Although Stick's statement is about the vastness of the world and Father Lantom's is about the nature of people, both speak to the idea that we are all inescapably interconnected. We cannot escape the world because the world is within us. As a result, each of us is a world within a world.[24] Strange as this idea may sound, there are those who argue that our bodies and minds exist as they are due to the problems we as a species have had to face over the course of evolution.[25] Bones and muscles, for example, are embodiments of the environmental constraints we have to overcome to move our body mass as a whole through the earth's gravity field, and teeth, throats, and stomachs embody the processes necessary to extract energy from food sources. In short, the processes that make up our bodies are inescapably connected to the world because they are embodiments of that world.

IT'S A PURPLE MAN'S WORLD

It turns out that we are embodiments of the social world as well. Parts of the brain that are involved in planning our own goals and preparing our own actions also are involved in perceiving the goals and actions of others.[26] This means that when we see another person complete a goal-directed action, such as picking up an amazing book about Daredevil, our brains are put in the planning states for doing the same thing ourselves. Interestingly, this interconnection we share with the goals and movements of others implies that we are all to some extent the Purple Man. Killgrave has hijacked the minds of others by releasing a pheromone. We do that simply by behaving.

If we humans are so socially interconnected, however, why don't we do everything we see others doing? The answer is the same in our world and in Daredevil's—we *inhibit* ourselves from doing what others are doing. In Hell's Kitchen, resisting Killgrave requires a lot of effort. When he first attempts to dominate Daredevil's will and fails, Killgrave is shocked and exclaims, "So! I've finally encountered someone who can resist my power!"[27] For us, inhibiting the influence of others begins immediately after birth as we learn to approach people we trust and avoid those we don't.[28]

HOW THE WORLD ACQUIRES ITS KILLGRAVE-LIKE POWERS

We learn approach-avoid behaviors toward other people as well as the world in general because the brain automatically associates the movements we make with our bodies with the effects our movements have on the world.[29] For example, the body movements of three-month-old infants are mostly spontaneous and don't appear to be goal-directed. However, if an infant's spontaneous leg movements are allowed to influence the movements of a mobile hanging above the infant (perhaps through a string-and-pulley system), the infant will begin to move its leg more. In addition, simply "seeing" the mobile later causes the infant to move its leg.[30]

This Killgrave-like influence of the environment is evident in the way Daredevil perceives the world. In addition to being aware of many more details than most, he often experiences those details in terms of the *actions* they seem to be calling for. One night, for example, he finds himself being kept awake by the wind, in which he hears "surrendering winter leaves that rustle and skitter like fairies, begging Matt to join in the dance."[31] While describing the rustle of leaves as an invitation to join a dance might read more like poetry than objective description, the author is implying that Daredevil actually perceives the rustling leaves in terms of the actions the sound is calling for, what psychologists refer to as *affordances*.[32]

Perceiving affordances means that we see things in terms of the behaviors they afford us. For example, to see a chair in terms of affordances is to see it in terms of possibly sitting in it or, if you like, standing on it. This is consistent with the idea that the brain associates our body movements with the effects they produce in the world. When we walk over leaves and make them rustle, the brain associates the walking movements with the rustling sound so that later, when we hear rustling leaves, we hear them in terms of the body movements that made the rustling happen in the first place. This explains how the world develops its Killgrave-like influence over us. Once we learn to make things happen in the world such as sit on chairs or walk and make leaves rustle, we then see chairs and hear rustling leaves in terms of sitting and walking, respectively. Again, it's a Purple Man's world.

If Daredevil truly perceives things in terms of affordances, focusing becomes terribly important. If he doesn't, all the infinite details of the environment will push him to behave in different ways at the same time, and he may find himself paralyzed, unable to act. This is exactly what happens when he wakes up for the first time after the accident that blinded him. Unfamiliar with the onslaught of details from the outside world, he throws his hands over his ears and panics.[33]

This action-oriented view of perception implies that when Daredevil is "focusing," he is really selecting which aspects of the outside world he will "let in" and allow to have their Killgrave-like influence over his actions. In short, Stick is right. The world is friggin' huge, and all we have to do to behave in it is let it in. Interestingly, when we read or watch Daredevil, we tend to feel that his way of perceiving the world is different from ours. We see the wavy, radar-like lines drawn in the comics, and we think, "Wow, that's pretty cool that he can pick out that one tiny group of details." As far as our own experiences are concerned, we don't feel like we're picking out details at all. We simply look or listen, and the world is there.

Regardless of how effortless our perceptions feel, however, research indicates that we see the world more the way Daredevil does than we think. If people are asked to compare two very similar images that quickly appear one after the other, they find it very difficult to notice *major* differences in the images (e.g., a jet that has a fuselage in one image but not in the other). This phenomenon is known as change blindness,[34] and it implies that just like Daredevil, we "see" the world in terms of what we - are *trying to do* (i.e., what we are looking for). It's as if, in order to let one aspect of the outside world exert its Killgrave-like influence over us, we have to keep all other aspects out or at least dampen their influence on our behavior. As a result, we don't really perceive changes in details we're not looking for. Rather, we simply *want* something, for example, to find our keys, and that want, what some might call an intention, a desire, or a goal, tunes our senses so that goal-relevant details can exert their Killgrave-like influence on our behavior.

STICK IS RIGHT AGAIN

In addition to being right about the hugeness of the world, Stick was right about the courage it takes to let it in, for being open to the worlds of others not only allows their behaviors to influence our own but allows their emotions to do the same thing. Research indicates that we experience the emotions of other people with the same parts of the brain we use to experience our own.[35] This emotional interconnectedness means that seeing someone express emotions puts us in the same emotional state, what researchers refer to as *emotional contagion*.[36] This explains why letting the world in takes courage. If we see people suffering, we suffer. Stick warns Matt about the need for courage because he is preparing him for the anguish he inevitably will encounter when he dives into the shadows of Hell's Kitchen to help those who suffer.

Stick's warning is important, for emotions can be paralyzing. This point is illustrated beautifully when Daredevil encounters the Purple Children, who have their father's ability to influence others' minds, plus the ability to take over their emotions. As the Purple Children pursue Daredevil, he reflects on the torrent of emotions they put him through. "They radiate pain—and grief—and rage—and loneliness—and despair—and there's no fighting it."[37] Eventually, Daredevil ends up in a sewer runoff, curled into a fetal position, unable to move.

Despite the ever-present risk of experiencing such empathetic suffering, Daredevil nonetheless engages the seedier side of Hell's Kitchen to help those who can't help themselves. When the Purple Man traps him and demands that he reveal the one thing he would never, ever do—so that the Purple Man can, of course, make him do it—Daredevil says the following, "The entire world goes to Hell. I know about it. I have the power to help, and I do nothing."[38] Although such a statement might smack of heroic hyperbole, in Daredevil's case it represents the bargain he has made with himself and the Killgrave-like powers of the world in which he lives. That is, one might say his story reflects an agreement to take on the suffering one necessarily encounters when helping the helpless as long as he is able to keep that suffering at bay by "focusing" on the suffering of others. If he loses that focus, the bargain is forfeit, and he will be defenseless against the torrent of suffering he has necessarily let into his world.

Of course, this is exactly what happens to him on his final day as he once again finds himself on his back, in the middle of the street, seemingly paralyzed by emotions. Bullseye is preparing to end Daredevil's life,[39] and the "Man without Fear" realizes he will never be able to help someone again. This loss of "focus" on the ability to reduce the suffering of others leaves him defenseless against the suffering he has embodied over the course of his life. No longer able to keep the bargain he has made with the Purple Man world he lives in, he utters the word *Mapone*—his daughter's name—and Bullseye takes his life.

One could call him a tragic figure. One could also call him a hero. What Daredevil's story truly seems to address, however, is the bargains we all have to make with the Purple Man powers of the world in which we live. "In each of us, there is a world, webbing out, reaching others."[40] Who do we let in? Who do we keep out? Who do we allow to be our Purple Man? Research in psychology[41] and neuroscience[42] indicates that this decision may lie at the root of how we distinguish our own identities from those of others.

THE DEFENSE'S CONCLUDING REMARKS

If it is true that we are worlds in world, maybe our thoughts were never supposed to be the "cause" of our actions. Maybe our thoughts have more to do with deciding which aspects of the world we will open ourselves up to and allow to exert their Killgrave-like influence over us. As the details of the worlds inside and outside of us continually change, the details of our openness change as well. As a result, we sometimes feel as though our thoughts cause events to happen, especially when a thought precedes an outcome, is consistent with the outcome, and seems to be the only cause of the outcome.

HAS THE JURY REACHED A DECISION?

Thought does matter, but it seems to be only one of the many details that have to be in place before we can produce the outcomes we want. Thus, instead of primacy, consistency, and exclusivity proving that conscious will is an illusion, perhaps they constitute evidence for just how complicated conscious will truly is. Details are everything. This is exactly why we conduct trials in courts before determining guilt—so that both sides, the prosecution and the defense, have the opportunity to present their take on the constellation of details that were ultimately responsible for why a crime occurred. In short, our legal systems reflects the understanding that we all make bargains with the Killgrave-like powers of the Purple Man world we live in every day. And the details of those bargains are always as complex as the worlds we make them with. Sorry, Karen, but Foggy is right: It's complicated.

NOTES

1. *Alias* #25 (2003).
2. Wegner (2002). p. 342.
3. James (1870). Diary entry published in Perry (1935, p. 323).
4. *Marvel's Daredevil*, episode 1–11, "The Path of the Righteous" (April 10, 2015).
5. *Daredevil* #4 (1964).
6. *Marvel's Jessica Jones*, episode 1–3, "AKA It's Called Whiskey" (November 20, 2015).
7. Wegner (2002).
8. Wegner (2002).
9. Langer and Roth (1975).
10. *Alias* #25 (2003).
11. Wegner & Wheatley (1999).
12. *Marvel's Daredevil*, episode 1–1, "Into the Ring" (April 10, 2015).
13. Kornhuber & Deecke (1965)
14. Libet (1985).
15. Wegner (2002).
16. Wegner (2002).
17. *Marvel Team-Up Annual* #4 (1981).
18. Wegner & Wheatley (1999).
19. *Marvel's Daredevil*, episode 2–3, "New York's Finest" (March 18, 2016).
20. Higgins (1987).
21. *Daredevil* #5 (1999).
22. *Marvel's Daredevil*, episode 1–7, "Stick" (April 10, 2015).
23. *Marvel's Daredevil*, episode 2–7, "Penny and Dime" (March 18, 2016).
24. Jordan (2000); Jordan et al. (2017).
25. Vandervert (1995).
26. Calvo-Merino et al. (2005).
27. *Daredevil* #4 (1964).
28. Kinsbourne & Jordan (1999).
29. Hommel et al. (2001).
30. Thelen & Fisher (1983)
31. *Daredevil: The Man without Fear* #2 (1993).
32. Gibson (1979).
33. *Marvel's Daredevil*, episode 1–1, "Into the Ring" (April 10, 2015).
34. Simons & Levin (1997).
35. Budell et al. (2010).
36. Barsade (2002).
37. *Daredevil* #9 (2015).
38. *Daredevil* #19 (2017).
39. *Daredevil: End of Days* #1 (2013).
40. *Marvel's Daredevil*, episode 2–7, "Penny and Dime" (March 18, 2016).
41. Brewer (1991).
42. Decety & Sommerville (2003).

CHAPTER 18

HAPPINESS IN HELL'S KITCHEN

MARA WOOD

*"A positive mood jolts us into an entirely different way of thinking
from a negative mood."*
—positive psychology founder Martin Seligman[1]

*"There's this whole happy-go-lucky swagger to his step lately,
which is great except—well, he's been through a lot recently."*
—Foggy Nelson[2]

*H*appiness guides heroic deeds, especially in the case of
the vigilante Matt Murdock. For superheroes exposed
to trauma early in life, the pursuit of happiness may seem like
a lost cause. Happiness itself and the benefits it brings may be
an important factor in effective heroic action. For example,
adaptation and mental health may be highly influenced by
happiness.[3] Matt Murdock (a.k.a. Daredevil) is not without his
life challenges. Since he is blinded at a young age, orphaned,

and constantly bombarded with negative life events, happiness is an elusive thing for the Daredevil in Hell's Kitchen. Despite all this, Murdock harnesses happiness in his life and becomes a better hero because of his positive outlook.

THEORIES OF HAPPINESS

Everyone may have some concept of happiness, but it is generally thought of as the cognitive and affective appraisal of one's life.[4] Happiness in essence is made up of three aspects: pleasure, engagement, and meaning.[5] Each aspect contributes to happiness in one way or another and has been derived from different theories of happiness. Pursuing all three aspects is akin to living a full life.[6]

Hedonism entails maximizing pleasure while minimizing pain.[7] This concept of happiness was revived during the Renaissance, when hedonistic happiness was encouraged by philosophers as long as the pleasure did not derive from artificial means.[8] Hedonism is a simple concept to grasp: Do more of what feels good. However, it does not fully explain all aspects of happiness. For example, happiness is felt at the completion of an advanced degree, though there may be minimal pleasure during the process of completion. A student will persevere through the stress and pain of studying to complete a degree with the hopes that the completion will lead to something he or she wants. Although heroism is not done for the sake of happiness, it would be hard to justify heroic (and dangerous) acts under the theory of hedonism. People pursue what brings them pleasure, and it is difficult to imagine that all the aspects of being a hero are pleasurable. Happiness therefore is not merely seeking out pleasure while avoiding pain.

Whereas hedonism deals primarily with immediate pleasurable activities, eudaimonia offers a slightly more complex view of happiness. Championed by Aristotle, *eudaimonia* essentially means being true to one's inner demon,[9] finding happiness by recognizing inner strengths, identifying virtues, building virtues up, and living on the basis of virtue.[10] In general, people who seek happiness through eudaimonic means are more satisfied than are those who seek happiness through hedonism only.[11] This theory of happiness better explains Matt's actions as Daredevil. He ties his happiness to helping those less fortunate than himself, and he acts on this virtue as a lawyer and as a superhero.[12] Well-being, an aspect of happiness, reflects more eudaimonic happiness than hedonistic happiness.[13] However, the distinction between hedonism and eudaimonia may exist only in philosophical terms. Objective definitions for these opposing views of happiness are not entirely conclusive, and there is some research that suggests that eudaimonic pursuits lead to hedonistic happiness.[14]

Object list theory proposes that happiness is achieved once the items on a list are accomplished.[15] These items range from concrete (buying a house) to abstract (living a fulfilled life). Each person's list is unique to his or her life, and the person sets the value of the items on the list. For Matt, his list can be assumed from the types of activities he engages in, such as volunteering with children from a school for the blind.[16] Although most people do not have a set list of items that would make them happy at the ready, an examination of a person's feelings and wishes illuminates what that person wants in life.[17] The items on a person's list must be self-concordant for the happiness gains to have the greatest impact.[18]

Despite sources of happiness being somewhat subjective, there are some common factors that lead to happiness. The largest factor is involvement in social events and the building of relationships with others.[19] Although Matt's social activities are limited by his demanding jobs, he still spends time with Foggy Nelson and goes on dates with a variety of women.[20] Other common sources of happiness include work, leisure, exercise, drugs, music, weather, and nature.[21] Being in a state of happiness can be measured by a person's physiological state, facial expression, and conscious experience.[22] Matt readily smiles in social situations, knowing that a smile is the easiest way to stave off negative emotion.[23] Emotional expressions are displayed more readily in the presence of others, accounting for the fact that happiness is more likely to be experienced around other people in social situations.[24]

The concept of happiness for each person is culture-bound; for example, self-sufficiency is a culture value that can also be valued as a means for happiness.[25] Societal values and resources correlate with the way happiness is defined in general by a culture.[26] Some factors, such as relationships with others and good health, have been found as correlates with happiness across cultures.[27] Relationships and health are two areas Matt spends a lot of time on, indicating that his happiness may not be entirely culture-bound.[28] Happiness also may have some gender differences; for example, men who cite material goods as sources of happiness have less intense positive emotions than do women who see material goods as sources of happiness.[29] Additionally, women tend to see relationships as a stronger source of positive affect than men commonly do.[30]

THE HAPPINESS EQUATION

The specifics of happiness differ between individuals, but there is a general "equation" that can be used to conceptualize happiness:

Happiness = Set Point + Life Circumstances + Volitional Activity

About 50 percent of happiness is determined by the set point, which includes personality and genetics. Circumstances

MEMORY MALLEABILITY: A SECRET OF THE OOZE

TRAVIS LANGLEY

Memory is an essential yet undependable thing. "As an attorney, I can tell you without hesitation that the most unreliable witness in any circumstance is memory," Matt Murdock muses. "The human brain is spectacular at playing tricks on itself to help people 'remember' what they want to remember. Sworn witnesses will bet everything, with all sincerity and zero doubt, swearing that a green light was red or that they heard sounds they couldn't possibly have."[31]

Psychologist Elizabeth Loftus built a career demonstrating the fallibility of eyewitness memory.[32] During one study in which she showed video of an auto accident, half her viewers (*experimental group*) were asked how fast the car was going when it passed a barn along the road. Those in the other half

(environment) determine roughly 10 percent, and volitional activity accounts for about 40 percent.[36] The happiness equation illustrates the amount of control a person has over his or her own happiness. The set point is generally stable over time and can be thought of as chronic or characteristic to the person.[37] Since genetics and personality are stable over time, these factors contribute to the set point. Circumstances are somewhat controllable, such as state of employment and place to live. No matter the circumstance, a person becomes accustomed to the new state.[38] This process, which is called (*control group*) were asked the same question but without any mention of the barn. A week later, some of the experimental group's members recalled seeing the barn but almost none of the control group members did. There was no barn.[33]

People who have read 1964's original *Daredevil #1* might recall seeing the canister that falls off the truck and injures young Matt or the radioactive waste that gives him super-senses. The scene, however, shows no such container or goo. The text refers vaguely to such details, as if the writer added them as an afterthought, when one witness to the accident declares, "But a cylinder fell from the truck. It struck his face! Is—is it radioactive?" Any readers who recall seeing cylinder or ooze in that particular story either vividly imagined them or retroactively inserted them into the memory after those elements appeared in one of the story's many retellings and variations.[34] The adult Matt knows a bit about why this happens: "That's just basic neuroscience. Recollections fade, like photos left in the sunlight."[35]

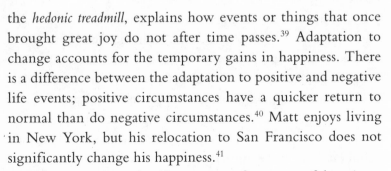

the *hedonic treadmill*, explains how events or things that once brought great joy do not after time passes.[39] Adaptation to change accounts for the temporary gains in happiness. There is a difference between the adaptation to positive and negative life events; positive circumstances have a quicker return to normal than do negative circumstances.[40] Matt enjoys living in New York, but his relocation to San Francisco does not significantly change his happiness.[41]

With approximately 60 percent of a state of happiness accounted for by factors that do not change or that we grow accustomed to, seeking happiness may seem futile. However, volitional activity can have a great impact on happiness. Volition takes effort on the part of a person and can include the practice of gratitude, thoughtful self-reflection, and positive motivational and attitudinal mindsets.[42] Changing circumstances such as place of residence and finding a new job may seem like the best way to increase happiness, but these life changes are temporary without intentional effort to change one's perspective.[43] Matt Murdock makes a conscious effort toward seeking happiness when he chooses to enjoy a holiday party rather than sit in contemplation in his office.[44] Gratitude and forgiveness are two volitional cognitive activities that can have a positive change on happiness.[45] When Matt learns about the circumstances surrounding his mother's departure, he readily forgives her.[46] Matt does not stop at forgiveness; he expresses gratitude toward his mother and all the work she has done since leaving her family as a nun and an activist.[47]

Working toward goals such as those associated with objective list happiness theories is a way that volitional activity affects levels of happiness. These goals, however, much have a degree of self-concordance; that is, they must reflect the person who sets them.[48] Matt partners with Foggy Nelson and establishes a law firm in New York. When Matt's role as Daredevil is revealed to the world, he makes a choice to adjust the way he practices law so that he may continue to pursue his goal of helping those who require legal advice.[49] The hedonic treadmill is avoided when a person actively pursues a volitional activity over a long period, always looking for ways to improve.[50] Matt shows enthusiasm in adjusting his approach to his practice and readily accepts the challenge of coaching clients in representing themselves in court.[51] Matt summarizes his choice to be happy in a thought he has while surveying his city: "For the first time in months I find myself in the familiar, paralyzing grip of overwhelming depression. Then I get over it."[52]

BENEFITS OF HAPPINESS

Positive affectivity is associated with greater job satisfaction, marital satisfaction, healthier lifestyles, and better coping strategies and is an influence on disease processes.[53] Positive emotions contribute to personal growth and development, especially in the area of social relationships.[54] Matt's relationships, especially the one he has with Foggy, benefit from continued positive affect.[55] Social relationships are particularly important in happiness. With social groups, the needs for affiliation and belonging are met. Additionally, social groups can help regulate and soothe negative affect, solve problems, give hope, and open the door for generosity and altruism.[56] Happy people are more cooperative, prosocial, charitable, and other-centered than unhappy people.[57] They also have positive constructs of themselves and others, prosocial and healthy behaviors, and good coping abilities when in distress.[58] Being happy is good for relationships; a happy mood leads a person to be more sensitive toward others.[59] Positive emotions correlate with relationships, indicating their importance to happiness.[60] Same-sex friendships matter to happiness, especially when the needs of those in the relationship are satisfied.[61] A friendship like the one Matt and Foggy share is correlated with happiness when positivity is shared in response to positive events, a feeling of mattering to the other exists, and satisfaction of psychological needs is met.[62] Matt and Foggy have been friends since law school, and they entered a partnership as professionals.[63] The strength of their relationship indicates that despite arguments and apparent differences, they are in fact happy in the relationship. In general, happy people are more likely to display empathy and altruism toward others than are people who are depressed.[64] Social support from family (or those one chooses to recognize as family) can lead to improved immune-system functioning and reactivity to stress.[65] In addition to relationships, health is one of the factors people most closely associate with happiness.[66] In general, happiness is positively correlated with improved mental and physical health.[67] As Foggy begins his treatment for cancer, Matt does his best to be positive and supportive, knowing that his friend needs to focus on the good things in life rather than his illness.[68]

Positive emotions also broaden the attention field, making an individual more aware of the physical and social environment surrounding him or her. In contrast, negative emotions narrow attention (which is good in flight-or-fight scenarios).[69] When in a state of positivity, people are also more creative, are open toward new people and ideas, and are poised for new

DAREDEVIL'S STRENGTHS

Regardless of the perspective on the origins of happiness, positive psychologists believe that happiness is tied to the use of an individual's strengths.[76] Martin Seligman, a notable positive psychologist, has identified six core virtues and corresponding strengths. Matt displays these strengths to some degree as a hero:

Wisdom and knowledge: creativity, curiosity, judgment, love of learning, perspective.
  * Matt's job as a lawyer requires him to creatively solve cases and see things from others' perspectives.[77]

Courage: bravery, perseverance, honesty, zest.
  * Matt's work as a vigilante and a lawyer puts him in danger. Despite the danger, he continues both lines of work.[78]

Humanity: love, kindness, social intelligence.
  * Matt spends his free time volunteering and with his friends.[79]

experiences.[70] Memory is also affected by mood; those in a positive mood are more likely to remember happy memories and positive words than are people in a negative mood.[71] Matt choses to focus on the happy moments with his father, such as his passion for boxing.[72] Matt hones his positive emotions by surveying Hell's Kitchen from his favorite spot in the city before rescuing others.[73] For the most part, the average person is moderately happy.[74] However, happiness can cloud an individual's self-examination of skills. Happy people overestimate their skills, whereas depressed people are far more accurate in their self-assessment of ability.[75]

Justice: teamwork, fairness, leadership.
  * Matt has an acute sense of justice that is separate from what is "law."[80]

Temperance: forgiveness, humility, prudence, self-regulation.
  * Matt is able to forgive his mother after learning about the reasons why she abandoned her family.[81]

Transcendence: appreciation of beauty and excellence, gratitude, hope, humor, spirituality.
  * Matt loves Hell's Kitchen and feels a deep connection to it and the people all around.[82]

Identified strengths can be used to pursue happiness if they are used in a way that brings pleasure, engagement, and meaning to a life.[83] The three aspects of happiness identified by Seligman—pleasure, engagement, and meaning—are all impacted by a person's adherence to the strengths and virtues he or she has.[84]

There are some other factors that are related to happiness that illustrate Matt's ability to find happiness despite negative life events. Education level is positively correlated with happiness, socioeconomic status, health, and longevity.[85] Matt is a lawyer, a profession that takes about seven years after high school to complete in addition to passing the bar exam.[86] Matt is highly educated and employed in a field for which he studied. People in skilled jobs display more happiness than people in unskilled jobs.[87] There is a moderate correlation between job satisfaction and happiness, and workers can develop an identity through their work.[88] Intrinsically rewarding work also involves well-developed skills and brings about social benefits.[89] Matt is in a unique position in that he essentially has two jobs. His job as a lawyer is obvious; he takes pride in his practice and continues to help people even after he cannot physically practice law in a courtroom. After getting disbarred in New York, he moves to California to continue working as a lawyer rather than staying in New York and pursuing a new career. Matt also "works" as Daredevil. This job requires extensive training and employs a set of skills that are well honed. At any time, Matt can put away his Daredevil persona and step away from being a superhero. The fact that he continues to be a superhero even after his identity is revealed implies that he finds some sort of reward in his actions and therefore a degree of joy.

FAKE IT UNTIL YOU MAKE IT

Matt Murdock's choice to be happy is not an easy one. It is a conscious decision on his part, a daily struggle to avoid succumbing to the despair and depression that lurk around the corner. In a particularly low moment for him, Matt reflects, "Turning my back on despair and depression these last few months is the hardest thing I've ever had to do, and I just have to stay strong."[90]

Happiness does not come easily. In Matt's case, he puts on a friendly face in order to convince others that he is in a much better place now.[91] Faking happiness in front of others does not work all the time, especially around Foggy.[92] However, the decision not to succumb to depression and seek moments of happiness plays into Matt's strengths of character. Matt may feel the burden of depression and despair from day to day, but he refuses to let a negative affect dictate his life.

NOTES

1. Seligman (2002), p. 38.
2. *Daredevil #5* (2011).
3. Lyubomirsky et al. (2005a).
4. Demir & Davidson (2012).
5. Seligman et al. (2004).
6. Seligman et al. (2004).
7. Peterson (2006).
8. Peterson (2006).
9. Peterson (2006).
10. Peterson (2006).
11. Peterson (2006).
12. *Daredevil #1* (2011).
13. Bojanowska & Zalewska (2016).
14. Kashdan et al. (2008).
15. Peterson (2006).
16. *Daredevil #7* (2012).
17. Peterson (2006).
18. Lyubomirsky et al. (2005b).
19. Argyle (1987).
20. *Daredevil #1* (2011); e.g., Kristen McDuffie in *Daredevil #12* (2012).
21. Argyle (1987).
22. Argyle (1987).
23. *Daredevil #7* (2011).
24. Argyle (1987).
25. Carr (2011).
26. Lyubomirsky et al. (2005a).
27. Bojanowska & Zalewska (2016).
28. *Daredevil #1* (2011).
29. Bojanowska & Zalewska (2016).
30. Bojanowska & Zalewska (2016).

31. *Daredevil* #6 (2014).
32. Zagorski (2005).
33. Loftus (1975).
34. e.g., *Daredevil* #53 (1969); *Daredevil* #164 (1980); *Daredevil: The Man without Fear* #1 (1993); *Marvel's Daredevil*, episode 1–1, "Into the Ring" (April 10, 2015); *Teenage Mutant Ninja Turtles* #1 (1984); *What If?* #28 (1981). Usually it's a glowing radioactive isotope in comics, not the liquid as depicted in film adaptations.
35. *Daredevil* #6 (2014).
36. Lyubomirsky et al. (2005b); Carr (2011).
37. Lyubomirsky et al. (2005b).
38. Lyubomirsky et al. (2005b).
39. Lyubomirsky et al. (2005b).
40. Luhmann et al. (2012).
41. *Daredevil* #1 (2011); *Daredevil* #1 (2014).
42. Lyubomirsky et al. (2005b).
43. Lyubomirsky et al. (2005b).
44. *Daredevil* #7 (2012).
45. Lyubomirsky et al. (2005b).
46. *Daredevil* #1 (2014).
47. *Daredevil* #1 (2014).
48. Lyubomirsky et al. (2005b).
49. *Daredevil* #3 (2011).
50. Lyubomirsky et al. (2005b).
51. *Daredevil* #3 (2011).
52. *Daredevil* #34 (2014).
53. Carr (2011).
54. Carr (2011).
55. *Daredevil* #12 (2012).
56. Carr (2011).
57. Lyubomirksy et al. (2005b).
58. Lyubomirsky et al. (2005a).
59. Lyubomirsky et al. (2005a).
60. Bojanowska & Zalewska (2016).
61. Demir & Davidson (2012).
62. Demir & Davidson (2012).
63. *Daredevil* #1 (2011).
64. Seligman (2002).
65. Carr (2011).
66. Bojanowska & Zalewska (2016).
67. Lyubomirsky et al. (2005a).
68. *Daredevil* #28 (2013).
69. Carr (2011).
70. Seligman (2002).
71. Argyle (1987).
72. *Daredevil* #17 (2012).
73. *Daredevil* #28 (2013).
74. Carr (2011).
75. Seligman (2002).
76. Seligman et al. (2004).
77. *Daredevil* #3 (2011).

78. *Daredevil* #12 (2012).
79. *Daredevil* #7 (2011).
80. *Daredevil* #6 (2011).
81. *Daredevil* #6 (2014).
82. *Daredevil* #1 (2011).
83. Seligman et al. (2004).
84. Seligman (2003).
85. Carr (2011).
86. Bureau of Labor Statistics (2015).
87. Carr (2011).
88. Carr (2011).
89. Carr (2011).
90. *Daredevil* #15 (2012).
91. *Daredevil* #7 (2012).
92. *Daredevil* #17 (2012).

BALANCE

TRAVIS LANGLEY

*"Even a happy life cannot be without a measure of darkness, and the
word happy would lose its meaning if it were not balanced by sadness."*
—psychoanalyst Carl Jung[1]

*"You have to think of it as more just than five senses. . . . Balance
and direction, micro-changes in air density, vibrations, blankets of
temperature variations. Mix all that with what I hear, subtle smells,
all the fragments form sort of an Impressionistic painting."*
—Matt Murdock[2]

We have more than five senses. Whether or not any psychic
senses also exist, our sensory array is richer than the
traditional five. Touch is treated as four separate senses because
the sensations of cold, warmth, pressure, and pain travel
through different sets of nerves to different bits of the brain.
We also have a *kinesthetic sense*, meaning a sense of motion, and

a *vestibular sense*, a sense of balance.[3] Matt Murdock's sense of balance is literally advanced, and yet like so many individuals, he struggles to find figurative balance in his life.

Lawyer by day, vigilante by night, he lives in the dichotomy of working both within the system and outside it, of both keeping and breaking the promise he made to use his brains instead of his fists, of serving the angels while dressed like a devil.[4] As he puts it, "As Daredevil, I get to save the world. As a lawyer, maybe I can fix it. I need them both. That's what I realized. The warrior and the lawyer. It doesn't work if I only have one."[5] People go to great lengths to make sense of their own contradictions.[6] We don't like to feel like hypocrites, yet balancing life's inherent paradoxes keep striking. Matt occasionally goes to one extreme or another to get away from his own contradictions: Sometimes he quits being Daredevil,[7] and sometimes he quits being Matt, letting his attorney alter ego play dead.[8] Those extremes often go hand in hand with the times when Matt immerses himself in bolstering his relationships with others as opposed to the times he cuts himself out of their lives. He also goes to extremes in his relationships, both pushing people away and pulling them back. Even the most stable figure his life, Foggy Nelson, periodically separates himself from Matt Murdock. The law partnership of Nelson & Murdock repeatedly breaks up and later forms again.[9]

At times he is mentally unbalanced, even experiencing hallucinations or catatonic withdrawal[10] but in oversimplified ways that bear too little resemblance to how real-world psychosis works and how people might recover when the stories are filled with so many better examples of genuine human nature worth exploring. Life is not simple—neither in terms of what human nature looks like nor how we might find solutions to the chaos in our existence. Extremes seem simple. They may help reduce how harshly we feel the seeming chaos, but at what cost? As simple as it might seem to take the same approach to solve every problem instead of analyzing situations and seeking new solutions every time, a single, simple solution will not solve it all.[11] When his law partner struggles to understand Daredevil's lifestyle, Matt tells him, "I'm an endless contradiction that'd never stand up to cross-examination, Foggy."[12] Matt keeps coming back from each extreme because his need for others, such as it is, remains. The scales of his personality need both Matt Murdock and Daredevil, and ultimately he believes in the scales of justice. He also happens to believe that they need help to balance.

Life's balancing act lasts as long as we do.

> *"Since losing my sight, my sense of balance is so acute that I could do this all day. . . ."*
> —Daredevil[13]

> *"Extremes are easy. Strive for balance."*
> —author Colin Wright[14]

NOTES

1. From a newspaper article quoted by Ferris (1963), p. 88.
2. *Marvel's Daredevil*, episode 1–5, "World on Fire" (April 10, 2015).
3. Goldstein & Brockmole (2017).
4. *Marvel's Daredevil*, episode 1–5, "World on Fire" (April 10, 2015).
5. *Daredevil* #21 (2017).
6. Festinger (1957); Festinger & Carlsmith (1959).
7. e.g., *Daredevil* #49 (1969); *Marvel's The Defenders* season 1 (August 18, 2017).
8. e.g., *Daredevil* #319–325 (1993–1994).
9. Starting in *Daredevil* #48 (1969).
10. e.g., *Daredevil* #347 (1996).
11. "I suppose it is tempting, if the only tool you have is a hammer, to treat everything as if it were a nail."—Maslow (1966), p. 15.
12. *Daredevil* #353 (1996).
13. *Daredevil* #3 (1964).
14. Quoted by Fall (2016).

ABOUT THE EDITOR

 **Travis Langley, PhD**, editor, is a psychology professor who teaches courses on crime, media, and mental illness at Henderson State University. He received his bachelor's from Hendrix College and his graduate degrees from Tulane University in New Orleans. Dr. Langley is the series editor and lead writer for the Popular Culture Psychology books on *The Walking Dead, Game of Thrones, Doctor Who, Star Wars, Star Trek, Supernatural, Westworld,* many superheroes, and more. He authored the acclaimed book *Batman and Psychology: A Dark and Stormy Knight. Psychology Today* carries his blog, "Beyond Heroes and Villains." Travis regularly speaks on media and heroism at universities, conferences, and conventions throughout the world. The documentary *Legends of the Knight* spotlighted how he uses fiction to teach real psychology, and he has appeared as an expert interviewee in programs such as Morgan Spurlock's *Superheroes Decoded, Necessary Evil: Super-Villains of DC Comics, Batman & Bill,* Robert Kirkman's *Secret History of Comics,* and Neil deGrasse Tyson's *StarTalk.*

Follow him as **@Superherologist** on Twitter, where he ranks among the ten most popular psychologists. Also keep up with him and this book series through **Facebook.com/ ThePsychGeeks**.

Stan Lee, who co-created Daredevil and wrote this volume's foreword, once said of Travis Langley: "This man's a genius!"

ABOUT THE CONTRIBUTORS

Travis Adams, MSW, received his master's degree from the University of Southern California and is currently a peer support specialist working with U.S. military veterans. He is a Marine Corps veteran who specializes in serving veterans who have been diagnosed with PTSD, anxiety, depression, substance use disorder, and other conditions. He uses various types of therapy to aid veterans in their recovery and has incorporated the use of pop culture into standardized treatment models. He co-authored a chapter in *Supernatural Psychology*. You can find Travis on Twitter: @themarine_peer.

Colt J. Blunt, PsyD, LP, has worked as a forensic examiner throughout his career and serves as a guest lecturer and trainer for a number of organizations and educational institutions. His academic interests include the intersection of psychology and law, including the study of criminal behavior. He previously contributed to *The Walking Dead Psychology: Psych of the Living Dead*, *Star Wars Psychology: Dark Side of the Mind*, *Game of Thrones Psychology: The Mind is Dark and Full of Terrors*, *Star Trek Psychology: The Mental Frontier*, and *Supernatural Psychology: Roads Less Traveled*.

Jenna Busch is a writer, host, and founder of Legion of Leia, a website to promote and support women in fandom. She co-hosted "Cocktails with Stan" with Daredevil creator and comic legend Stan Lee, hosted Most Craved, has appeared in the film *She Makes Comics*, and has been a guest on ABC's *Nightline*, *Attack of the Show*, NPR, Al Jazeera America, and multiple episodes of *Tabletop with Wil Wheaton*. Busch has co-authored chapters in *Star Wars Psychology*, *Game of Thrones Psychology*, *Star Trek Psychology*, *Doctor Who Psychology*, *Captain America vs. Iron Man Psychology*, *Supernatural Psychology*, *Wonder Woman Psychology*, and *Supernatural Psychology*, and worked as an editorial assistant on most volumes in this series. Her work has appeared all over the web. She can be reached on Twitter @JennaBusch.

Erin Currie, PhD, LP, is an instructor, therapist, and consultant by day. Driven to use her psychology superpowers for good, she founded the consulting practice MyPsychgeek, LLC, to help people develop their own superpowers through professional and team development. By night she gives her inner geek free rein to write about the psychological factors that influence her favorite characters. She also wrote for *Game of Thrones Psychology, Doctor Who Psychology, Wonder Woman Psychology,* and *Supernatural Psychology.*

Jim Davies is a professor of cognitive science at Carleton University and author of the book *Riveted: The Science of Why Jokes Make Us Laugh, Movies Make Us Cry, and Religion Makes Us Feel One with the Universe.* He contributed chapters to *Star Wars Psychology: The Dark Side of the Mind, Star Trek Psychology: The Mental Frontier,* and *Doctor Who Psychology: A Madman with a Box.*

Larisa A. Garski, MA, LMFT, is a licensed marriage and family therapist. She works with geeks, superheroes, and their families at Empowered Therapy in Chicago, IL. Larisa blogs on geek wellness and related topics for Blue Box Counseling (blueboxcounseling.com). She has co-authored chapters in *Supernatural Psychology: Roads Less Traveled.* Larisa and her research partner, Justine Mastin, LMFT, are currently developing a book on geek-focused narrative therapy. Larisa can be reached at empoweredtherapy.org.

Christine Hanefalk, MScEng, has been writing regularly about Daredevil for over ten years at her website *The Other Murdock Papers.* She has also contributed to the book *The Devil is in the Details: Examining Matt Murdock and Daredevil.* Christine's professional background is in biotech engineering, though she has spent most of her career in governmental affairs. She currently resides just north of Stockholm, Sweden, with her cats Murdock and Elektra.

Jeffrey Henderson has lectured and taught courses on storyboarding/visual storytelling/film direction at the Art Center College of Design in Pasadena, CA, and The Savannah College of Art & Design/ SCAD. An award-winning actor, director, writer, voiceover artist, illustrator, and musician, his original work includes *Star Wars: The Sable Corsair* (Lucasfilm's Audience Choice award-winner). He has worked as a storyboard/concept artist for *The Dark Knight*, *Fargo*, Sam Raimi's *Spider-Man* films, *Destiny*, *Injustice 2*, and the Dishonored series. Find him at PlanetHenderson.com, his Threadless shop at PlanetHenderson. Threadless.com, and @PlanetHenderson on his Twitter and Instagram.

Jeremy Johnson, PhD, is an assistant professor in Art Education at the University of Nebraska at Omaha. His research and creative activities address the need to create inclusive art experiences both in the classroom and in the gallery for individuals with disabilities, specifically those with visual impairments. Jeremy has been a self-proclaimed comic geek since his early years. He lives in Omaha with his wife and seven children.

Lisa Johnson, PhD, is the Director of Student Support Services and instructor at Nebraska Methodist College in Omaha, Nebraska. Her published research focuses on the social experiences and identity development of individuals with disabilities, as well as inclusive educational practices. She and her husband live in Omaha with their seven children with whom they enjoy fostering a love of all things comics.

J. Scott Jordan, PhD, is a cognitive psychologist who studies the roots of cooperative behavior. He often uses popular culture in his classes in order to illustrate the relevance of social-cognitive psychology to daily life. He has contributed chapters to *Captain American vs. Iron Man: Freedom, Security, Psychology*; *Wonder Woman Psychology: Lassoing the Truth*; *Star Trek Psychology: The Mental Frontier*; and *Supernatural Psychology: Roads Less Traveled*. He is extremely proud of his international comic book collection.

Jordan P. LaBouff, PhD, is an associate professor of psychology and honors at the University of Maine and an associate editor for the *Archive for the Psychology of Religion*. His research focuses on understanding the social situations that lead people to be more helpful, more generous, and less prejudiced. Outside of his research, he pursues justice on roller skates, volunteering as a referee for roller derby across New England and the Canadian Maritimes.

Rebecca M. Langley, MS, LPC, is a therapist who has worked with chronically mentally ill populations, at-risk youth, and adolescents in long-term foster care. She has been licensed as a professional counselor since 2007. Now a full-time psychology instructor at Henderson State University, Rebecca teaches courses such as abnormal psychology, developmental psychology, and infancy and childhood. Rebecca contributed to the book *Wonder Woman Psychology: Lassoing the Truth*. Her therapeutic method has been eclectic because, like the psychologist who created Wonder Woman, she does not believe in one-size-fits-all treatment.

Justine Mastin, MA, LMFT, is the owner of Blue Box Counseling in Minneapolis. She specializes in working with clients who self-identify as being outside the mainstream, such as those in the geek, secular, and LGBTQ communities. Justine is also the fearless leader of YogaQuest, a business that blends geek narratives with yoga. In addition to her work in her office/studio, she appears at pop culture conventions around the country, teaching yoga and speaking on geek wellness topics. She has co-authored chapters in *Supernatural Psychology: Roads Less Traveled*. Justine takes a holistic approach to healing: mind, body, and fandom. Follow her on Twitter @mindbodyfandom.

Leandra Parris, PhD, is an assistant professor of school psychology at Illinois State University. Her expertise is in the areas of crisis intervention, peer victimization, trauma-informed care, and Joss Whedon TV shows. She is the creator of the Trauma-Informed Program for Promoting Success (TIPPS), the Coping with Bullying Scale for Children, and a thorough Pinterest board dedicated to Ursula, the Sea Witch. Specializing in social and emotional assessment, Dr. Parris enjoys using her skills in arguments about morality, motivation, and character development.

Craig Pohlman, PhD, is a neurodevelopmental psychologist who helps struggling learners find success. He has written several books, including *How Can My Kid Succeed in School?* which helps parents and educators understand and help students with learning challenges. Craig is the CEO of Southeast Psych, a private practice and media company based in Charlotte, NC. He wrote chapters for *Star Wars Psychology: Dark Side of the Mind* and *Star Trek Psychology: The Mental Frontier.* He regularly contributes to Shrink Tank and Psych Bytes. Follow him on Twitter: @DrCraigPohlman.

Janina Scarlet, PhD, is a licensed clinical psychologist, a scientist, and a full-time geek. She uses superhero therapy to help patients with anxiety, depression, chronic pain, and PTSD at the Center for Stress and Anxiety Management. Dr. Scarlet is the author of *Superhero Therapy* and *Therapy Quest* with Little Brown Book Group and has written for all volumes in this Popular Culture Psychology series. She can be reached via her website at www.superhero-therapy.com or on Twitter: @shadowquill.

William Sharp, PsyD, is a certified psychoanalyst who teaches at Northeastern University with a private practice in Brookline, MA. His textbook, *Talking Helps,* is one of the few addressing the "impossible profession" of psychoanalytically informed counseling. He enjoys using popular media to explain complex psychoanalytic topics in his psychology courses. You can follow him on Twitter: @DrWilliamSharp.

Laura Vecchiolla, PsyD, is a clinical psychologist and professor in Chicago, Illinois. She uses the empowering themes of myth and shadow in therapy to help others on their journey toward growth and healing. When she is not out slaying her own dragons, she is pursuing her academic interests, which include the mythopoetic nature of the psyche and the curative powers of stories. She contributed to *Star Wars Psychology: Dark Side of the Mind, Game of Thrones Psychology: The Mind is Dark and Full of Terrors,* and *Wonder Woman Psychology: Lassoing the Truth.*

Eric D. Wesselmann, PhD, is an associate professor of psychology at Illinois State University. He publishes research on various topics, such as social exclusion, stigma, and religion/spirituality. He has been a comic fan since grade school and loves that he now gets to read comics and consider it "work." When not at work, he and his spouse train their three little superheroes at home to be the best heroes they can be. He has contributed to the majority of volumes in the Popular Culture Psychology series.

Mara Wood, PhD, is a licensed psychologist and a school psychology specialist whose research focus is on comics and their educational and therapeutic application to youth. She has contributed to the books *The Walking Dead Psychology, Star Wars Psychology,* and *Captain America Psychology* for Sterling as well as *A Galaxy Here and Now: Historical and Cultural Readings of Star Wars.* She co-edited *Wonder Woman Psychology: Lassoing the Truth.* She shares her daily musings on Twitter as @MegaMaraMon.

Jennifer L. Yen, MD, is a board certified child, adolescent, and adult psychiatrist in Houston, Texas. She serves as Clinical Assistant Professor of Psychiatry at Baylor College of Medicine, and is also in private practice. She is the health editor for *CKW Luxe,* a local philanthropic magazine focused on promoting positive and healthy living. Dr. Yen is the author of the Amazon bestselling YA fantasy series, *The Avalon Relics,* and is currently working on several new books that encourage discussions about diversity, culture, and mental health. Connect with her on Twitter and Instagram @JenYenWrites.

SPECIAL CONTRIBUTOR

Stan Lee is known to millions as the man whose superheroes propelled Marvel to its preeminent position in the comic book industry. His co-creations include Spider-Man™*, the Avengers™, X-Men™, Iron Man™, the Incredible Hulk™, and the Fantastic Four™, as well as hundreds of others. He introduced Spider-Man™ as a syndicated newspaper strip that became the most successful of all syndicated adventure strips and has appeared in more than 500 newspapers worldwide. Stan was named Chairman Emeritus of Marvel, as well as a member of the Editorial Board of Marvel Comics.

Stan became the Chairman & Chief Creative Officer of POW! Entertainment, a multimedia entertainment company based in Beverly Hills, CA, which he founded with production partner Gill Champion and Arthur Lieberman. POW! has debuted several titles in the publishing sphere, including Stan's graphic memoir *Amazing Fantastic Incredible* with Simon & Schuster; the first two books of the *Zodiac* trilogy with Disney Publishing; *Soldier Zero, Traveler,* and *Starborn* with Boom Comics; *Romeo and Juliet: The War* with 1821 Comics; and *Stan Lee and the Mighty 7* with Archie Comics and Genius Brands International. Additionally, *Stan Lee and the Mighty 7* premiered as an animated TV movie broadcast on the Hub. Stan has been involved in developing feature film projects, including *Annihilator, Prodigal,* and *Replicator & Antilight,* as well as TV projects including *Stan Lee's Lucky Man* and *Hellana.* He released his first-ever Indian superhero, *Chakra: The Invincible,* which debuted on Cartoon Network in India and can be watched on the Rovio ToonsTV app, and continued working on a number of potential superhero franchises.

---

* All trademarks indicated above are owned by Marvel Entertainment, LLC.

REFERENCES

COMIC BOOK REFERENCES

Alias #22–23 (2003). "The Secret Origin of Jessica Jones." Script: B. M. Bendis. Art: M. Gaydos.

Alias #25 (2003). "Purple," part 2. Script: B. M. Bendis. Art: M. Gaydos, M. Bagley, M. Hollingsworth, & D. White.

Amazing Fantasy #15 (1962). "Spider-Man!" Script: S. Lee. Art: S. Ditko.

Batman #404–407 (1987). "Batman: Year One." Script: F. Miller. Art: D. Mazzucchelli.

Batman/Daredevil (2000). "King of New York." Script: A. Grant. Art: E. Barreto & K. Bruzenak.

Batman: The Dark Knight Returns (1986). Script: F. Miller. Art: F. Miller, K. Janson, & L. Varley. New York, NY: DC Comics.

Daredevil #1 (1964). "The Origin of Daredevil." Script: S. Lee. Art: B. Everett, S. Ditko, & S. Brodsky.

Daredevil #3 (1964). "The Owl, Ominous Overlord of Crime!" Script: S. Lee. Art: J. Orlando & V. Colletta.

Daredevil #4 (1964). "Killgrave, the Unbelievable Purple Man!" Script: S. Lee. Art: J. Orlando & V. Colletta.

Daredevil #5 (1964). "The Mysterious Masked Matador." Script: S. Lee. Art: W. Wood.

Daredevil #6 (1965). "Trapped by The Fellowship of Fear." Script: S. Lee. Art: W. Wood & S. Rosen.

Daredevil #8 (1965). "The Stiltman Cometh!" Script: S. Lee. Art: W. Wood.

Daredevil #9 (1965). "That He May See!" Script: S. Lee. Art: W. Wood.

Daredevil #10 (1965). "While the City Sleeps!" Script: W. Wood. Art: S. Powell & W. Wood.

Daredevil #48 (1969). "Farewell to Foggy!" Script: S. Lee. Art: G. Colan & G. Klein.

Daredevil #49 (1969). "Daredevil Drops Out." Script: S. Lee. Art: G. Colan & G. Klein.

Daredevil #53 (1969). "As It Was in the Beginning." Script: S. Lee & R. Thomas. Art: G. Colan & G. Klein.

Daredevil #87 (1972). "From Stage Left, Enter: Elektro" Script: G Conway. Art: G. Colan & T. Palmer.

Daredevil #88 (1972). "Call Him: Killgrave!" Script: G. Conway. Art: G. Colan, T. Palmer, & J. Costa.

Daredevil #97 (1972). "He Who Saves." Script: S. Gerber. Art: G. Colan & E. Chua.

Daredevil #100 (1973). "Mind Storm." Script: S. Gerber. Art: G. Colan & E. Chua.

Daredevil #108 (1974). "The Beetle Strikes by Night." Script: S. Gerber. Art: B. Brown & P. Gulacy.

Daredevil #114 (1974). "A Quiet Night in the Swamp." Script: S. Gerber. Art: B. Brown & V. Colletta.

Daredevil #119 (1975). "They're Tearing Down Fogwell's Gym!" Script: T. Isabella. Art: B. Brown & D. Heck.

Daredevil #120 (1975). "And a HYDRA New Year!" Script: L. Wein. Art: B. Brown & V. Colletta.

Daredevil #124 (1975). "In the Clutches of the Copperhead." Script: M. Wolfman. Art: G. Colan & K. Janson.

Daredevil #158 (1979). "A Grave Mistake!" Script: R. McKenzie. Art: F. Miller & K. Janson.

Daredevil #166 (1980). "Till Death Do Us Part!" Story: R. McKenzie & F. Miller. Art: F. Miller & K. Janson.

Daredevil #167 *(1980)*. ". . . The Mauler!" Script: D. Michelinie. Art: F. Miller.

Daredevil #164 (1980). "Exposé." Script: R. McKenzie. Art: F. Miller & K. Janson.

Daredevil #168 (1981). "Elektra." Script: F. Miller. Art: F. Miller, K. Johnson, D. R. Martin, & J. Rosen.

Daredevil #170 (1981). "The Kingpin Must Die!" Script: F. Miller. Art: F. Miller & K. Janson.

Daredevil #175 (1981). "Gantlet." Script: F. Miller. Art: F. Miller & K. Janson.

Daredevil #177 (1981). "Where Angels Fear to Tread." Script: F. Miller. Art: K. Janson.

Daredevil #191 (1981). "Roulette." Script: F. Miller. Art: K. Janson.

Daredevil #178 (1982). "Paper Chase." Script: F. Miller. Art: F Miller & K. Janson.

Daredevil #180 (1982). "The Damned." Script: F. Miller. Art: F. Miller & K. Jansen.

Daredevil #181 (1982). "Last Hand." Script: F. Miller. Art: F. Miller & K. Jansen.

Daredevil #182 (1982). "She's Alive." Script: F. Miller. Art: F. Miller & K. Jansen.

Daredevil #183 (1982). "Child's Play." Writers: R. McKenzie & F. Miller. Art: F. Miller & K. Jansen.

Daredevil #185 (1982). "Guts." Script: F. Miller. Art: K. Janson.

Daredevil #186 (1982). "Stilts." Script: F. Miller. Art: K. Janson.

Daredevil #187 (1982). "Overkill." Script: F. Miller. Art: F. Miller & K. Jansen.

Daredevil #188 (1982). "The Widow's Bite." Script: F. Miller. Art: K. Janson.

Daredevil #189 (1982). "Siege." Script: F. Miller. Art: F. Miller & K. Jansen.

Daredevil #190 (1983). "Resurrection." Script: F. Miller. Art: K. Janson.

Daredevil #191 (1983). "Roulette." Script: F. Miller. Art: F. Miller & T. Austin.

Daredevil #223 (1985). Script: D. O'Neil & J. Shooter. Art: D. Mazzucchelli & K. DeMulder.

Daredevil #227 (1986). "Apocalypse." Script: F. Miller. Art: D. Mazzucchelli.

Daredevil #228 (1986). "Purgatory." Script: F. Miller. Art: D. Mazzucchelli.

Daredevil #229 (1986). "Pariah." Script: F. Miller. Art: D. Mazzucchelli.

Daredevil #231 (1986). "Saved." Script: F. Miller. Art: D. Mazzucchelli.

Daredevil #232 (1986). "God and Country." Script: F. Miller. Art: D. Mazzucchelli.

Daredevil #254 (1988). "Typhoid." Script: A. Nocenti. Art: J. Romita Jr. & A. Williamson.

Daredevil #263 (1989). "In Bitterness Not Far from Death . . ." A. Nocenti. Art: J. Romita Jr. & A. Williamson.

Daredevil #266 (1989). "A Beer with the Devil." Story: A. Nocenti & J. Romita Jr. Art: J. Romita Jr. & A. Williamson.

Daredevil #319 (1993). "Fall from Grace, Prologue." Script: D. G. Chichester. Art: S. McDaniel, H. Collazo, & H. Candelario.

Daredevil #325 (1994). "Fall from Grace, Finale: Salvation for the Damned." Script: D. G. Chichester. Art: S. McDaniel & H. Collazo.

Daredevil #347 (1995). "Inferno, Part Three." Script: J. M. DeMatteis. Art: R. Wagner & B. Reinhold.

Daredevil #348 (1996). "Purgatorio." Script: J. M. DeMatteis. Art: C. Nord & B. Reinhold.

Daredevil #352 (1996). "Smoky Mirrors." Script: B. Raab. Art: S. McManus.

Daredevil #353 (1996). "The Devil's Work!" Script: K. Kesel. Art: C. Nord & M. Ryan.

Daredevil #1 (1998). "Guardian Devil, Part One: And a Child Shall Lead Them All!" Script: K. Smith. Art: J. Quesada & J. Palmiotti.

Daredevil #2 (1998). "Guardian Devil Part 2: The Unexamined Life." Script: K. Smith. Art: J. Quesada & J. Palmiotti.

Daredevil #4 (1999). "Guardian Devil, Part Four: The Devil's Distaff." Script: K. Smith. Art: J. Quesada & J. Palmiotti.

Daredevil #5 (1999). "Guardian Devil, Part Five: Devil's Despair." Script: K. Smith: Art: J. Quesada & J. Palmiotti.

Daredevil #6 (1999). "Guardian Devil, Part Six: The Devil's Divested." Script: K. Smith. Art: J. Quesada & J. Palmiotti.

Daredevil #7 (1999). "Guardian Devil, Part Seven: The Devil's Demon." Script: K. Smith. Art: J. Quesada & J. Palmiotti.

Daredevil #8 (1999). "Guardian Devil, Part Eight! The Devil's Deliverance." Script: K. Smith. Art: J. Quesada & J. Palmiotti.

Daredevil #26 (2001). "Underboss, Part 1." Script: B. M. Bendis. Art: A. Maleev.

Daredevil #41 (2003). "Lowlife, Part 1." Script: B. M. Bendis. Art: A. Maleev.

Daredevil #43 (2003). "Lowlife Part 3." Script: B. M. Bendis. Art: A. Maleev.

Daredevil #58 (2004). "The King of Hell's Kitchen, Part 3." Script: B. M. Bendis. Art: A. Maleev.

Daredevil #62 (2004). "The Widow Part 2." Script: B. M. Bendis. Art: A. Maleev.

Daredevil #69 (2005). "Golden Age Part 4." Script: B. M. Bendis. Art: A. Maleev.

Daredevil #74 (2005). "Decalogue Part 4." Script: B. M. Bendis. Art: A. Maleev.

Daredevil #93 (2007). "The Devil Takes a Ride, Conclusion." Script: E. Brubaker.
Art: M. Lark & S. Gaudiano.

Daredevil #100 (2007). "Without Fear," part 1. Script: E. Brubaker. Art: M. Lark,
M. Djurdjevic, M., J. Romita, G. Colan, B. Sienkiewicz, A. Maleev, L. Bermejo,
S. Gaudiano, & A. Milgrom.

Daredevil #105 (2008). "Without Fear," part 6. Script: E. Brubaker. Art: M. Lark,
P. Azaceta, & S. Gaudiano.

Daredevil #114 (2009). "Lady Bullseye, Part Four." Script: E. Brubaker. Art: M. Lark &
S. Gaudiano.

Daredevil #1 (2011). "Man w/o Fear." Script: M. Waid. Art: P. Rivera.

Daredevil #3 (2011). "Sound and Fury." Script: M. Waid. Art: P. Rivera.

Daredevil #5 (2011). Script: M. Waid. Art: M. Martin.

Daredevil #6 (2011). Script: M. Waid. Art: M. Martin.

Daredevil #114 (2009). "Lady Bullseye, Part Four." Script: E. Brubaker. Art: M. Lark &
S. Gaudiano.

Daredevil #7 (2012). "Daredevil Faces Off with Five Crime Organizations at Once."
Script: M. Waid. Art: P. Rivera.

Daredevil #8 (2012). "The Devil and the Details, Part 2 of 2." Script: M. Waid. Art: Kano.

Daredevil #11 (2012). "The Omega Effect (Part 3)." Script: M. Waid. Art: M. Checchetto.

Daredevil #12 (2012). Script: M. Waid. Art: C. Samnee.

Daredevil #15 (2012). Script: M. Waid. Art: C. Samnee.

Daredevil #17 (2012). "The Great Divide." Script: M. Waid. Art: M. Allred.

Daredevil #1 (2013). "End of Days (Part 1 of 8)." Script: B. Bendis & D. Mack.
Art: K. Janson & B. Sienkiewicz.

Daredevil #21 (2013). "Locked Room Murder Trial Continues!" Script: M. Waid.
Art: C. Samnee.

Daredevil #24 (2013). "Savage Wilders Attack City." Script: M. Waid. Art: C. Samnee &
J. Rodriguez.

Daredevil #28 (2013). "Help Wanted." Script: M. Waid. Art: C. Samnee.

Daredevil #34 (2013). "The Devil Went Down to Kentucky." Script: M. Waid. Art: J.
Rodriguez.

Daredevil #0.1 (2014). "Road Warrior." Script: M. Waid. Art: P. Krause.

Daredevil #1–4 (2014). [Untitled]. Script: M. Waid. Art: C. Samnee.

Daredevil #5 (2014). "Daredevil." Script: M. Waid. Art: C. Samnee & J. Rodriguez.

Daredevil #6 (2014). "Sisters Act!" Story: M. Waid & J. Rodriguez. Art: J. Rodriguez &
A. Lopez.

Daredevil #6 (2014). "Blind Man Sees?" Story: M. Waid & J. Rodriguez. Art: J. Rodriguez
& A. Lopez.

Daredevil #7 (2014). "Nun to Be Found!" Story: M. Waid & J. Rodriguez. Art: J. Rodriguez
& A. Lopez.

Daredevil #9–10 (2014). Script: M. Waid. Art: C. Samnee.

Daredevil #10 (2014). Script: M. Waid. Art: C. Samnee.

Daredevil #34 (2014). Script: M. Waid. Art: J. Rodriguez.

Daredevil #9 (2015). "West-Case Scenario." Script: M. Waid. Art: C. Samnee & A. Lopez.

Daredevil #15 (2015). "Worlds Collide." Script: M. Guggenheim. Art: P. Krause.

Daredevil #16 (2015). [Untitled]. Script: M. Waid. Art: C. Samnee.

Daredevil #7 (2016). Script: C. Soule. Art: M. Buffagni.

Daredevil #9 (2016). "Blind Man's Bluff, Part II." Script: C. Soule. Art: G. Sudzuka.

Daredevil #19 (2017). "Purple (Part 3)." Script: C. Soule. Art: M. Laming.

Daredevil #21 (2017). "Supreme, Part 1." Script: C. Soule. Art: G. Sudzuka.

Daredevil #25 (2017). "Supreme: Conclusion." Script: C. Soule. Art: A. Morgan.

Daredevil #595 (2017). "Mayor Fisk, Part 1." Script: C. Soule. Art: S. Landini.

Daredevil and Batman (1997). "An Eye for an Eye." Script: Dan G. Chichester.
Art: S. McDaniel & D. Fisher.

Daredevil: Battlin' Jack Murdock #3 (2007). "Round 3." Story: C. Di Giandomenico &
Z. Wells. Art: C. Di Giandomenico.

Daredevil: Battlin' Jack Murdock #4 (2007). "Round 4." Story: C. Di Giandomenico &
Z. Wells. Art: C. Di Giandomenico.

Daredevil: Love & War (1986). Script: F. Miller. Art: B. Sienkiewicz.

Daredevil: Reborn #1 (2010). "Reborn Chapter 1." Script: A. Diggle. Art: D. Gianfelice.

Daredevil: Redemption #1 (2005). „Redemption Part 1." Script: D. Hine. Art: M. Gaydos.

Daredevil: The Man without Fear #1–5 (1993–1994). [Untitled]. Script: F. Miller. Art: J. Romita Jr. & A. Williamson.

Daredevil vs. Punisher: Means and Ends #1 (2005). "Good Deeds, Bad Seeds." Script: D. Lapham. Art: D. Lapham.

Daredevil vs. Punisher: Means and Ends #3 (2005). "Victory, Now!" Script: D. Lapham. Art: D. Lapham.

Daredevil vs. Punisher: Means and Ends #4 (2005). "Over the Line." Script: D. Lapham. Art: D. Lapham.

Daredevil vs. Punisher: Means and Ends #5 (2005). "The Unraveling!" Script: D. Lapham. Art: D. Lapham.

Daredevil v. Punisher: Means and Ends #6 (2005). "The Second Chance . . ." Script: D. Lapham. Art: D. Lapham.

Detective Comics #33 (1939). "The Legend of the Batman—Who He is and How He Came to be!" Script: B. Kane & B. Finger. Art: B. Kane & S. Moldoff. New York, NY: National Comics.

Elektra #18 (2003). "Going Home." Script: L. Hama. Art: M. Deodato Jr. & S. Koblish.

Elektra: Assassin #1 (1986). "Chapter 1: Hell and Back." Script: F. Miller. Art: B. Sienkiewicz.

Elektra: Root of Evil #2 (1995). "Murderer's Bible." Script: D. G. Chichester. Art: S. McDaniel & H. Collazo.

The Elektra Saga #1 (1984). "The Wall." Script: F. Miller. Art: F. Miller & K. Johnson.

The Elektra Saga #2 (1984). "The Gauntlet." Script: F. Miller. Art: F. Miller & K. Johnson.

The Elektra Saga #3 (1984). "Last Hand." Script: F. Miller. Art: F. Miller & K. Johnson.

The Elektra Saga #4 (1984). "Resurrection." Script: F. Miller. Art: F. Miller & K. Johnson.

Luke Cage, Hero for Hire #1 (1972). "Out of Hell—a Hero!" Script: A. Goodwin. Art: G. Tuska & B. Graham.

Marvel Knights #1 (2000). "The Burrowers." Script: C. Dixon. Art: E. Baretto & K. Jansen.

Marvel Knights #15 (2001). "The Unreal World." Script: C. Dixon. Art: E. Barreto & N. DeCastro.

Marvel Knights #3 (2000). "The Destroyers." Script: C. Dixon. Art: E. Baretto & K. Jansen.

Marvel Preview #2 (1974). "The Punisher: America's Greatest Crime Destroyer!" Script: G. Conway. Art: G. Morrow & T. DeZuniga.

Marvel Premiere #15 (1974). "The Fury of Iron Fist!" Script: R. Thomas. Art: G. Kane & D. Giordano.

Marvel Team-Up Annual #4 (1981). "Pawns of the Purple Man!" Script: F. Miller. Art: H. Trimpe & M. Esposito.

Original Sin #2 (2014). "Bomb Full of Secrets." Script: J. Aaron. Art: M. Deodato.

Punisher War Journal #1 (2006). Script: M. Fraction. Art: A. Olivetti.

Punisher War Journal #4 (2007). Script: M. Fraction. Art: A. Olivetti.

Silver Streak Comics #6 (1940). "The Daredevil, Master of Courage." Script: D. Rico. Art: J. Binder. New York, NY: Lev Gleason.

Silver Streak Comics #7 (1940). "Daredevil Battles the Claw, Part 1." Script & Art: J. Cole.

Teenage Mutant Ninja Turtles #1 (1984). [Untitled.] Script: P. Laird. Art: K. Eastman. Dover, NH: Mirage Studios.

The Amazing Spider-Man #96 (1971). ". . . And Now, the Goblin!" Script: S. Lee. Art: G. Kane & F. Giacola.

The Amazing Spider-Man #98 (1971). "The Goblin's Last Gasp!" Script: S. Lee. Art: G. Kane, F. Giacola, & T. Mortellaro.

The Amazing Spider-Man #121 (1973). "The Night Gwen Stacy Died." Script: G. Conway. Art: G. Kane, J. Romita, Jr., & T. Mortellaro.

The Amazing Spider-Man #129 (1974). Script: G. Conway. Art: R. Andru, F. Giacoia, D. Hunt, & J. Costanza.

The Amazing Spider-Man #197 (1979). "The Kingpin's Midnight Massacre!" Script: M. Wolfman. Art: K. Pollard & J. Mooney.

The Amazing Spider-Man #396 (1994). "Back from the Edge, Part 3: Deadmen." Script: J. M. DeMatteis. Art: M. Bagley & L. Mahlstedt.

The Defenders #1 (2017). "So I Told Him, I'll Sell You." Script: B. M. Bendis. Art: D. Marquez.

The Defenders #2 (2017). "@#$% Agh!" Script: B. M. Bendis. Art: D. Marquez.

The Defenders #7 (2017). Script: B. M. Bendis. Art: D. Marquez.

The Punisher: Year One #4 (1995). Script: D. Abnett & A. Lanning. Art: D. Eaglesham, S. Koblish, C. Jorgensen, B. Oakley, & V. Evans.

The Punisher: Born #1 (2003). "The First Day." Script: G. Ennis. Art: D. Robertson, T. Palmer, P. Mounts, & R. Wooten.

The Punisher: Born #4 (2003). "The Last Day." Script: G. Ennis. Art: D. Robertson, T. Palmer, P. Mounts, R. Wooten, & W. Walkuski.

The Punisher: Intruder (1989). Script: M. Baron. Art: B. Reinhold, W. Schubert, & L. Lessman.

The Punisher MAX #6 (2004). "In the Beginning: Conclusion." Script: G. Ennis. Art: L. Larosa, T. Palmer, D. White, R. Gentile, & T. Bradstreet.

The Punisher: The Tyger #1 (2000). Script: G. Ennis. Art: J. Severin.

Ultimate Marvel Team-Up #8 (2001). "Spider-Man & the Punisher & Daredevil (Part III)." Script: B. M. Bendis. Art: Bill Sienkiewicz.

Watchmen #1–12 (1986–1987). Script: A. Moore. Art: D. Gibbons.

What If? #28 (1981). "Matt Murdock, Agent of . . . S.H.I.E.L.D." Script: M. W. Barr & F. Miller. Art: F. Miller & K. Janson.

X-Men #116 (1978). "To Save the Savage Land." Story: C. Claremont & J. Byrne. Art: J. Byrne & T. Austin.

Other References

Abbot, N., & Cameron, L. (2014). What makes a young assertive bystander? The effect of intergroup contact, empathy, cultural openness, and in-group bias on assertive bystander intentions. *Journal of Social Issues, 70(1)*, 167–182.

Adkisson, J. (2006). *Lost eye: Coping with monocular vision after enucleation or eye loss from cancer, accident, or disease.* Bloomington, IN: iUniverse.

Ainsworth, M. D. S., & Bell, S. M. (1970). Attachment, exploration, and separation: Illustrated by the behavior of one-year-olds in a strange situation. *Child Development, 41(1)*, 49–67.

Alaniz, J. (2014). *Death, disability, and the superhero: The silver age and beyond.* Jackson, MS: University Press of Mississippi.

Algoe, S. B., & Haidt, J. (2009). Witnessing excellence in action: The 'other-praising' emotions of elevation, gratitude, and admiration. *Journal of Positive Psychology, 4(2)*, 105–127.

Allison, S. T., & Goethals, G. R. (2016). Hero worship: The elevation of the human spirit. Journal for the Theory of Social Behaviour, 46(2), 187–210.

American Psychiatric Association (2013). *Diagnostic and statistical manual of mental disorders* (5th ed.) (DSM-5). Washington, DC: American Psychiatric Association.

Anderson, S. W., Bechara, A., Damasio, H., Tranel, D., & Damasio, A. R. (1999). Impairment of social and moral behavior related to early damage in human prefrontal cortex. *Nature Neuroscience*, 2(11), 1032–1037.

Aquino, K., McFerran, B., & Laven, M. (2011). Moral identity and the experience of moral elevation in response to acts of uncommon goodness. *Journal of Personality & Social Psychology, 100(4)*, 703–718.

Araneda, R., Renior, L. A., Rombaux, P., Cuevas, I., & De Volder, A. G. (2016). Cortical plasticity and olfactory function in early blindness. *Frontiers in Systems Neuroscience, 10*, ArtID 75.

Argyle, M. (1987). *The psychology of happiness.* London, UK: Methuen.

Arnold, D. H., Wegener, S. V., Brown, F., & Mattingley, J. B. (2012). Precision of synesthetic color matching resembles that for recollected colors rather than physical colors. *Journal of Experimental Psychology: Human Perception & Performance, 38(5)*, 1078–10 84.

Asch, S. E. (1955). Opinions and social pressure. *Readings about the Social Animal, 193(5)*, 17-26.

Asch, S. E. (1956). Studies of independence and conformity: I. A minority of one against a unanimous majority. *Psychological Monographs: General and Applied, 70(9)*, 1–70.

Asghari, V., Sanyal, S., Buchwaldt, S., Paterson, A., Jovanovic, V., & Van Tol, H. H. (1995). Modulation of intracellular cyclic AMP levels by different human dopamine D4 receptor variants. *Journal of Neurochemistry, 65(3)*, 1157–1165.

Bal, P. M., & Veltkamp, M. (2013). How does fiction reading influence empathy? An experimental investigation on the role of emotional transportation. *PloS one, 8*(1), e55341.

Bandura, A. (1962). *Social learning through imitation.* Lincoln, NE: University of Nebraska Press.

Bandura, A. (1977). *Social learning theory.* New York, NY: General Learning Press.

Bandura, A., Ross, D., & Ross, S. A. (1963). Imitation of film-mediated aggressive models. *Journal of Abnormal & Social Psychology, 66*(1), 3–11.

Bandura, A., Underwood, B., & Fromson, M. E. (1975). Disinhibition of aggression through diffusion of responsibility and dehumanization of victims. *Journal of Research in Personality, 9*(4), 253–269.

Barboza, G. E., & Dominguez, S. (2017). Longitudinal growth of post-traumatic stress and depressive symptoms following a child maltreatment allegation: An examination of violence exposure, family risk and placement type. *Children & Youth Services Review, 81*(C), 368–378.

Barker, D., Quennerstedt, M., & Annerstedt, C. (2015) Inter-student interactions and student learning in health and physical education: a post-Vygotskian analysis, *Physical Education & Sport Pedagogy, 20*(4), 409–426.

Barker, S. (2004/2008). *Life of Evel: Evel Knievel.* London, UK: HarperSport.

Baron, R. S., Baron, P. H., & Miller, N. (1973). The relation between distraction and persuasion. *Psychological Bulletin, 80*(4), 310–323.

Barron, B. (2003). When smart groups fail. *Journal of the Learning Sciences, 12*(3), 307–359.

Barsade, S. G. (2002). The ripple effect: Emotional contagion and its influence on group behavior. *Administrative Science Quarterly, 47*(4), 644–675.

Bee, H. L. (1992). *The developing child.* London, UK: HarperCollins.

Belzeaux, R., Loundou, A., Azorin, J., Naudin, J., & Ibrahim, E. C. (2014). Longitudinal monitoring of the serotonin transporter gene expression to assess major depressive episode evolution. *Neuropsychobiology, 70*(4), 220–227.

Beaulieu-Lefebvre, M., Schneider, F. C., Kupers, R., & Ptito, M. (2011). Odor perception and odor awareness in congenital blindness. *Brain Research Bulletin, 84*(3), 206–209.

Beers, P. J., Boshuizen, H. P. A., Kirschner, P. A., & Gijselaers, W. H. (2005). Computer support for knowledge construction in collaborative learning environments. *Computers in Human Behavior, 21*, 623–643.

Bell, B. E., & Loftus, E. F. (1985). Vivid persuasion in the courtroom. *Journal of Personality Assessment, 49*(6), 659–664.

Biography (n.d.). *Jack Nicholson.* Biography: https://www.biography.com/people/jack-nicholson-9423081.

Blatt, S. J., & Levy, K. N. (2003). Attachment theory, psychoanalysis, personality development, and psychopathology. *Psychoanalytic Inquiry, 23*(1), 102–150.

Bogart, K. R., Rottenstein, A., Lund, E. M., & Bouchard, L. (2017). Who self-identifies as disabled? An examination of impairment and contextual predictors. *Rehabilitation Psychology*, no pagination specified.

Bojanowska, A., & Zalewska, A. M. (2016). Lay understanding of happiness and the experience of well-being: Are some conceptions of happiness more beneficial than others? *Journal of Happiness Studies, 17*(2), 793–815.

Bosson, J. K., Weaver, J. R., & Prewitt-Freilino, J. L. (2012). Concealing to belong, revealing to be known: Classification expectations and self-threats among persons with concealable stigmas. *Self & Identity, 11*(1), 114–135.

Botwin, M. D., Buss, D. M., & Shackleford, T. K. (1997). Personality and mate preferences: Five factors in mate selection and marital satisfaction. *Journal of Personality, 65*(1), 107–136.

Bourdain, A. (2001). *Typhoid Mary: An urban historical.* New York, NY: Bloomsbury.

Bowlby, J. (1988). *A secure base: Parent-child attachment and healthy human development.* New York, NY: Basic.

Boyes, A. (2013). *50 characteristics of healthy relationships.* Psychology Today: https://www.psychologytoday.com/blog/in-practice/201301/50-characteristics-healthy-relationships.

Braithwaite, D.O., Wackernagel Bach, B., Baxter, L.A., DiVerniero,R., Hammonds, J. R., Hosek, A. M., Willer, E. K., & Wolf, B. M., (2010). Constructing family: A typology of voluntary kin. *Journal of Social & Personal Relationships, 27*(3), 388–407.

Bresin, K., & Gordon, K. H. (2013). Aggression as affect regulation: Extending catharsis theory to evaluate aggression and experiential anger in the laboratory and daily life. *Journal of Social & Clinical Psychology, 32*(4), 400–423.

Bretherton, I. (1992). The origins of attachment theory: John Bowlby and Mary Ainsworth. *Developmental Psychology, 28*(5), 759–775.

Brewer, M. B. (1991). The social self: On being the same and different at the same time. *Personality & Social Psychology Bulletin, 17*(5), 475–482.

Brockner, J., Greenberg, J., Brockner, A., Bortz, J., Davy, J., & Carter, C. (1986). Layoffs, equity theory, and work performance: Further evidence of the impact of survivor guilt. *Academy of Management Journal, 29*(2), 373–384.

Broadbent, D. E. (1959). *Perception and communication. New York, NY: Oxford University Press.*

Brown, J. (1999). Bowen family systems theory and practice: Illustration and critique. *Australian & New Zealand Journal of Family Therapy, 20*(2), 94–103.

Buckley, C. (2007). *Why our hero leapt onto the tracks and we might not.* New York Times. http://www.nytimes.com/2007/01/07/weekinreview/07buckley.html?mcubz=0.

Butler, E. K. (2017). *Extreme air sports.* Mankato, MN: Capstone.

Budell, L., Jackson, P., & Rainville, P. (2010). Brain responses to facial expressions of pain: Emotional or motor mirroring? *Neuroimage, 53*(1), 355–363.

Bull, R., Rathborn, H., & Clifford, B. R. (1983). The voice recognition accuracy of blind listeners. *Perception, 12*(2), 223–226.

Bureau of Labor Statistics (2015). *Occupational outlook handbook.* Bureau of Labor Statistics: https://www.bls.gov/ooh/legal/lawyers.htm#tab-1.

Burton, N. (2012). *Hide and seek: The psychology of self-deception.* London, UK: Acheron.

Bushman, B. J., & Whitaker, J. L. (2010). Like a magnet: Catharsis beliefs attract angry people to violent games. *Psychological Science, 21*(6), 790–792.

Buss, D. M. (1985). Human mate selection. *American Scientist, 73,* 47–51.

Calhoun, L. G., & Tedeschi, R. G. (2006). The foundations of posttraumatic growth: An expanded framework. In L. G. Calhoun & R. G. Tedeschi (Eds.), *Handbook of posttraumatic growth: Research and practice* (pp. 3–23). Mahwah, NJ: Erlbaum.

Calhoun, L. G., & Tedeschi, R. G. (2013). *Posttraumatic growth in clinical practice.* New York, NY: Brunner Routledge.

Calvo-Merino, B., Glaser, D. E., Grèzes, J., Passingham, R. E., & Haggard, P. (2005). Action observation and acquired motor skills: An fMRI study with expert dancers. *Cerebral Cortex, 15*(8), 1243–1249.

Carr, A. (2011). *Positive psychology: The science of happiness and human strengths* (2nd ed.). New York, NY: Routledge.

Catholic Church (1995). *Catechism of the Catholic Church* (1995). New York, NY: Doubleday.

Cavalieri, J., & Cohn, M. (1982). The Denny O'Neil interview. In M. Cohn (Ed.), *The Daredevil chronicles* (pp. 37–41). Albany, NY: FantaCo.

Celesia, G. G. (2010). Visual perception and awareness: A modular system. *Journal of Psychophysiology, 24*(2), 62–67.

Centers for Disease Control & Prevention (2008, April 9). *Prevalence of self-reported postpartum depressive symptoms—17 states, 2004–2005.* CDC: https://www.cdc.gov/mmwR/preview/mmwrhtml/mm5714a1.htm.

Cleavans, E. L. (1983). On maturity. *Modern Psychoanalysis, 8*(2): 131–133.

Cleckley, H. M. (1941/1976). *The mask of sanity: An attempt to clarify some issues about the so-called psychopathic personality.* Maryland Heights, MO: Mosby.

Cobrinik, L. H., Fisch, M. L., Levy, S., Lichtenberg, P., Romm, F., & Rudner, S. (1953). Loyalty oaths and anti-intellectualism. *American Psychologist, 8*(11), 707.

Coughlan, G., Igou, E. R., van Tilburg, W. A., Kinsella, E. L., & Ritchie, T. D. (in press). On boredom and perceptions of heroes: A meaning-regulation approach to heroism. *Journal of Humanistic Psychology.*

Cuevas, I., Rombaux, P., De Volder, A. G., & Renier, L. (2009). Odour discrimination and identification are improved in early blindness. *Neuropsychologia, 47*(14), 3079–3083.

Dagher, A. (2014). Alcohol and the paradox of self-control. *Biological Psychiatry, 76*(9), 674–675.

Daily Mail (2007, September 11). *Mugger attacks blind man . . .who turns out to be a judo world champion.* Daily Mail: http://www.dailymail.co.uk/news/article-481200/Mugger-attacks-blind-man--turns-judo-world-champion.html.

Darley, J. M., & Latané, B. (1970). *The unresponsive bystander: Why doesn't he help?* New York, NY: Appleton Century Crofts.

Danckert, J., & Culham, J. C. (2010). Reflections on blindsight: Neuroimaging and behavioural explorations clarify a case of reversed localisation in the blind field of a patient with hemianopia. *Canadian Journal of Experimental Psychology, 64*(2), 86–101.

Davies, J. (2014, August 14). *What do blind people actually see?* Nautilis: http://nautil.us/blog/what-do-blind-people-actually-see.

Decety, J., & Sommerville, J. A. (2003). Shared representations between self and other: A social cognitive neuroscience view. *Trends in Cognitive Sciences, 7*(12), 527–533.

DeLong, C. M., Au, W. W. L., Harley, H. E., Roitblat, H. L., & Pytka, L. (2007). Human listeners provide insights into echo features used by dolphins (*Tursiops truncatus*) to discriminate among objects. *Journal of Comparative Psychology, 121*(3), 306–319.

Demir, M., & Davidson, I. (2012). Toward a better understanding of the relationship between friendship and happiness: Perceived responses to capitalization attempts, feelings of mattering, and satisfaction of basic psychological needs in same-sex best friendships as predictors of happiness. *Journal of Happiness Studies, 14*(2), 525–550.

Denzler, M., & Förster, J. (2012). A goal model of catharsis. *European Review of Social Psychology, 23*(1), 107–142.

Deutsch, J. A., & Deutsch, D. (1963). Attention and some theoretical considerations. *Psychological Review, 70*(1), 80–90.

Dixon, W. E., Jr. (2015). Anti-intellectualism and the fracking of psychology. *Training & Education in Professional Psychology, 9*(4), 286–291.

Doidge, N. (2016). *The brain's way of healing: Remarkable discoveries and recoveries from the frontiers of neuroplasticity.* New York, NY: Penguin.

Dorella, A. (2010). Halloween. Zucche e streghe, santi de defunti [Halloween. Pumpkins and witches, and saints and the dead.] *Giornale Stiorico Del Centro Studi di Psicologia e Letteratura, 6*(1), 195–221.

Down, I. M., Downs, D. S., Schaefer, E. W., Beiler, J. S., & Weisman, C. S. (2013). Postpartum anxiety and maternal-infant health outcomes. *Pediatrics, 131*(4). http://pediatrics.aappublications.org/content/early/2013/02/26/peds.2012-2147?sid=82b744e7-0fb3-424d-b155-43229c10a021.

Dusek, J. B. (1987). *Adolescent development and behavior.* Englewood Cliffs, NJ: Prentice-Hall.

Easterbrook, J. A. (1959). The effect of emotion on cue utilization and the organization of behaviour. *Psychological Review, 66*(3), 183–201.

Easterbrook, J. A. (1959). The effect of emotion on cue utilization and the organization of behaviour. *Psychological Review, 66*(3), 183–201.

Eberhart, N. K., Auerbach, R. P., Bigda-Peyton, J., & Abela, J. R. Z. (2011). Maladaptive schemas and depression: Tests of stress generation and diathesis-stress models. *Journal of Social & Clinical Psychology, 30*(1), 7–104.

Edison, T. (2013). *What do blind people see?* The Tommy Edison Experience: https://www.youtube.com/watch?v=ZDHJRCtv0WY.

Eng, W., Heimberg, R. G., Hart, T. A., Schneier, F. R., & Liebowitz, M. R. (2001). Attachment in individuals with social anxiety disorder: The relationship among adult attachment styles, social anxiety, and depression. *Emotion, 1*(4), 365–380.

Erikson, E. (1950/2012). *Childhood and society.* New York, NY: Norton.

Erikson, E. H. (Ed.). (1963). *Youth: Change and challenge.* New York, NY: Basic.

Exline, J. J. (2013). Religious and spiritual struggles. In K. I. Pargament, J. J. Exline, & J. W. Jones (Eds.), *APA handbook of psychology, religion, and spirituality* (Vol. 1: Context, theory, and research) (pp. 459–475). Washington, DC: American Psychological Association.

Exline, J. J., Grubbs, J. B., & Homolka, S. J. (2015). Seeing God as cruel or distant: Links with divine struggles involving anger, doubt, and fear of God's disapproval. *International Journal for the Psychology of Religion, 25*(1), 29–41.

Exline, J. J., Pargament, K. I., Grubbs, J. B., & Yali, A. M. (2014). The Religious and Spiritual Struggles Scale: Development and initial validation. *Psychology of Religion & Spirituality, 6*(3), 208–222.

Exline, J. J., Park, C. L., Smyth, J. M., & Carey, M. P. (2011). Anger toward God: social-cognitive predictors, prevalence, and links with adjustment to bereavement and cancer. *Journal of Personality & Social Psychology, 100*(1), 129–148.

Exline, J. J., Worthington Jr., E. L., Hill, P., & McCullough, M. E. (2003). Forgiveness and justice: A research agenda for social and personality psychology. *Personality & Social Psychology Review, 7*(4), 337–348.

Eysenck, S., & Zuckerman, M. (1978). The relationship between sensation-seeking and Eysenck's dimensions of personality. *British Journal of Psychology, 69*(4), 483–487.

Fall, P. (2016, February 21). *A recipe for balance in a distraction-filled world.* Redesigning Your Life: http://redesigning-your-life.com/2016/02/recipe-for-balance/.

Farhadian, C. E., & Emmons, R. A. (2009). The psychology of forgiveness in the world religions. In A. Kalayjian & R. F. Paloutzian (Eds.), *Forgiveness and reconciliation* (pp. 55–70). New York: Springer.

Farley, F. H. (1971). Measures of individual differences in stimulation seeking and the tendency toward variety. *Journal of Consulting & Clinical Psychology, 37*(3), 394–396.

Feinman, J. (2014). *Everything you need to know about American law* (4th ed.). Oxford, UK: Oxford University Press.

Felitti, V. J., Anda, R. F., Nordenberg, D., Williamson, D. F., Spitz, A. M., Edwards, V., Koss, M. P., & Marks, J. S. (1998). Relationship of childhood abuse and household dysfunction to many of the leading causes of death in adults. *American Journal of Preventive Medicine, 14*(4), 245–258.

Ferris, T. P. (1963). *What Jesus did.* New York, NY: Oxford University Press.Festinger, L. (1957). *A theory of cognitive dissonance.* Stanford, CA: Stanford University Press.

Festinger, L. (1957). *A theory of cognitive dissonance.* Stanford, CA: Stanford University Press.

Festinger, L, & Carlsmith, J. M. (1959). Cognitive consequences of forced compliance. *Journal of Abnormal & Social Psychology, 58*(2), 203–211.

Fincham, F. D. (2000). The kiss of the porcupines: From attributing responsibility to forgiving. *Personal Relationships, 7*(1), 1–23.

Fiske, S. T. (2009). From dehumanization and objectification to rehumanization. *Annals of the New York Academy of Sciences, 1167*(1), 31–34.

Fiske, S. T., Harris, L. T., & Cuddy, A. J. (2004). Why ordinary people torture enemy prisoners. *Science, 306*(5701), 1482–1483.

Fleming, J. S. (2004). *Psychological perspectives on human development.* Southwest Psychometrics and Psychology Resources: http://swppr.org/textbook/contents.html.

Forber-Pratt, A. J., & Zape, M. P. (2017). Disability identity development model: Voices from the ADA-generation. *Disability and Health Journal, 10*(2), 350–355.

Franco, Z. E., Blau, K., & Zimbardo, P. G. (2011). Heroism: a conceptual analysis and differentiation between heroic action and altruism. *Review of General Psychology, 15*(2), 99–113

Freud, S. (1908/1948). The relation of the poet to day-dreaming. In *Collected papers, 4,* pp. 173–83. London, UK: Hogarth.

Freud, S. (1909/1955). Analysis of a phobia in a 5-year-old boy. In J. Strachey (Trans. & Ed.), *The standard edition of the complete works of Sigmund Freud* (Vol. X, pp. 1–149). London, UK: Hogarth.

Freud, S. (1920/2001). Psychogenesis of a case of homosexuality in a woman. In J. Strachey (Trans. & Ed.), *The standard edition of the complete works of Sigmund Freud* (Vol. XVIII, pp. 147–172). London, UK: Vintage.

Freud, S. (1923/1990). *The ego and the id.* New York, NY: Norton.

Frimer, J. A. (2016). Groups create moral superheroes to defend sacred values. In J. P. Forgas, L. Jussim, & P. A. M. Van Lange (Eds), *The social psychology of morality* (pp. 304–315). New York, NY: Routledge.

Fromm, E. (1941). *Escape from freedom.* New York, NY: Holt, Rinehart & Winston.

Fromm, E. (1964). *The heart of man.* New York, NY: Harper & Row.

Fulker, D. W., Eysenck, S. B., & Zuckerman, M. (1980). A genetic and environmental analysis of sensation seeking. *Journal of Research in Personality, 14*(2), 261–281.

Gallagher, B. (2015). *Daredevil's powers are more realistic than you think.* Nautilis: http://nautil.us/blog/daredevils-powers-are-more-realistic-than-you-think.

Garland-Thomson, R. (2009). *Staring: How we look.* Oxford, UK: Oxford University Press.

Gazo, A. & McDaniel, S.A. (2015). Families by choice and the management of low income through social supports. *Journal of Family Issues, 36*(3), 371-395.

Gibney, P. (2006). The double bind: Still crazy making after all these years. *Psychotherapy in Australia, 12*(3), 48-55.

Gibson, J. J. (1979). *The ecological approach to visual perception*. Dallas, TX: Houghton Mifflin.

Glicksohn, J., & Abulafia, J. (1998). Embedding sensation seeking within the big three. *Personality & Individual Differences, 25*(6), 1085–1099.

Glover, H. (1984). Survival guilt and the Vietnam veteran. *Journal of Nervous & Mental Disease, 172*(7), 393–397

Goelman, D. (1988, June 14). *Erikson, in his own old age, expands his view of life*. New York Times: http://www.nytimes.com/books/99/08/22/specials/erikson-old.html?mcubz=0.

Goethals, G. R., & Allison, S. T. (2012). Making heroes: The construction of courage, competence, and virtue. In J. M. Olson & M. P. Zanna (Eds.), *Advances in experimental social psychology*, (Vol. 46, pp. 183–235). San Diego, CA: Elsevier.

Goffman, E. (1986). *Stigma: Notes on the management of spoiled identity*. New York, NY: Touchstone.

Gold, K. J., Singh, V., Marcus, S. M., & Palladino, C. L. (2012). Mental health, substance use and intimate partner problems among women and postpartum suicide victims in the National Violent Death Reporting System. *General Hospital Psychiatry, 34*(2), 139–145.

Goldberg, L. (2014, March 24). *Marvel's Netflix drama "Daredevil" taps new showrunner (exclusive)*. The Hollywood Reporter: https://www.hollywoodreporter.com/live-feed/steven-deknight-set-as-daredevil-703693.

Goldman, C. (2012). *Bullied: What every parent, teacher, and kid needs to know about ending the cycle of fear*. New York, NY: Harper Collins.

Goldreich, D., & Kanics, I. M. (2003). Tactile acuity is enhanced in blindness. *Journal of Neuroscience, 23*(8), 3439–3445.

Goldstein, E. B., & Brockmole, J. R. (2017). *Sensation and perception* (10th ed.). Boston, MA: Cengage.

Goleman, D. (1996). *Vital lies, simple truths: The psychology of self-deception*. New York, NY: Simon & Schuster.

Govrin, A. (2016). Blurring the threat of "otherness": Integration by conversion in psychoanalysis and CBT. *Journal of Psychotherapy Integration, 26*(1), 78–90.

Gougoux, F., Zatorre, R. J., Lassonde, M., Voss, P., & Lepore, F. (2005). A functional neuroimaging study of sound localization: Visual cortex activity predicts performance in early-blind individuals. *PLoS Biology, 3*(2), e27.

Gray, K., & Wegner, D. M. (2010). Blaming God for our pain: Human suffering and the divine mind. *Personality & Social Psychology Review, 14*(1), 7–16.

Gross, R. D., & Humphreys, P. (1992). *Psychology: The science of mind and behavior*. London, UK: Hodder & Stoughton.

Grossman, D. (2009). *On killing: The psychological cost of learning to kill in war and society*. New York, NY: Back Bay.

Haidt, J. (2003). The moral emotions. In R. J. Davidson, K. R. Scherer, & H. H. Goldsmith (Eds.), *Handbook of Affective Sciences* (pp. 852–870). New York, NY: Oxford University Press.

Haidt, J. (2008). Morality. *Perspectives on Psychological Science, 3(1), 65–72*.

Halpern, D.F. & Collaer, M.L. (2005). Sex differences in visuospatial abilities: More than meets the eye. In P. Shah and A. Miyake (Eds.) *The Cambridge handbook of visuospatial thinking* (pp. 170–212). Cambridge University Press: Cambridge, MA.

Hanefalk, C. (2011, October 9). *A history of the radar sense—present time*. The Other Murdock Papers: http://www.theothermurdockpapers.com/2011/10/radar-sense-present-time/.

Hanefalk, C. (2016, March 6). *All that booze—Daredevil season one revisited, part 3*. The Other Murdock Papers: http://www.theothermurdockpapers.com/2016/03/all-that-booze-daredevil-season-one-revisited-part-3/.

Haney, C., Banks, W. C., & Zimbardo, P. G. (1973). Study of prisoners and guards in a simulated prison. *Naval Research Reviews, 9*, 1–17.

Hareli, S., & Eisikovits, Z. (2006). The role of communicating social emotions accompanying apologies in forgiveness. *Motivation & Emotion, 30*(3), 189–197.

Hatchard, T., Mioduszewski, O., Zambrana, A., O'Farrell, E., Caluyong, M., Poulin, P. A., & Smith, A. M. (2017). Neural changes associated with mindfulness-based stress reduction (MBSR): Current knowledge, limitations, and future directions. *Psychology & Neuroscience, 10*(1), 41–56.

Heath, A. C., & Martin, N. G. (1990). Psychoticism as a dimension of personality: A multivariate genetic test of Eysenck and Eysenck's psychoticism construct. *Journal of Personality & Social Psychology, 58*(1), 111–121.

Heirene, R. M., Shearer, D., Roderique-Davies, G., Mellalieu, S. D. (2016). Addiction in extreme sports: An exploration of withdrawal states in rock climbers. *Journal of Behavioral Addictions, 5*(2), 332–341.

Hendin, H., & Haas, A. P. (1991). Suicide and guilt as manifestations of PTSD in Vietnam combat veterans. *American Journal of Psychiatry, 148*(5), 586–591.

Henning, K. R., & Frueh, B. C. (1997). Combat guilt and its relationship to PTSD symptoms. *Journal of Clinical Psychology, 53*(8), 801–808.

Hero Construction Company (2015, January 21). *Philip Zimbardo and Matt Langdon at the Hero Round Table 2014.* The Hero Construction Company: https://www.youtube.com/watch?v=ujtkIaAfiSM.

Henry, J. F., & Sherwin, B. B. (2012). *Behavioral Neuroscience, 126*(1), 73–85.

Higgins, E. T. (1987). Self-discrepancy: A theory relating self and affect. *Psychological Review, 94*(3), 319–340.

Hodben, K. L., & Olson, J. M. (1994). From jest to antipathy: Disparagement humor as a source of dissonance-motivated attitude change. *Basic & Applied Social Psychology, 15*(3), 239–249.

Hommel, B., Müsseler, J., Aschersleben, G., & Prinz, W. (2001). The theory of event coding (TEC): A framework for perception and action planning. *Behavioral & Brain Sciences, 24*(5), 849–937.

Hooper, L.M., Marotta, S.A., & Lanthier, R.P. (2007). Predictors of growth and distress following childhood parentification: A retrospective exploratory study. *Journal of Child & Family Studies, 17*(5), 693–705.

Howarth, E. (1986). What does Eysenck's psychoticism scale really measure? *British Journal of Psychology, 77*(pt. 2), 223–227.

Hubbard, T. L. (2010). Auditory imagery: Empirical findings. *Psychological Bulletin, 136*(2), 302–329.

Hull, A. M., Alexander, D. A., & Klein, S. (2002). Survivors of the Piper Alpha oil platform disaster: long-term follow-up study. *British Journal of Psychiatry, 181*(5), 433–438.

Huo, Y., Huang, L., Zhang, D., Yao, Y., Fang, Y., Zhang, C., & Luo, X. (2016). Identification of SLC25A37 as a major depressive disorder risk gene. *Journal of Psychiatric Research, 83*, 168–175.

Israel, S., Weisel, O., Ebstein, R. P., & Bornstein, G. (2012). Oxytocin, but not vasopressin, increases both parochial and universal altruism. *Psychoneuroendocrinology, 37*(8), 1341–1344.

Iversen, K. D., Ptito, M. Møller, P., & Kupers, R. (2015). Enhanced chemosensory detection of negative emotions in congenital blindness. *Neural Plasticity*, ArtID 469750.

Janoff-Bulman, R. (2012). Conscience: The dos and don'ts of moral regulation. In M. Mikulincer & P. R. Shaver (Eds.) *The social psychology of morality: Exploring the causes of good and evil* (pp. 131–148). Washington, DC: American Psychological Association.

Jastreboff, P. J., & Jastreboff, M. M. (2000). Tinnitus Retraining Therapy (TRT) as a method for treatment of tinnitus and hyperacusis patients. *Journal of the American Academy of Audiology, 11*, 162–177.

Jeong S., & Hwang, Y. (2016). Media multitasking effects on cognitive vs. attitudinal outcomes: A meta-analysis. *Human Communication Research, 42*(4), 599–618.

Jinpa, T. (2016). *A fearless heart: How the courage to be compassionate can transform our lives.* New York, NY: Random House.

Johnson, A. (1991). *Owning your own shadow: Understanding the dark side of the psyche.* San Francisco, CA: Harper.

Johnson, D. R. (2012). Transportation into a story increases empathy, prosocial behavior, and perceptual bias toward fearful expressions. *Personality & Individual Differences, 52*(2), 150–155.

Johnson, M. S. (2003) interviewed in *"Daredevil: HBO First Look Special."* Daredevil: Director's Cut Blu-ray bonus feature.

Johnson, R. D., & Downing, L. L. (1979). Deindividuation and valence of cues: Effects on prosocial and antisocial behavior. *Journal of Personality & Social Psychology, 37*(9), 1532-1538.

Johnson, S. B., Blum, R. W., & Giedd, J. N. (2009). Adolescent maturity and the brain: The promise and pitfalls of neuroscience research in adolescent health policy. *Journal of Adolescent Health, 45*(3), 216–221.

Jones, R. V. (1978). *Most secret war: British Scientific Intelligence 1939–1945.* Hamish Hamilton, London.

Jordan, J. S. (2000). The world in the organism: Living systems are knowledge. *Psycoloquy, 11*(113), Article 18.

Jordan, J. S., Cialdella, V. T., Dayer, A., Langley, M. D., & Stillman, Z. (2017). Wild bodies don't need to perceive, detect, capture, or create meaning: They ARE meaning. *Frontiers in Psychology, 8,* Article 1149.

Judge, M. (2014, April 2). *Daredevil: A Catholic in comics.* CNS News: http://www. catholicnews.com/services/englishnews/2014/daredevil-a-catholic-in-comics.cfm.

Jung, C. (1953/1966). *Two essays on analytical psychology.* Princeton, NJ: Princeton University Press.

Jung, C. (1956/1976). *Symbols of transformation* (2nd ed.). Princeton, NJ: Princeton University Press.

Jung, C. (1959/1973). *Four archetypes: Mother, rebirth, spirit, trickster.* Princeton, NJ: Princeton University Press.

Jung, C. (1959/1978). *Aion.* Princeton, NJ: Princeton University Press.

Jung, C. (1995). *Dream analysis: Notes of the seminar given in 1928–30.* London, UK: Routledge.

Jung, C. G. (1913). The theory of psychoanalysis. *Psychoanalytic Review, 1*(1), 1–40.

Jung, C. G., & Jaffé, A. (1989). *Memories, dreams, reflections.* New York, NY: Vintage.

Jung, J. R. (2000). *Psychology of alcohol and other drugs: A research perspective.* Thousand Oaks, CA: SAGE.

Juvonen, J., & Murdock, T. B. (1995). How to promote social approval: Effects of audience and achievement outcome on publicly communicated attributions. *Journal of Educational Psychology, 85*(2), 365–376.

Juvonen, J., Nishina, A., & Grahma, S. (2000). Peer harassment, psychological adjustment, and school functioning in early adolescence. *Journal of Educational Psychology,* 92(2), 349–359.

Kandel, D. B. (1978). Similarity in real-life adolescent friendship pairs. *Journal of Personality & Social Psychology, 36*(3), 306–312.

Kärnekull, S. C., Arshamian, A., Nilsson, M. E., & Larsson, M. (2016). From perception to metacognitioun: Auditory and olfactory functions in early blind, late blind, and sighted individuals. *Frontiers in Psychology, 7,* ArtID 1450.

Kashdan, T. B., Biswas-Diener, R., & King, L. A. (2008). Reconsidering happiness: The costs of distinguishing between hedonics and eudaimonia. *Journal of Positive Psychology, 3*(4), 219–233.

Keane, M. B. (2013). *Fever.* New York, NY: Scribner.

Keller, H. (1933). Three days to see. *Atlantic Monthly, 151*(1), 35–42.

Kellogg, W. (1962). Sonar system of the blind: New research measures their accuracy in detecting the texture, size, and distance of objects "by ear." *Science, 137* (3528), 399–404.

Keltner, D., & Haidt, J. (1999). Social functions of emotions at four levels of analysis. *Cognition & Emotion, 13*(5), 505–521.

Kerr, W. (1954). The anti-intellectual mania. *American Psychologist, 9*(5), 196–197.

Kim, S. (2014). *Without you, there is no us: Undercover among the sons of North Korea's elite.* New York, NY: Penguin.

Kinsbourne, M., & Jordan, J. S. (2009). Embodied anticipation: A neurodevelopmental interpretation. *Discourse Processes, 46*(2–3), 103–126.

Kinsella, E. L., Igou, E. R., & Ritchie, T. D. (in press). Heroism and the pursuit of a meaningful life. *Journal of Humanistic Psychology.*

Kinsella, E. L., Ritchie, T. D., & Igou, E. R. (2015l). Lay perspectives on the social and psychological functions of heroes. *Frontiers in Psychology, 6,* 1–12.

Kinsella, E. L., Ritchie, T. D., & Igou, E. R. (2015b). Zeroing in on heroes: a prototype analysis of hero features. *Journal of Personality & Social Psychology, 108*(1), 114–127.

Klasen, F., Oettingen, G., Daniels, J., & Adam, H. (2010). Multiple trauma and mental health in former Ugandan child soldiers. *Journal of Traumatic Stress, 23(5)*, 573–581.

Klein, M. (2002). *Love, guilt and reparation: And other works 1921–1945.* New York, NY: Simon & Schuster.

Knippenberg, S., Damoiseaux, J., Bol, Y., Hupperts, R., Taylor, B. V., Ponsonby, A., Dwyer, T., Simpson, S., & van der Mei, I. A. F. (2014). Higher levels of reported sun exposure, and not vitamin D status, are associated with less depressive symptoms and fatigue in multiple sclerosis. *Neurologica Scandinavica, 129*(2), 123–131.

Kohlberg, L. (1984). *The psychology of moral development: The nature and validity of moral stages.* San Francisco, CA: Harper & Row.

Koritar, E. (2017). Shining a psychoanalytic light on alienation, otherness, and xenophobia. *American Journal of Psychoanalysis, 77*(4), 341–346.

Kornhuber, H. H., & Deecke, L. (1965). Hirnpotentialaenderungen bei Willkuerbewegungen und passive Bewegungen des Menchen: Bereitschaftspotential und reafferente Ptentiale. *Pflugers Archiv für Gesamte Psycholgie, 284*, 1–17.

Kovács, M., Stauder, A., & Szedmák, S. (2003). Severity of allergic complaints: The importance of depressed mood. *Journal of Psychosomatic Research, 54*(6), 549–557.

Krousel-Wood, M., Islam, T., Muntner, P., Holt, E., Joyce, C. Morisky, D. E., Webber, L. S., & Frohlich, E. D. (2010). Association of depression with antihypertensive medication adherence in older adults: Cross-sectional and longitudinal findings with CoSMO. *Annals of Behavioral Medicine, 40*(3), 248–257.

Kumashiro, K. (2002). *Troubling education: Queer activism and anti-oppressive.*

Kupers, R., Beaulieu-Lefebvrre, M., Schneider, F. C., Kassuba, T., Paulson, O. B., Siebner, H. R., & Ptito, M. (2011). Neural correlates of olfactory processing in congenital blindness. *Neuropsychologia, 49*(7), 2037–2044.

Lalvani, P. (2015). Disability, stigma, and otherness: Perspectives of parents and teachers. *International Journal of Disability, 62*(4), 379–393.

Lampe, L. (2015). Social phobia and avoidant personality disorder: Similar but different? *Journal of Personality Disorders, 29*(1), 115–130.

Langer, E. J., & Roth, J. (1975). Heads I win, tails it's chance: The illusion of control as a function of the sequence of outcomes in a purely chance task. *Journal of Personality & Social Psychology*, 32(6), 951–955.

Langley, T. (2012). *Batman and psychology: A dark and stormy knight.* New York, NY: Wiley.

Langley, T. (2017, September 30). *Why does the Man without Fear become a loner among heroes?* Psychology Today: https://www.psychologytoday.com/blog/beyond-heroes-and-villains/201709/why-does-the-man-without-fear-become-loner-among-heroes.

Latané, B., & Rodin, J. (1969). A lady in distress: Inhibiting effects of friends and strangers on bystander intervention. *Journal of Experimental Social Psychology, 5*(2), 189–202.

Laurent, H. K., & Ablow, J. C. (2012). A cry in the dark: Depressed mothers show reduced neural activation to their own infant's cry. *Social Cognitive & Affective Neuroscience, 7*(2), 125–134.

Lavie, N. (1995). Perceptual load as a necessary condition for selective attention. *Journal of Experimental Psychology: Human Perception & Performance, 21*(3), 451–468.

Lerner, M. J. (1970). The desire for justice and reactions to victims. In J. Macaulay & L. Berkowitz (Eds.), *Altruism and helping behavior* (pp. 205–229). New York, NY: Academic Press.

Levine, D. N., Warach, J., & Farah, M. (1985). Two visual systems in mental imagery Dissociation of "what" and "where" in imagery disorders due to bilateral posterior cerebral lesions. *Neurology, 35*(7), 1010–1018.

Libet, B. (1985). Unconscious cerebral initiative and the role of conscious will in voluntary action. *Behavioral & Brain Sciences, 8*(4), 529–539.

Lindroos, O. F. C., Riittinen, M. A., Multanen, J. V., & Bergström, R. M. (1984). Overstimulation, occipital/somesthetic cerebral cortical depth, and cortical asymmetry in mice. *Developmental Psychobiology, 17*(5), 547–554.

Linton, S. (1998). *Claiming disability: Knowledge and identity.* New York, NY: NYU Press.

Loftus, E. F. (1975). Leading questions and the eyewitness report. *Cognitive Psychology, 7*(4), 560–572.

Loo, R. (1979). A psychometric investigation of the Eysenck Personality Questionnaire. *Journal of Personality Assessment, 43*(1), 54–58.

Loria, K. (2016, September 9). *8 of the most dangerous adventure sports.* Business Insider: http://www.businessinsider.com/adventure-extreme-sports-injury-concussion-rates-2016-9/#skiing-people-who-ski-report-high-numbers-of-concussions-according-to-the-study-though-part-of-that-is-due-to-the-large-number-of-skiers-skiers-also-face-an-especially-high-risk-for-acl-tears-and-other-knee-injuries-1.

Lorenzo-Luaces, L. (2015). Heterogeneity in the prognosis of major depression: From the common cold to a highly debilitating and recurrent illness. *Epidemiology & Psychiatric Sciences, 24*(6), 466–472.

Luhmann, M., Hofmann, W., Eid, M., & Lucas, R. E. (2012). Subjective well-being and adaptation to life events: A meta-analysis on differences between cognitive and affective well-being. *Journal of Personality & Social Psychology, 102*(3), 592–615.

Lyubomirsky, S., King, L., & Diner, E. (2005a). The benefits of frequent positive affect: Does happiness lead to success? *Psychological Bulletin, 131*(6), 803–855.

Lyubomirsky, S., Sheldon, K. M., & Schkade, D. (2005b). Pursuing happiness: The architecture of sustainable change. *Review of General Psychology, 9*(2), 111–131.

Macchio, R. (1994). Introduction. In R. Machio (Ed.), *Daredevil: The Man Without Fear Trade Paperback* (pp. 4–5). New York, NY: Marvel.

Machiavelli, N. (1532/2017). *The prince* [Kindle edition]. Seattle, WA: AmazonClassics.

Malone, P. M., Kier, K. L., Stanovich, J. E., & Malone, M. J. (2014). *Drug information: A guide for pharmacists* (5th ed.). New York, NY: McGraw-Hill.

Mar, R. A., & Oatley, K. (2008). The function of fiction is the abstraction and simulation of social experience. *Perspectives on Psychological Science, 3*(3), 173–192.

Marchetti, I. Everaert, J., Dainer-Best, J., Loeys, T., Beevers, C. G., & Koster, E. H. W. (2018). Specificity and overlap of attention and memory biases in depression. *Journal of Affective Disorders, 225,* 404–412.

Marques, M. D., Elphinstone, B., Critchley, C. R., & Eigenberger, M. E. (2017). A brief scaling for measuring anti-intellectualism. *Personality & Individual Differences, 114,* 167–174.

Martinez-Pilkington, A. (2007). Shame and guilt: The psychology of sacramental confession. *Humanistic Psychologist, 35*(2), 203–218.

Maslow, A. H. (1966). *The psychology of science: A reconnaissance.* New York, NY: Harper & Row.

May, R. (1955). A psychological approach to anti-intellectualism. *Journal of Social Issues, 11(3),* 41–47.

Merrick, M. T., Ports, K. A., Ford, D. C., Afifi, T. O., Gershoff, E. T., & Grogan-Kaylor, A. (2017). Unpacking the impact of adverse childhood experiences on adult mental health. *Child Abuse & Neglect, 69,* 10–19.

McClelland, D. C. (1975). *Power: The inner experience.* New York, NY: Irvington-Wiley.

McCullough, M. E. (2000). Forgiveness as human strength: Theory, measurement, and links to well-being. *Journal of Social & Clinical Psychology, 19*(1), 43–55.

McGoldrick, M., Gerson, R., & Shellenberger, S. (1999). *Genograms: Assessment and intervention* (2nd ed.). New York: Norton.

Memon, A., Vrij, A., & Bull, R. (2003). *Psychology and law: Truthfulness, accuracy, and credibility* (2nd ed.). New York, NY: Wiley.

Merabet, L., & Pascual-Leone, A. (2009). Neural reorganization following sensory loss: the opportunity of change, *Nature Reviews Neuroscience, 11* (1), 44–52.

Michaud, S., & Aynesworth, H. (1983/1999). *The only living witness: The true story of serial sex killer Ted Bundy* (revised ed.). Irving, TX: Authorlink.

Milgram, S. (1963). Behavioral study of obedience. Journal of Abnormal & Social Psychology, 67(4), 371–378.

Milgram, S. (1963). Behavioral study of obedience. *Journal of Abnormal & Social Psychology, 67*(4), 371–378.

Miller, A. G. (Ed.). (2016). *The social psychology of good and evil.* New York, NY: Guilford.

Miller, E. S., Chu, C., Gollan, J., & Gossett, D. R. (2013). Obsessive-compulsive symptoms during the postpartum period: A prospectus report. *Journal of Reproductive Medicine, 58*(3–4), 115–122.

Miller, F. (2012) interviewed in "Men without fear: Creating Daredevil." *Daredevil: Director's Cut* Blu-ray bonus feature.

Miner, B. (2015, May 18). *Daredevil and the Devil.* The Catholic Thing: https://www. thecatholicthing.org/2015/05/18/daredevil-and-the-devil/.

Minuchin, S., & Fishman, H.C. (1981/2002). *Family therapy techniques.* Cambridge, MA: Harvard University Press.

Moisala, M., Salmela, V., Hietajärvi, L., Salo, E., Carlson, S., Salonen, O., Lonka, K., Hakkarainen, K., Salmela-Aro, K., Alho, K. (2016). Media multitasking is associated with distractibility and increased prefrontal activity in adolescents and young adults. *NeuroImage, 134,* 113–121.

Mortlock, A. (2015). Toddlers' use of peer rituals at mealtime: Symbols of togetherness and otherness. *International Journal of Early Years Education, 23*(4), 426–435.

Mossakowska-Wójcik, J., Orzechowska, A., Talarowska, M., Szemraj, J., & Galecki, P. (2018). The importance of TCF4 gene in the etiology of recurrent depressive disorders. *Progress in Neuro-Psychopharmacology & Biological Psychiatry, 80*(C), 304–308.

Murray, H. A. (1948). *Explorations in personality: A clinical and experimental study of fifty men of college age.* New York, NY: Oxford University Press.

Murray-Swank, A. B., McConnell, K. M., & Pargament, K. I. (2007). Understanding spiritual confession: A review and theoretical synthesis. *Mental Health, Religion & Culture, 10*(3), 275–291.

Nadal, K. L., Hamit, S., Lyons, O., Weinberg, A., & Corman, L. (2013). Gender microaggressions: Perceptions, processes, and coping mechanisms of women. In M. A. Paludi (Ed.), *The psychology of business success* (pp. 193–220). Santa Barbara, CA: Praeger.

Neil, J. & Kniskern, D. (1982/1989). *From psyche to system: The evolving therapy of Carl Whitaker* (2nd ed.). New York, NY: Guilford.

Nelson, R., & Kriegsfeld, L. J. (2017). *An introduction to behavioral endocrinology* (5th ed.). Cary, NC: Sinauer.

Oliver, M. (1996). *Understanding disability: From theory to practice.* New York, NY: St Martin's.

Oliver, M. B., Hartmann, T., & Woolley, J. K. (2012). Elevation in response to entertainment portrayals of moral virtue. *Human Communication Research, 38*(3), 360–378.

Olson, D. H. & Markoff, R. (1994). *Marriage and the family: Diversity and strengths.*

Opp, R. E., & Samson, A. Y. (1989). Taxonomy of guilt for combat veterans. *Professional Psychology: Research & Practice, 20*(3), 159–165.

Pelletier, M. (n.d.). *The science of Daredevil: 5 scientific explanations for Daredevil's abilities.* Nuskool: https://www.nuskool.com/learn/lesson/the-science-of-daredevil-5-scientific-explanations-for-daredevils-abilities-3/.

Pagé, S., Sharp, A., Landry, S. P., & Champoux, F. (2016). Short-term visual deprivation can enhance spatial release from masking. *Neuroscience Letters, 628,* 167–170.

Panno, J. (2004). *Cancer: The role of genes, lifestyle, and environment.* New York, NY: Facts on File.

Patten, S. B. (2013). Major depression epidemiology from a diathesis-stress conceptualization. *Psychiatry, 13*(ArtID), 19.

Perry, R. B. (1935). *The thought and character of William James: As revealed in unpublished correspondence and notes, together with his published writings. Vol. 1, Inheritance and vocation; Vol. 2, Philosophy and psychology.* Oxford, UK: Little, Brown.

Pervin, L. A. (1996). *The science of personality.* Oxford, UK: Wiley.

Peterson, C. (2006). *A primer in positive psychology.* New York, NY: Oxford University Press.

Piaget, J. (1954). *The construction of reality in the child.* New York, NY: Basic.

Piaget, J. (1974). *The origins of intelligence in children.* (M. Cook, trans.). New York, NY: International University Press.

Pohlman, C. (2008). *Revealing minds: Assessing to understand and support struggling learners.* San Francisco, CA: Jossey-Bass.

Pope, C. J., Xie, B., Sharma, V., & Campbell, M. K. (2013). A prospective study of thoughts of self-harm and suicidal ideation during the postpartum period in women with mood disorders. *Archives of Women's Mental Health, 16*(6), 483–488.

Puryear, L. J. (2007). *Understanding your moods when you're expecting: Emotions, mental health, and happiness—before, during, and after pregnancy.* New York, NY: Houghton Mifflin.

Raby, K. L., Labella, M. H., Martin, J., Carlson, E. A., & Roisman, G. I. (2017). Childhood abuse and neglect and insecure attachment states of mind in adulthood: Prospective, longitudinal evidence from a high-risk sample. *Development & Psychopathology, 29*(2), 347–363.

Rader, C. M., & Tellegen, A. (1987). An investigation of synesthesia. *Journal of Personality & Social Psychology, 52*(5), 981–987.

Ray, L. A., MacKillop, J., Hesterberg, K., Bryan, A., McGeary, J., & Hutchinson, K. E. (2009). The dopamine D4 receptor (DRD4) gene exon III polymorphism, problematic alcohol use, and novelty seeking: Direct and mediated effects. *Addiction Biology, 14*(2), 238–244.

Reissland, J., & Manzey, D. (2016). Serial or overlapping processing in multitasking as individual preferences: Effects of stimulus preview on task switching and concurrent dual-task performance. *Acta Psychoogica, 168,* 27–40.

Rentzsch, K., Schütz, A., & Schröder-Abé, M. (2011). Being labeled *nerd*: Factors that influence the social acceptance of high-achieving students. *Journal of Experimental Education, 79*(2), 143–168.

Rhodes, A., & Segre, L. (2014). Perinatal depression: A review of U.S. legislation and law. *Archives of Women's Mental Health, 16*(4), 259–270.

Röder, B., Teder-Sälejärvi, W., Sterr, A. Rösler, F., Hillyard, S. A., & Neville, H. J. (1999). Improved auditory spatial tuning in blind humans. *Nature, 400,* 162–166.

Rosenblum, L., Gordon, M., & Jarquin, L. (2000). Echolocating distance by moving and stationary listeners, *ecological psychology, 12*(3), 181–206.

Rosenfield, M., & Logan, N. (Eds.). *Optometry: Science, techniques, and clinical management.* Oxford, UK: Butterworth & Heinemann.

Rubin, L. C. (2013). Are superhero stories good for us? Reflections from clinical practice. In R. S. Rosenberg (Ed.) *Our superheroes, ourselves* (pp. 37–52). New York, NY: Oxford University Press.

Ryan, B. (2017, July 25). *The true story behind the role of Devil's Advocate in the Catholic Church.* uCatholic: http://www.ucatholic.com/blog/the-history-of-the-devils-advocate/.

Sanderson, P. (1982). The Frank Miller/Klaus Janson interview. In M. Cohn (Ed.), *The Daredevil chronicles* (pp. 9–27). Albany, NY: FantaCo.

Schnall, S., & Roper, J. (2012). Elevation puts moral values into action. *Social Psychological & Personality Science, 3*(3), 373–378.

Schwartz, S. A. (2014). From one to the many: the social implications of nonlocal perception. *Explore: The Journal of Science & Healing, 10*(3), 146–149.

Schwenn, O., Hundorf, I., Moll, B., Pitz, S., & Mann, W. J. (2002). Do blind persons have a better sense of smell than normal sighted people? *Klinische Monatsblatter für Augenheilkunde, 219*(9), 649–654.

Screenocean (2012, May 30). *The boy who sees without eyes.* YouTube: https://www.youtube.com/watch?v=TeFRkAYb1uk.

Seligman, M. E. P. (1972). Learned helplessness. *Annual Review of Medicine, 23*(1), 307–412.

Seligman, M. E. P. (1998). Building human strength: Psychology's forgotten mission. *APA Monitor, 74*(1), 1–9.

Seligman, M. E. P. (2002). *Authentic happiness: Using the new positive psychology to realize your potential for lasting fulfillment.* New York, NY: Free Press.

Seligman, M. E. P. (2003). Positive psychology: Fundamental assumptions. *The Psychologist, 16*(3), 125–127.

Seligman, M. E. P., Parks, A. C., & Steen, T. (2004). A balanced psychology and a full life. *Philosophical Transactions of the Royal Society B: Biological Sciences, 359*(1449), 1379–1381.

Shaffer, L. S. (1977). The Golden Fleece: Anti-intellectualism and social science. *American Psychologist, 32*(10), 814–823.

Shapiro, D. (2014). Survivor guilt. *Families, Systems, & Health, 32*(3), 354.

Shields, B. (2006). *Down came the rain: My journey through postpartum depression.* New York, NY: Hachette.

Siebers, T. (2008). *Disability theory.* Ann Arbor, MI: University of Michigan Press.

Simons, D. J., & Levin, D. T. (1997). Change blindness. *Trends in Cognitive Sciences, 1*(7), 261–267.

Skitka, L. J. (2010). The psychology of moral conviction. *Social & Personality Psychology Compass, 4*(4), 267–281.

Skitka, L. J. (2012). Moral convictions and moral courage: Common denominators of good and evil. In M. Mikulincer & P. R. Shaver (Eds.) *The social psychology of morality: Exploring the causes of good and evil* (pp. 349–365). Washington, DC: American Psychological Association.

Smith, K. (2012) interviewed in "Men without fear: Creating Daredevil." *Daredevil: Director's Cut* Blu-ray bonus feature.

Smokowski, P.R., Reynolds, A.J., & Bezcruzko, N. (1999). Resilience and protective factors in adolescents: An autobiographical perspective from disadvantaged youth. *Journal of School Psychology, 37*(4), 425–448.

Sokol, J. T. (2009). Identity development throughout the lifetime: An examination of Ericksonian theory. *Graduate Journal of Counseling Psychology, 1*(2), 1–11.

Solomon, M. F. (2003). Connection, disruption, repair: Treating the effects of attachment trauma on intimate relationships. In M. F. Solomon & D. J. Siegel (Eds.), *Healing trauma: Attachment, mind, body, and brain*. New York, NY: Norton.

Spector, F., & Maurer, D. (2013). Synesthesia: A new approach to understanding the development of perception. *Psychology of Consciousness: Theory, Research, & Practice, 1*(S), 108–129.

Spilka, B., & Ladd, K. L. (2013). *The psychology of prayer: A scientific approach*. New York, NY: Guilford.

Spotnitz, H. (1995). *Treatment of the narcissistic neuroses*. Rev. ed. New York, NY: Jason Aronson.

Springer, L., Stanne, M. E., & Donovan, S. S. (1999). Effects of small-group learning on undergraduates in science, mathematics, engineering, and technology: A meta-analysis. *Review of Educational Research, 69*(1), 21–51.

Sroufe, A. & Siegel, D. (2011). The verdict is in: The case for attachment theory. *Psychotherapy Networker, 35*, 1–12.

Stafford, A. (2017). *The science of being a hero*. The Age: http://www.theage.com.au/national/the-science-of-being-a-hero-20170201-gu3gbt.

Stein, M. (1996). *Jung on evil*. Princeton, NJ: Princeton University Press.

St. Petersburg–USA Orphanage Research Team (2005). Characteristics of children, caregivers, and orphanages for young children in St. Petersburg, Russian Federation. *Journal of Applied Developmental Psychology, 26*(5), 477–506.

Stevenson, R. J., & Tomiczek, C. (2007). Olfactory-induced synesthesias: A review and model. *Psychological Bulletin, 133*(2), 294–309.

Stewart, D. E., & Vigod, S. (2016). Postpartum depression. *New England Journal of Medicine, 375*(22), 2177–2186.

Stinton, N., Atif, M. A., Barkat, N., & Doty, R. L. (2010). Influence of smell loss on taste function. *Behavioral Neuroscience, 124*(2), 256–264.

Stroffregen, T. A., & Pittenger, J. B. (1995). Human echolocation as a basic form of perception and action. *Ecological Psychology, 7*(3), 181–216.

Stumpf, C. (1883/1890). *Psychology of tone*. Leipzig, Germany: Hirzel.

Susman, J. L. (1996). Postpartum depressive disorders. *Journal of Family Practice, 43*(6, Sup.), S17–S24.

Tangney, J. P., Stuewig, J., & Mashek, D. J. (2007). Moral emotions and moral behavior. *Annual Review of Psychology, 58*, 345–372.

Tatala, M. (2009). The role of personal adjustment to developmental crises in improving quality of life. *International Journal of Psychology & Counseling, 1*(10), 187–193.

Taylor, J. G. (1966). Perception generated by training echolocation. *Canadian Journal of Psychology, 20*(1), 64–81.

Teichmann, A. L., Nieuwenstein, M. R., & Rich, A. N. (2017). Digit–color synaesthesia only enhances memory for colors in a specific context: A new method of duration thresholds to measure serial recall. *Journal of Experimental Psychology: Human Perception & Performance, 43*(8), 1494-1503.

Teng, S., Sommer, V., Pantazis, D., & Oliva, A. (2016). Hearing scenes: A neuromagnetic signature of perceived auditory spatial extent. *BioRxiv*, 061762.

Thakrar, B. T., & Robinson, N. J. (2009). Isotretinoin and the risk of depression. *Journal of Clinical Psychiatry, 70*(10), p. 1475.

Thaler, L., Arnott, S. R., & Goodale, M. A. (2011). Neural correlates of natural human echolocation in early and late blind echolocation experts. *PLoS One 6*(5), e20162.

Thelen, E., & Fisher, D. M. (1983). The organization of spontaneous leg movements in newborn infants. *Journal of Motor Behavior, 15*(4), 353–372.

Thompson, C. (1955). Anti-intellectualism in the individual. *Journal of Social Issues, 11*(3), 48–50.

Tokuhama-Espinosa, T. (2010). *The new science of teaching and learning: Using the best of mind, brain, and education science in the classroom.* New York, NY: Teachers College.

Trani, J., Ballard, E., & Peña, J. B. (2016). Stigma of persons with disabilities in Afghanistan: Examining the pathways from stereotyping to mental distress. *Social Science & Medicine, 153,* 258–265.

Trikojat, K., Luksch, H., Rösen-Wolff, A. Plessow, F., Schmitt, J., & Buscke-Kirschbaum, A. (2017). "Allergic mood"—depressive and anxiety symptoms in patients with seasonal allergic rhinitis (SAR) and their association to inflammatory, endocrine, and allergic markers. *Brain, Behavior, & Immunity, 65,* 202–209.

Van Ackeren, M. J., Barbero, F. M., Mattioni, S., & Bottini, R. (2017, September 8). Neuronal populations in the occipital cortex of the blind synchronize to the temporal dynamics of speech. *BioRxiv,* p. 186338.

Van Bommel, M., van Prooijen, J. W., Elffers, H., & Van Lange, P. A. (2012). Be aware to care: Public self-awareness leads to a reversal of the bystander effect. *Journal of Experimental Social Psychology, 48*(4), 926–930.

Van Dam, D. S., van Nierop, M., Viechtbauer, W., Velthrost, E., van Winkel, R., Bruggeman, R., Cahn, W., de Haan, L., Kahn, R. S., Meijer, C. J., Myin-Germeys, I., van Os, J., & Wiersma, D. (2015). Childhood abuse and neglect in relation to the presence of persistence of psychotic and depressive symptomatology. *Psychological Medicine, 45*(7), 1363–1377.

Vandervert, L. (1995) Chaos theory and the evolution of consciousness and mind: A thermodynamic-holographic resolution to the mind-body problem. *New Ideas in Psychology, 13*(2), 107–127.

Van Geert, P. (1998). A dynamic systems model of basic developmental mechanisms: Piaget, Vygotsky, and beyond. *Psychological Review, 105*(4), 634–677.

Van Slyke, J. (2013). *Post-traumatic growth.* Naval Center for Combat and Operational Stress Control: https://archive.org/details/PTGWhitePaperFinal.

Ventura, J. D. (2005). *Law for dummies.* New York, NY: Wiley.

Vianello, M., Galliani, E. M., & Haidt, J. (2010). Elevation at work: The effects of leaders' moral excellence. *Journal of Positive Psychology, 5*(5), 390–411.

Violanti, J. M., & Aron, F. (1994). Ranking police stressors. *Psychological Reports, 75,* 824–826.

Voorpostel, M. (2013). Just like family: Fictive kin relationships in the Netherlands. *Journals of Gerontology, Series B: Psychological Sciences & Social Sciences, 68*(5), 816–824.

Vygotsky, L. S. (1978). *Mind in society: The development of higher psychological processes.* Cambridge, MA: Harvard University Press.

Wallmeier, L., Geßele, N., & Wiegrebe, L. (2013). Echolocation versus echo suppression in humans. *Proceedings of the Royal Society of London B: Biological Sciences, 280*(1769), 20131428.

Watters, A. J., Gotlib, I. H., Harris, A. W. F., Boyce, P. M., & Williams, L. M. (2013). Using multiple methods to characterize the phenotype of individuals with a family history of major depressive disorder. *Journal of Affective Disorders, 150*(2), 474–480.

Wegner, D. M. (2002) *The illusion of conscious will,* London, UK: MIT Press.

Wegner, D. M., & Wheatley, T. (1999). Apparent mental causation: Sources of the experience of will. *American Psychologist, 54*(7), 480–492.

Weiner, B. (2006). *Social motivation, justice, and the moral emotions.* Mahwah, NJ: Erlbaum.

White, W. C., Jr. (1975). Validity of the Overcontrolled-Hostility (O-H) scale: A brief report. *Journal of Personality Assessment, 39*(6), 587–590.

Wilde, O. (1883/2007) The Duchess of Padua. In H. Trayler (Ed.), *The collected works of Oscar Wilde* (pp. 407–482). Ware, Hertfordshire, UK: Wordsworth.

Wilson, J. P., Drożdek, B., & Turkovic, S. (2006). Posttraumatic shame and guilt. *Trauma, Violence, & Abuse, 7*(2), 122–141.

Wishart, D. Somoray, K., & Rowland, B. (2017). Role of thrill and adventure seeking in risky work-related driving behaviours. *Personality & Individual Differences, 104,* 362–367.

Woo, S. M., & Keatinge, C. (2016). *Diagnosis and treatment of mental disorders across the lifespan* (2nd ed.). New York, NY: Wiley.

Worthington, Jr., E. L. (2003). *Forgiving and reconciling: Bridges to wholeness and hope.* Downers Grove, IL: InterVarsity.

Wundt, W. (1862/1961). Contributions to the theory of sensory perception. In T. Shipley (Ed.), *Classics in psychology.* New York, NY: Philosophical Library.

Wylie, M. S., & Turner, L. (2011). The attuned therapist. *Psychotherapy Networker, 35(2),* 1–19.

Xu, Y., Qi, J., Yang, Y., & Wen, X. (2016). The contribution of lifestyle factors to depressive symptoms: A cross-sectional study in Chinese college students. *Psychiatry Research, 245,* 243–249.

Yang, Y., & Raine, A. (2009). Prefrontal structural and functional brain imaging findings in antisocial, violent, and psychopathic individuals: A meta-analysis. *Psychiatry Research: Neuroimaging, 174*(2), 81–88.

Yar, M. A. (2015, January 22). *Top 10 most dangerous jobs in the world.* Geek's Top Ten: http://geekstopten.com/most-dangerous-jobs-in-world/.

Zagorski, N. (2005). Profile of Elizabeth Loftus. *Proceedings of the National Academy of Sciences of the United States of America, 102*(39), 13721–13723.

Zajonc, R. B. (1965, July 16). Social facilitation. *Science, 149*(3681), 269–274.

Zimbardo, P. (2007). *The Lucifer effect: Understanding how good people turn evil.* New York, NY: Random House.

Zimbardo, P. G. (1971). *The psychological power and pathology of imprisonment.* A statement prepared for the U.S. House of Representatives Committee on the Judiciary, Subommittee No. 3: Hearings on Prison Reform. San Francisco, CA.

Zimmerman, M., McGlinchey, J. B., Young, D., & Chelminski, I. (2006). Diagnosing major depressive disorder: VII. Family history as a diagnostic criterion. *Journal of Nervous & Mental Disease, 194*(9), 704–707.

Zuckerman, M. (1971). Dimensions of sensation seeking. *Journal of Consulting & Clinical Psychology, 36*(1), 45–52.

Zuckerman, M. (1979). *Sensation seeking: Beyond the optimal level of arousal.* Hillsdale, NJ: Erlbaum.

Zuckerman, M. (1994). *Behavioral expressions and biosocial bases of sensation seeking.* Cambridge, MA: Cambridge University Press.

Zuckerman, M., & Link, K. (1968). Construct validity for the Sensation Seeking Scale. *Journal of Consulting & Clinical Psychology, 32*(4), 45–52.

Zuckerman, M., Eysenck, S., & Eysenck, H. J. (1978). Sensation seeking in England and America: Cross-cultural, age, and sex comparisons.

Zuckerman, M., Kolin, E. A., Price, L, & Zoob, I. (1964). Development of a sensation-seeking scale. Journal of Consulting Psychology, 28(6), 477–482.

INDEX